OXFORD WORLD'S CLASSICS

IBSEN: FOUR MAJOR PLAYS

HENRIK IBSEN was born in 1828, the son of a Norwegian merchant, who suffered financial setbacks during the boy's childhood, causing him to be apprenticed to an apothecary at the age of 15. In 1850 Ibsen came to Christiania (Oslo) with the intention of studying at the university there, but soon abandoned this idea in order to devote himself to writing. His first play, *Catiline*, aroused little interest, but his second, *The Burial Mound*, was staged, and not unsuccessfully. He held posts as producer and resident dramatist in theatres in Bergen and Christiania successively, but his politics in the latter post were severely criticized, and in 1864 he embarked on a long period of self-imposed exile abroad with his wife and their only child, Sigurd. Recognition of Ibsen's true genius came after the publication in 1866 of the dramatic poem *Brand*, and he was at last awarded an annual grant by the Norwegian Parliament to devote himself to writing. From 1868 to 1891 he lived mainly in Dresden, Munich, and Rome, and during this period wrote most of the prose plays which established his European reputation. *A Doll's House* (1879) went through three editions within four months of publication (and was the first substantial Ibsen production in London, ten years later). *Ghosts* (1881) and *Hedda Gabler* (1890) also aroused storms of controversy, but Ibsen's position as a dramatist of world-wide stature was by now unassailable. He returned to live in Norway in 1891, and his seventieth birthday was the occasion of national celebrations. His literary career was terminated by a stroke in 1900, and he died on 23 May 1906.

JAMES MCFARLANE, editor of the Oxford Ibsen, was Emeritus Professor of European Literature at the University of East Anglia until his death in 1999. His publications include several critical studies of modern European and Scandinavian literature.

OXFORD WORLD'S CLASSICS

For over 100 years Oxford World's Classics have brought readers closer to the world's great literature. Now with over 700 titles—from the 4,000-year-old myths of Mesopotamia to the twentieth century's greatest novels—the series makes available lesser-known as well as celebrated writing.

The pocket-sized hardbacks of the early years contained introductions by Virginia Woolf, T. S. Eliot, Graham Greene, and other literary figures which enriched the experience of reading. Today the series is recognized for its fine scholarship and reliability in texts that span world literature, drama and poetry, religion, philosophy and politics. Each edition includes perceptive commentary and essential background information to meet the changing needs of readers.

OXFORD WORLD'S CLASSICS

==

HENRIK IBSEN

Four Major Plays

==

A Doll's House · Ghosts
Hedda Gabler · The Master Builder

Translated by
JAMES McFARLANE
and
JENS ARUP

With an Introduction by
JAMES McFARLANE

OXFORD
UNIVERSITY PRESS

OXFORD

UNIVERSITY PRESS

Great Clarendon Street, Oxford OX2 6DP

Oxford University Press is a department of the University of Oxford.
It furthers the University's objective of excellence in research, scholarship,
and education by publishing worldwide in

Oxford New York

Athens Auckland Bangkok Bogotá Buenos Aires Calcutta
Cape Town Chennai Dar es Salaam Delhi Florence Hong Kong Istanbul
Karachi Kuala Lumpur Madrid Melbourne Mexico City Mumbai
Nairobi Paris São Paulo Singapore Taipei Tokyo Toronto Warsaw

with associated companies in Berlin Ibadan

Oxford is a registered trade mark of Oxford University Press
in the UK and in certain other countries

Published in the United States
by Oxford University Press Inc., New York

British Library Cataloguing in Publication Data

Data available

Library of Congress Cataloging in Publication Data

Data available

ISBN–13: 978–0–19–283387–7
ISBN–10: 0–19–283387–1

13

Printed in Great Britain by
Clays Ltd, St Ives plc

CONTENTS

INTRODUCTION

In an age when literature addressed itself to the debating of problems, Henrik Ibsen waited for question time and cast his dramas in an interrogative mould. 'I do but ask,' he at one point insisted, 'my call is not to answer.' In its totality his creative career fits almost exactly into the second half of the nineteenth century: his first prentice drama was published in the early spring of 1850, and his final 'dramatic epilogue' appeared in the last December days of 1899. It is however from the second half of this career, and from the last quarter of the century, that the four plays in this volume are drawn. They form part of that incomparable series of twelve investigative 'dramas of contemporary life' which filled these years—a period of sustained creative endeavour unparalleled in the history of the modern theatre and one which gave a whole new impetus and direction to the drama of the twentieth century.

The series began in 1877 with the publication of *Pillars of Society*; and it was largely through its immediate (and multiple) translation into German and its rapid and sensational success in the German theatre that Ibsen began to reach out to a wider European public. But it was the next two plays in the series—*A Doll's House* (1879) and *Ghosts* (1881)—which on their appearance and during the following years and decades were to bring the name of Ibsen inescapably to the attention of the world. The two plays belong inherently together. Indeed, not only did Ibsen himself define *A Doll's House* as 'an introduction to or preparation for *Ghosts*' but he also and more explicitly asserted that '*Ghosts* had to be written. . . . After Nora, Mrs. Alving had of necessity to come.' Together these two plays provoked a storm of outraged controversy that penetrated far beyond the confines of the theatre proper into the leader columns of the Western press and the drawing rooms of polite society.

In much the same way that *A Doll's House* and *Ghosts* thus complement each other, so the other two plays in this volume—*Hedda Gabler* (1890) and *The Master Builder* (1892)—share a common dramatic purpose. As numbers eight and nine in the duodecimal series, they are similarly contiguous. Nevertheless in the intervening years between the two pairs—years in which there appeared *An Enemy of the People* (1882),

The Wild Duck (1884), *Rosmersholm* (1886) and *The Lady from the Sea* (1888)—a distinct shift in the author's preoccupations is evident: from the social to the visionary, from the naturalistic to the symbolic, from the problematical to the psychological, from the demonstrative to the evocative. At the same time, this shift remains firmly located within one unifying progression; and it is useful to see the two *pairs* of plays as relating to each other in a way not dissimilar from the way the individual plays within the pair do. It is not without relevance in this respect that when in later life Ibsen wrote a brief preface to the collected edition of his works, he commended the whole corpus of his authorship as 'a continuing and cohesive whole'.

Most of the work on *A Doll's House* was done while Ibsen was resident in Rome in 1879, though the final revisions to it were made while holidaying in Amalfi later that summer. A few notes and jottings from the previous autumn indicate that from the very first Ibsen was intent on writing a drama which would highlight the anomalous position of women in the prevailingly male-dominated society. 'A woman [he wrote] cannot be herself in contemporary society; it is an exclusively male society with laws drafted by men, and with counsel and judges who judge feminine conduct from the male point of view.' In these notes he claimed to be able to identify two kinds of conscience, one in man and a completely different one in woman; and he pointed to the inevitable confusion over matters of right and wrong that inescapably follows when a woman is judged by man's law, and when in consequence her natural instincts are brought into conflict with the notions of authority she has grown up with.

That the defining starting-point in the genesis of the play should have been a 'problem' of this kind came as a response to the vigorous promptings of his friend and fellow Scandinavian, the critic Georg Brandes. A few years previously, Brandes had insisted that the only way in which a work of literature could show itself as a living and vital thing was 'by subjecting problems to debate'. When in the course of the winter of 1879–80 *A Doll's House* was played in all three Scandinavian capital cities, it was the *problem* treated there that provoked the most intense public discussion. Such furious controversy did the play arouse—it was reported from Stockholm—'that many a social invitation . . . during that winter bore the words: "You are requested not to mention Ibsen's *Doll's House*!" ' In Germany the same vehement public argument followed, exacerbated by the fact that the eminent actress cast for the role of Nora refused in a storm of publicity to play the part of such a monster unless the ending were altered and a more conciliatory one substituted.

It took several years before the play eventually reached the London stage. But when finally on 7 June 1889 *A Doll's House* was produced at the Novelty Theatre, it was—in the words of Harley Granville-Barker —'the most dramatic event of the decade'; and William Archer remarked that if fame were to be measured by mileage of newspaper comment, then Henrik Ibsen had become the most famous man in the English literary world, so much had Nora's departure from her doll's house exercised the mind of contemporary men and women. Although in many circles there was widespread public hostility to the play, there was also a measure of vocal and influential support; and with this came that polarization into 'Ibsenist' and 'anti-Ibsenist' conviction which dominated the cultural scene in Britain in the early 1890s.

By comparison, *Ghosts* was in its impact more subversive, though no less influential. On its publication in Scandinavia, it was so vehemently attacked in the press that its sales in book form were seriously affected. In this new play the 'problem' was an extension of the one that had served *A Doll's House*: the exploration in dramatic form of the fate of contemporary woman to whom society denied any reasonable opportunity for self-fulfilment in a male world. This time Ibsen's jottings asked: 'These women of the modern age, mistreated as daughters, as sisters, as wives, not educated in accordance with their talents, debarred from following their real mission, deprived of their inheritance, embittered in mind—these are the ones who supply the mothers for the next generation. What will result from this?' Now the institution of marriage and the nature of the obligations it imposed on the woman partner were subjected to even sterner and more uncompromising scrutiny in a drama remarkable for the concentration and tautness of its structural design. Ibsen was from the very first in no doubt as to the audaciousness of his theme and the starkness of his treatment of it, especially its readiness to introduce topics about which polite society was normally at pains to preserve a decent reticence. He was determined 'that a few frontier posts should be moved', as he put it, even though he was aware that this would doubtless bring a storm about his ears. In this he was not disappointed. The Scandinavian establishment—in the form of the leading theatres of the three capital cities—repudiated his play completely: indeed, in the Norwegian capital of Christiania it had to wait more than eighteen years for a production at the National Theatre, and at Copenhagen's Royal Theatre even longer. In Germany,

the police authorities refused permission for 'public' performances for
many years, whilst in Britain the first fully public performance licensed
by the Lord Chamberlain was not until 1914.

In contrast to this a whole series of private and so-called independent
theatres throughout Europe seized on the play as one which most
triumphantly embodied their ideas of what 'contemporary' drama
should be. Conspicuous among these were the Meiningen Court
Theatre, the 'Freie Bühne' (which selected this play for its opening
production in Berlin on 29 September 1889), Antoine's 'Théâtre Libre'
in Paris, and J. P. Grein's Independent Theatre in London. The reaction
of the press to the first London production on 13 March 1891 was
memorably recorded by William Archer in the anthology of cuttings
which he compiled on that occasion:

'Ibsen's positively abominable play called *Ghosts* . . . An open drain; a loathsome
sore unbandaged; a dirty act done publicly; a lazar house with all its windows
open . . . Candid foulness . . . Offensive cynicism . . . Ibsen's melancholy and
malodorous world . . . Absolutely loathsome and fetid . . . Gross almost putrid
indecorum . . . Literary carrion . . . Crapulous stuff.'

In an entirely quantitative sense, therefore, it was primarily the
'problem' element in Ibsen that preoccupied the contemporary public;
though not everyone saw as clearly as did Shaw that these two plays
were not indicative but interrogative. In his confidently assertive study
of Ibsen, *The Quintessence of Ibsenism*, Shaw disarmingly indicated the
folly of making confident assertion, especially about *A Doll's House*
and *Ghosts*:

'When you have called Mrs. Alving an emancipated woman or an unprincipled
one, Alving a debauchee or a victim of society, Nora a fearless and noble-
hearted woman or a shocking little liar and an unnatural mother, Helmer a
selfish hound or a model husband and father, according to your bias, you
have said something which is at once true and false, and in both cases perfectly
idle.

The tradition so established has proved within the wider European
context to be remarkably persistent; and among those who were
subsequently to make what Brecht was to call 'the great attempts to
give the problems of the age a theatrical structure' one would probably
wish to include the names of Hauptmann, Shaw, Wedekind, Gorky,
Kaiser and O'Neill as well as that of Brecht himself. It is a tradition
which has acknowledged a *truthful* vision as its prime commitment:

truth, fearlessly recognized and boldly declared, was the supreme objective; truth, however unexpected or unpalatable it might be to received ideas, was the overriding imperative.

In the group of plays of which *A Doll's House* and *Ghosts* are the defining achievements, Ibsen's attention was thus chiefly drawn to those problems stemming from the inhibitions set upon individual freedom and self-realization by social and institutional forces: by commercial hypocrisy, religious intolerance, political expediency, and all the accumulated pressures of conventional morality and established authority. With the passing of time, he became more and more engrossed by the ways of the individual mind, by the clash of personal temperament, by the endless and tragic conflict between the calls of duty and the search for happiness within the individual psyche. Ibsen's plays of the nineties, beginning with *Hedda Gabler* and *The Master Builder*, are often best resolved when read as studies of interlocking and interpersonal relationships. Increasingly his preoccupations were less with public abuses than with private dilemma and anguish, more with what was individual and personal than with what was typical and representative; and with this went a compulsive curiosity about the nature of the tensions, the manifold attractions and repulsions, that hold a shifting and essentially dynamic situation together in moment-to-moment equilibrium: temperamental and sexual incompatibility; personal magnetism and hypnotic force: the undertow of the unconscious mind; the persuasive force of dreams and visions.

On its appearance *Hedda Gabler* was a sad disappointment to many, including even some of Ibsen's most ardent admirers. The reason was precisely because of this shift of focus. Expecting the usual Ibsenist exposure of establishment folly, the castigation of some social abuse, the best they could find in the play was a piece of admittedly brilliant but essentially pointless dramatic portraiture, 'the story of . . . un état d'âme', as Henry James put it at the time.

Once again it is Ibsen's own notebooks that provide the corrective. There, in a wealth of preliminary jottings for the play, we read: 'The demonic thing about Hedda is that she wants to exert an influence over another person'; and again: 'The despairing thing about [Lövborg] is that he wants to control the world, but cannot control himself.' Whereupon, taking our cue from this, we see that *Hedda Gabler* is most convincingly read as the record of a series of personal campaigns for control and domination: over oneself, over others, and over one's world. Hedda, Lövborg, Brack, Thea Elvsted are all plausibly interpreted along these lines; even Tesman and Aunt Julle are responsive to this reading.

The Master Builder, no less than *Hedda Gabler*, is the product of a mind deeply preoccupied with the nature of power, particularly the power of one mind to influence and impose itself upon another. But whereas *Hedda Gabler* is a study in the demonic—Ibsen's own term—*The Master Builder* is a study in the erotic. Potency, the capacity to exert some inherent power, is the theme to which the events of the drama constantly relate. In a basic sexual sense in the first instance: the nature of the power of the male mind over the female, and vice versa. And then by extension into the areas of artistic and professional potency. And ultimately to the sheerly personal potency of individual charisma. Potency, the possession of it, the loss of it, the search for and the wonder at it, the stimulation of and the submission to it are the drama's central concerns, the recurrent forms and images of which cluster and combine into patterns of often unexpected complexity. As when Solness—first by simple force of his hypnotic personality, and then by a more overtly sexual domination—imposes his will on Kaja, then by extension exploits this relationship to maintain by oblique methods a supremacy in the generation battle with youth (in the person of Ragnar), in order ultimately to preserve a kind of surrogate potency in his profession as builder and designer.

At the core of the drama there is of course the hauntingly complex relationship between Solness and Hilde: between man and woman, between youth and age, between a guilt-ridden and remorseful spirit and an aggressively amoral and essentially pagan will. This encounter with Hilde is something to which Solness responds with a hope born of desperation and indeed despair: a hope that he may once again be assisted towards the reassertion of his variously threatened potencies. But in the final consummation it is only Hilde who enjoys an unambiguous triumph, who wins the struggle for possession. 'My ... my ... master builder!' is her last exultant cry.

If *A Doll's House* and *Ghosts* were the plays which by their *succès de scandale* transformed Ibsen from a dramatic author of modest Scandinavian reputation into one of European stature, it was the plays and productions of the nineties that gave him undisputed international status. Ibsen was responsible for a totally new phenomenon—the concerted launching of a single literary or dramatic work in a whole range of the cultural capitals of Europe. These were the years when the publication of a new Ibsen play sent profound cultural reverberations throughout Europe and the world. Within two years of its initial publication in Scandinavia, *Hedda Gabler* had been translated and published in Germany (three times), in Russia (three times), in England and America (twice), in France and in the Netherlands, and shortly afterwards was additionally translated into Italian, Spanish and Polish; moreover, within a year of its composition, it had been played in Munich, Berlin, Helsinki, Stockholm, Copenhagen, Christiania, Rotterdam, London and Paris, and in the following year in St. Petersburg and in Rome. *The Master Builder* had within a year been translated and published in German (thrice), English (twice), French, Italian and Russian; and within three years it had been played not only in many places in Scandinavia (including Finland), but also in London, Manchester, Chicago, Berlin, Leipzig, Paris, Rome, Brussels and Amsterdam. Never before had a dramatic author so dominated the theatres of the world or so monopolized public debate.

After all this has been noted, it would nevertheless be wrong to think of Ibsen's achievement as being wholly or even predominantly attributable to his genius as a 'problem' dramatist. Whilst acknowledging that this was the aspect of his authorship that was most stridently remarked upon, one must also be aware that accompanying it went an equally obsessive and dedicated concern on his part to explore the previously unapprehended subtleties of *prose* dialogue. After the completion of his great verse dramas *Brand* and *Peer Gynt* (in 1866 and 1867 respectively), Ibsen quite deliberately gave himself to the strenuous exploration of what he called 'the far more difficult art' of prose. Never again for the rest of his life did he attempt to use verse as a medium for his drama. The result was the creation of a mode of communication which, behind a façade of what at first sight might seem to be little more than the spare commonplaces of everyday speech, was nevertheless able to convey nuances and profundities of which prose had never been thought capable. This achievement did not go unremarked in his own day; and one now sees that it was precisely those who were themselves among the most sensitive practitioners of language—writers such as Henry James, Maeterlinck, Hofmannsthal, James Joyce, Rilke— who were most immediately seized by this aspect of Ibsen's achievement. Like Maeterlinck, who was conscious in these dramas of what he called a 'dialogue du second degré', they were fascinated by the elusive undertones in Ibsen's dramatic dialogue; they detected a second unspoken reality behind the more immediate surface of the words. Of *The Master Builder*, and particularly of those long (and, to some of

Ibsen's contemporary audiences, forbidding) conversations between Hilde and Solness, Maeterlinck wrote: 'Le poète a tenté de mêler dans une même expression le dialogue intérieur et extérieur. Il règne dans ce drame somnambulique je ne sais quelles puissances nouvelles. Tout ce qui s'y dit cache et découvre à la fois les sources d'une vie inconnue.' Or as Rilke put it more comprehensively, the onward path of Ibsen's authorship was 'an ever more desperate search for visible correlations of the *inwardly* seen'. And, one might add, audible correlations of the inwardly heard. Alongside the 'problematic' tradition inspired by the truth of his vision, his art also in this way gave impetus to that line of development in modern European drama for which the oblique, the implied, the subdued, the elusive, the symbolic are of the essence.

SELECT BIBLIOGRAPHY

1. COLLECTED WORKS IN ENGLISH TRANSLATION

There is no lack of editions of Ibsen's plays: these are of greater or lesser comprehensiveness. William Archer (ed.), *The Collected Works of Henrik Ibsen*, 12 vols (London, 1906–12), was the first comprehensive collection in English translation to be published, and the version by which Ibsen became generally known in the English-speaking world. James McFarlane (ed.), The Oxford Ibsen, 8 vols (London, 1960–77), includes the complete plays, together with Ibsen's notes, jottings and earlier draft versions, as well as critical introductions and other editorial commentary.

2. LETTERS

The Correspondence of Henrik Ibsen, ed. Mary Morison (London, 1905)
Speeches and New Letters, tr. Arne Kildal (London, 1911)
Ibsen: Letters and Speeches, ed. Evert Sprinchorn (New York, 1964; London, 1965)

3. BIOGRAPHIES

Henrik Jæger, *The Life of Henrik Ibsen*, tr. Clara Bell (London, 1890)
Edmund Gosse, *Ibsen* (London, 1907)
Halvdan Koht, *The Life of Ibsen* (London, 1931; rev. ed. New York, 1971)
Adolph E. Zucker, *Ibsen the Master Builder* (London, 1929)
Bergliot Ibsen, *The Three Ibsens*, tr. G. Schjelderup (London, 1951)
Michael Meyer, *Henrik Ibsen*, 3 vols (London, 1967–71)
Hans Heiberg, *Ibsen: A Portrait of the Artist*, tr. Joan Tate (London, 1969)

4. CRITICISM (in chronological order)

George Bernard Shaw, *The Quintessence of Ibsenism* (London, 1891; second augmented ed., London, 1913)
George Bernard Shaw, *Our Theatres in the Nineties*. 3 vols (London, 1932)
Hermann J. Weigand, *The Modern Ibsen: a reconsideration* (New York, 1925)

Brian W. Downs, *Ibsen: the intellectual background* (Cambridge, 1946)

M. C. Bradbrook, *Ibsen the Norwegian* (London, 1948)

P. F. D. Tennant, *Ibsen's Dramatic Technique* (Cambridge, 1948)

Brian W. Downs, *A Study of Six Plays by Ibsen* (Cambridge, 1950)

Raymond Williams, *Drama from Ibsen to Eliot* (London, 1952); 2nd rev. ed. *Drama from Ibsen to Brecht* (London, 1969)

John Northam, *Ibsen's Dramatic Method: a study of the prose dramas* (London, 1953)

F. L. Lucas, *The Drama of Ibsen and Strindberg* (London, 1962)

M. J. Valency, *The Flower and the Castle* (New York, 1964)

Rolf Fjelde (ed.), *Twentieth-century Views on Ibsen* (New York, 1965)

James McFarlane (ed.), *Henrik Ibsen*. Penguin critical anthology (London, 1970)

Michael Egan (ed.), *Ibsen: the Critical Heritage* (London, 1972)

Charles R. Lyons, *Henrik Ibsen: the Divided Consciousness* (S. Illinois, 1972)

John Northam, *Ibsen, a Critical Study* (Cambridge, 1973)

Brian Johnston, *The Ibsen Cycle* (Boston, 1975)

Einar Haugen, *Ibsen's Drama* (Minneapolis, 1979)

Edvard Beyer, *Henrik Ibsen* (London, 1979)

Errol Durbach (ed.), *Ibsen and the Theatre* (London, 1980)

Brian Johnston, *To the Third Empire. Ibsen's Early Drama* (Minneapolis, 1980)

Richard Hornby, *Patterns in Ibsen's Middle Plays* (London, 1981)

John S. Chamberlain, *Ibsen: The Open Vision* (London, 1982)

Errol Durbach, *Ibsen the Romantic* (London, 1982)

John Northam (tr. and ed.), *Ibsen's Poems* (Oslo, 1986)

Charles R. Lyons (ed.), *Critical Essays on Henrik Isben* (Boston, 1987)

James McFarlane, *Ibsen and Meaning: Studies, essays and prefaces 1953–87* (Norwich, 1989)

Robin Young, *Time's Disinherited Children: Childhood, Regression and Sacrifice in the plays of Henrik Ibsen* (Norwich, 1989)

Brian Johnston, *Text and Supertext in Ibsen's Drama* (Pennsylvania, 1989)

Frederick J. Marker and Lise-Lone Marker, *Ibsen's Lively Art: A performance study of the major plays* (Cambridge, 1989)

Charles R. Lyons, *'Hedda Gabler.' Gender, Role and World* (Boston, 1991)

Contemporary Approaches to Ibsen (ed. Daniel Haakonsen, Bjørn Hemmer, Vigdis Ystad et al.), vols. I–VII (Oslo, 1966–91)

The Cambridge Companion to Ibsen (ed. James McFarlane) (Cambridge, 1994)

CHRONOLOGY OF HENRIK IBSEN

1828   20 March Born in Skien, a small timber port about 150 kilometres
       south-west of Christiania (now Oslo), the second son in a family of six
       children

1835   June The Ibsen family moves out of town to a smaller house at Venstøp

1843   Leaves Skien for Grimstad to work as an apothecary's apprentice

1846   9 October A servant girl in the household bears him an illegitimate son

1850   12 April His first play, *Catiline*, published, privately and unsuccessfully
       28 April Arrives in Christiania in the hope of studying at the university
       26 September *The Burial Mound* performed at the Christiania Theatre

1851   26 October Takes up an appointment at the theatre in Bergen as pro-
       ducer and 'dramatic author'

1852   Study tour of theatres in Hamburg, Copenhagen and Dresden

1853   2 January *St John's Night* performed at the Bergen theatre

1855   2 January *Lady Inger* performed

1856   2 January *The Feast at Solhoug* performed

1857   2 January *Olaf Liljekrans* performed
       11 August Moves to a post at the Norwegian Theatre in Christiania

1858   25 April *The Vikings at Helgeland* published
       18 June Marries Suzannah Thoresen

1859   His son (and only legitimate child) Sigurd born

1861   Accused of neglect and inefficiency in his post at the Norwegian Theatre

1862   31 December *Love's Comedy* published

1863   October *The Pretenders* published

1864   Leaves Norway and travels via Copenhagen, Lübeck, Berlin and Vienna
       to Italy, where he remains resident until 1868

1866   15 March *Brand* published. Awarded an annual grant by the Norwegian
       Parliament

1867   14 November *Peer Gynt* published

1868   October Takes up residence in Dresden

1869   30 September *The League of Youth* published
       October–December Travels to Egypt and the Middle East and attends
       the opening of the Suez Canal, as Norway's representative

1871   3 May His collected *Poems* published

1873   16 October *Emperor and Galilean* published

1874   July–September Summer visit to Norway. Invites Edvard Grieg to com-
       pose incidental music for *Peer Gynt*

1875   April Moves from Dresden to Munich for the sake of his son's education

1877   11 October *Pillars of Society* published

1878   Returns to Italy 'for the winter', but remains largely resident there (in Rome) until 1885

1879   4 December *A Doll's House* published

1881   12 December *Ghosts* published

1882   28 November *An Enemy of the People* published

1884   11 November *The Wild Duck* published

1885   June–September Summer visit to Norway
       October Takes up residence once again in Munich

1886   23 November *Rosmersholm* published

1887   9 January Berlin performance of *Ghosts* creates a sensation
       July–October Summer visit to Denmark and Sweden

1888   28 November *The Lady from the Sea* published

1889   7 June *A Doll's House* performed in London—the first substantial Ibsen production in England

1890   December *Hedda Gabler* published

1891   13 March J. T. Grein's Independent Theatre performs *Ghosts* in London to a storm of criticism
       July Leaves Munich for Norway and takes up permanent residence there

1892   11 October His son Sigurd marries Bjørnson's daughter Bergliot
       December *The Master Builder* published

1894   December *Little Eyolf* published

1896   12 December *John Gabriel Borkman* published

1898   Collected editions of his works in Norwegian and German begin publication

1899   19 December *When We Dead Awaken* published

1900   15 March Suffers a stroke, and is unable to do any further literary work

1906   23 May Dies, and is given a public funeral

A DOLL'S HOUSE

[Et dukkehjem]

PLAY IN THREE ACTS

(1879)

Translated by James McFarlane

CHARACTERS

TORVALD HELMER, a lawyer

NORA, his wife

DR. RANK

MRS. KRISTINE LINDE

NILS KROGSTAD

ANNE MARIE, the nursemaid

HELENE, the maid

The Helmers' three children

A porter

The action takes place in the Helmers' flat.

ACT ONE

A pleasant room, tastefully but not expensively furnished. On the back wall, one door on the right leads to the entrance hall, a second door on the left leads to HELMER'S *study. Between these two doors, a piano. In the middle of the left wall, a door; and downstage from it, a window. Near the window a round table with armchairs and a small sofa. In the right wall, upstage, a door; and on the same wall downstage, a porcelain stove with a couple of armchairs and a rocking-chair. Between the stove and the door a small table. Etchings on the walls. A whatnot with china and other small objets d'art; a small bookcase with books in handsome bindings. Carpet on the floor; a fire burns in the stove. A winter's day.*

The front door-bell rings in the hall; a moment later, there is the sound of the front door being opened. NORA *comes into the room, happily humming to herself. She is dressed in her outdoor things, and is carrying lots of parcels which she then puts down on the table, right. She leaves the door into the hall standing open; a* PORTER *can be seen outside holding a Christmas tree and a basket; he hands them to the* MAID *who has opened the door for them.*

NORA. Hide the Christmas tree away carefully, Helene. The children mustn't see it till this evening when it's decorated. [*To the* PORTER, *taking out her purse.*] How much?

PORTER. Fifty öre.

NORA. There's a crown. Keep the change.

[*The* PORTER *thanks her and goes.* NORA *shuts the door. She continues to laugh quietly and happily to herself as she takes off her things. She takes a bag of macaroons out of her pocket and eats one or two; then she walks stealthily across and listens at her husband's door.*]

NORA. Yes, he's in.

[*She begins humming again as she walks over to the table, right.*]

HELMER [*in his study*]. Is that my little sky-lark chirruping out there?

NORA [*busy opening some of the parcels*]. Yes, it is.

HELMER. Is that my little squirrel frisking about?

NORA. Yes!

HELMER. When did my little squirrel get home?

NORA. Just this minute. [*She stuffs the bag of macaroons in her pocket and wipes her mouth.*] Come on out, Torvald, and see what I've bought.

HELMER. I don't want to be disturbed! [*A moment later, he opens the door and looks out, his pen in his hand.*] 'Bought', did you say? All that? Has my little spendthrift been out squandering money again?

NORA. But, Torvald, surely this year we can spread ourselves just a little. This is the first Christmas we haven't had to go carefully.

HELMER. Ah, but that doesn't mean we can afford to be extravagant, you know.

NORA. Oh yes, Torvald, surely we can afford to be just a little bit extravagant now, can't we? Just a teeny-weeny bit. You are getting quite a good salary now, and you are going to earn lots and lots of money.

HELMER. Yes, after the New Year. But it's going to be three whole months before the first pay cheque comes in.

NORA. Pooh! We can always borrow in the meantime.

HELMER. Nora! [*Crosses to her and takes her playfully by the ear.*] Here we go again, you and your frivolous ideas! Suppose I went and borrowed a thousand crowns today, and you went and spent it all over Christmas, then on New Year's Eve a slate fell and hit me on the head and there I was. . . .

NORA [*putting her hand over his mouth*]. Sh! Don't say such horrid things.

HELMER. Yes, but supposing something like that did happen . . . what then?

NORA. If anything as awful as that did happen, I wouldn't care if I owed anybody anything or not.

HELMER. Yes, but what about the people I'd borrowed from?

NORA. Them? Who cares about them! They are only strangers!

HELMER. Nora, Nora! Just like a woman! Seriously though, Nora, you know what I think about these things. No debts! Never borrow! There's always something inhibited, something unpleasant, about a home built on credit and borrowed money. We two have managed to stick it out so far, and that's the way we'll go on for the little time that remains.

NORA [*walks over to the stove*]. Very well, just as you say, Torvald.

HELMER [*following her*]. There, there! My little singing bird mustn't go drooping her wings, eh? Has it got the sulks, that little squirrel of mine? [*Takes out his wallet.*] Nora, what do you think I've got here?

NORA [*quickly turning round*]. Money!

HELMER. There! [*He hands her some notes*]. Good heavens, I know only too well how Christmas runs away with the housekeeping.

NORA [*counts*]. Ten, twenty, thirty, forty. Oh, thank you, thank you, Torvald! This will see me quite a long way.

HELMER. Yes, it'll have to.

NORA. Yes, yes, I'll see that it does. But come over here, I want to show you all the things I've bought. And so cheap! Look, some new clothes for Ivar . . . and a little sword. There's a horse and a trumpet for Bob. And a doll and a doll's cot for Emmy. They are not very grand but she'll have them all broken before long anyway. And I've got some dress material and some handkerchiefs for the maids. Though, really, dear old Anne Marie should have had something better.

HELMER. And what's in this parcel here?

NORA [*shrieking*]. No, Torvald! You mustn't see that till tonight!

HELMER. All right. But tell me now, what did my little spendthrift fancy for herself?

NORA. For me? Puh, I don't really want anything.

HELMER. Of course you do. Anything reasonable that you think you might like, just tell me.

NORA. Well, I don't really know. As a matter of fact, though, Torvald . . .

HELMER. Well?

NORA [*toying with his coat buttons, and without looking at him*]. If you did want to give me something, you could . . . you could always . . .

HELMER. Well, well, out with it!

NORA [*quickly*]. You could always give me money, Torvald. Only what you think you could spare. And then I could buy myself something with it later on.

HELMER. But Nora. . . .

NORA. Oh, please, Torvald dear! Please! I beg you. Then I'd wrap the money up in some pretty gilt paper and hang it on the Christmas tree. Wouldn't that be fun?

HELMER. What do we call my pretty little pet when it runs away with all the money?

NORA. I know, I know, we call it a spendthrift. But please let's do what I said, Torvald. Then I'll have a bit of time to think about what I need most. Isn't that awfully sensible, now, eh?

HELMER [*smiling*]. Yes, it is indeed—that is, if only you really could hold on to the money I gave you, and really did buy something for yourself with it. But it just gets mixed up with the housekeeping and frittered away on all sorts of useless things, and then I have to dig into my pocket all over again.

NORA. Oh but, Torvald. . . .

HELMER. You can't deny it, Nora dear. [*Puts his arm round her waist.*] My pretty little pet is very sweet, but it runs away with an awful lot of money. It's incredible how expensive it is for a man to keep such a pet.

NORA. For shame! How can you say such a thing? As a matter of fact I save everything I can.

HELMER [*laughs*]. Yes, you are right there. Everything you *can*. But you simply can't.

NORA [*hums and smiles quietly and happily*]. Ah, if you only knew how many expenses the likes of us sky-larks and squirrels have, Torvald!

HELMER. What a funny little one you are! Just like your father. Always on the look-out for money, wherever you can lay your hands on it; but as soon as you've got it, it just seems to slip through your fingers. You never seem to know what you've done with it. Well, one must accept you as you are. It's in the blood. Oh yes, it is, Nora. That sort of thing is hereditary.

NORA. Oh, I only wish I'd inherited a few more of Daddy's qualities.

HELMER. And I wouldn't want my pretty little song-bird to be the least bit different from what she is now. But come to think of it, you look rather ... rather ... how shall I put it? ... rather guilty today. . . .

NORA. Do I?

HELMER. Yes, you do indeed. Look me straight in the eye.

NORA [*looks at him*]. Well?

HELMER [*wagging his finger at her*]. My little sweet-tooth surely didn't forget herself in town today?

NORA. No, whatever makes you think that?

HELMER. She didn't just pop into the confectioner's for a moment?

NORA. No, I assure you, Torvald. . . !

HELMER. Didn't try sampling the preserves?

NORA. No, really I didn't.

HELMER. Didn't go nibbling a macaroon or two?

NORA. No, Torvald, honestly, you must believe me. . . !

HELMER. All right then! It's really just my little joke. . . .

NORA [*crosses to the table*]. I would never dream of doing anything you didn't want me to.

HELMER. Of course not, I know that. And then you've given me your word. . . . [*Crosses to her.*] Well then, Nora dearest, you shall keep your little Christmas secrets. They'll all come out tonight, I dare say, when we light the tree.

NORA. Did you remember to invite Dr. Rank?

HELMER. No. But there's really no need. Of course he'll come and have dinner with us. Anyway, I can ask him when he looks in this morning. I've ordered some good wine. Nora, you can't imagine how I am looking forward to this evening.

NORA. So am I. And won't the children enjoy it, Torvald!

HELMER. Oh, what a glorious feeling it is, knowing you've got a nice, safe job, and a good fat income. Don't you agree? Isn't it wonderful, just thinking about it?

NORA. Oh, it's marvellous!

HELMER. Do you remember last Christmas? Three whole weeks beforehand you shut yourself up every evening till after midnight making flowers for the Christmas tree and all the other splendid things you wanted to surprise us with. Ugh, I never felt so bored in all my life.

NORA. I wasn't the least bit bored.

HELMER [*smiling*]. But it turned out a bit of an anticlimax, Nora.

NORA. Oh, you are not going to tease me about that again! How was I to know the cat would get in and pull everything to bits?

HELMER. No, of course you weren't. Poor little Nora! All you wanted was for us to have a nice time—and it's the thought behind it that counts, after all. All the same, it's a good thing we've seen the back of those lean times.

NORA. Yes, really it's marvellous.

HELMER. Now there's no need for me to sit here all on my own, bored to tears. And you don't have to strain your dear little eyes, and work those dainty little fingers to the bone. . . .

NORA [*clapping her hands*]. No, Torvald, I don't, do I? Not any more. Oh, how marvellous it is to hear that! [*Takes his arm.*] Now I want to tell you how I've been thinking we might arrange things, Torvald. As soon as Christmas is over. . . . [*The door-bell rings in the hall.*] Oh, there's the bell. [*Tidies one or two things in the room.*] It's probably a visitor. What a nuisance!

HELMER. Remember I'm not at home to callers.

MAID [*in the doorway*]. There's a lady to see you, ma'am.

NORA. Show her in, please.

MAID [*to* HELMER]. And the doctor's just arrived, too, sir.

HELMER. Did he go straight into my room?

MAID. Yes, he did, sir.

[HELMER *goes into his study. The* MAID *shows in* MRS. LINDE, *who is in travelling clothes, and closes the door after her.*]

MRS. LINDE [*subdued and rather hesitantly*]. How do you do, Nora?

NORA [*uncertainly*]. How do you do?

MRS. LINDE. I'm afraid you don't recognize me.

NORA. No, I don't think I... And yet I seem to.... [*Bursts out suddenly.*] Why! Kristine! Is it really you?

MRS. LINDE. Yes, it's me.

NORA. Kristine! Fancy not recognizing you again! But how was I to, when... [*Gently.*] How you've changed, Kristine!

MRS. LINDE. I dare say I have. In nine... ten years....

NORA. Is it so long since we last saw each other? Yes, it must be. Oh, believe me these last eight years have been such a happy time. And now you've come up to town, too? All that long journey in wintertime. That took courage.

MRS. LINDE. I just arrived this morning on the steamer.

NORA. To enjoy yourself over Christmas, of course. How lovely! Oh, we'll have such fun, you'll see. Do take off your things. You are not cold, are you? [*Helps her.*] There now! Now let's sit down here in comfort beside the stove. No, here, you take the armchair, I'll sit here on the rocking-chair. [*Takes her hands.*] Ah, now you look a bit more like your old self again. It was just that when I first saw you.... But you are a little paler, Kristine... and perhaps even a bit thinner!

MRS. LINDE. And much, much older, Nora.

NORA. Yes, perhaps a little older... very, very little, not really very much. [*Stops suddenly and looks serious.*] Oh, what a thoughtless creature I am, sitting here chattering on like this! Dear, sweet Kristine, can you forgive me?

MRS. LINDE. What do you mean, Nora?

NORA [*gently*]. Poor Kristine, of course you're a widow now.

MRS. LINDE. Yes, my husband died three years ago.

NORA. Oh, I remember now. I read about it in the papers. Oh, Kristine, believe me I often thought at the time of writing to you. But I kept putting it off, something always seemed to crop up.

MRS. LINDE. My dear Nora, I understand so well.

NORA. No, it wasn't very nice of me, Kristine. Oh, you poor thing, what you must have gone through. And didn't he leave you anything?

MRS. LINDE. No.

NORA. And no children?

MRS. LINDE. No.

NORA. Absolutely nothing?

MRS. LINDE. Nothing at all . . . not even a broken heart to grieve over.

NORA [*looks at her incredulously*]. But, Kristine, is that possible?

MRS. LINDE [*smiles sadly and strokes* NORA'S *hair*]. Oh, it sometimes happens, Nora.

NORA. So utterly alone. How terribly sad that must be for you. I have three lovely children. You can't see them for the moment, because they're out with their nanny. But now you must tell me all about yourself. . . .

MRS. LINDE. No, no, I want to hear about you.

NORA. No, you start. I won't be selfish today. I must think only about your affairs today. But there's just one thing I really must tell you. Have you heard about the great stroke of luck we've had in the last few days?

MRS. LINDE. No. What is it?

NORA. What do you think? My husband has just been made Bank Manager!

MRS. LINDE. Your husband? How splendid!

NORA. Isn't it tremendous! It's not a very steady way of making a living, you know, being a lawyer, especially if he refuses to take on anything that's the least bit shady—which of course is what Torvald does, and I think he's quite right. You can imagine how pleased we are! He starts at the Bank straight after New Year, and he's getting a big salary and lots of commission. From now on we'll be able to live quite differently . . . we'll do just what we want. Oh, Kristine, I'm so happy and relieved. I must say it's lovely to have plenty of money and not have to worry. Isn't it?

MRS. LINDE. Yes. It must be nice to have enough, at any rate.

NORA. No, not just enough, but pots and pots of money.

MRS. LINDE [*smiles*]. Nora, Nora, haven't you learned any sense yet? At school you used to be an awful spendthrift.

NORA. Yes, Torvald still says I am. [*Wags her finger.*] But little Nora isn't as stupid as everybody thinks. Oh, we haven't really been in a position where I could afford to spend a lot of money. We've both had to work.

MRS. LINDE. You too?

NORA. Yes, odd jobs—sewing, crochet-work, embroidery and things like that. [*Casually.*] And one or two other things, besides. I suppose you know that Torvald left the Ministry when we got married. There weren't any prospects of promotion in his department, and of course he needed to earn more money than he had before. But the first year he wore himself out completely. He had to take on all kinds of extra jobs, you know, and he found himself working all hours of the day and night. But he couldn't go on like that; and he became seriously ill. The doctors said it was essential for him to go South.

MRS. LINDE. Yes, I believe you spent a whole year in Italy, didn't you?

NORA. That's right. It wasn't easy to get away, I can tell you. It was just after I'd had Ivar. But of course we had to go. Oh, it was an absolutely marvellous trip. And it saved Torvald's life. But it cost an awful lot of money, Kristine.

MRS. LINDE. That I can well imagine.

NORA. Twelve hundred dollars. Four thousand eight hundred crowns. That's a lot of money, Kristine.

MRS. LINDE. Yes, but in such circumstances, one is very lucky if one has it.

NORA. Well, we got it from Daddy, you see.

MRS. LINDE. Ah, that was it. It was just about then your father died, I believe, wasn't it?

NORA. Yes, Kristine, just about then. And do you know, I couldn't even go and look after him. Here was I expecting Ivar any day. And I also had poor Torvald, gravely ill, on my hands. Dear, kind Daddy! I never saw him again, Kristine. Oh, that's the saddest thing that has happened to me in all my married life.

MRS. LINDE. I know you were very fond of him. But after that you left for Italy?

NORA. Yes, we had the money then, and the doctors said it was urgent. We left a month later.

MRS. LINDE. And your husband came back completely cured?

NORA. Fit as a fiddle!

MRS. LINDE. But . . . what about the doctor?

NORA. How do you mean?

MRS. LINDE. I thought the maid said something about the gentleman who came at the same time as me being a doctor.

NORA. Yes, that was Dr. Rank. But this isn't a professional visit. He's our best friend and he always looks in at least once a day. No, Torvald has never had a day's illness since. And the children are fit and healthy, and so am I. [*Jumps up and claps her hands.*] Oh God, oh God, isn't it marvellous to be alive, and to be happy, Kristine! . . . Oh, but I ought to be ashamed of myself . . . Here I go on talking about nothing but myself. [*She sits on a low stool near* MRS. LINDE *and lays her arms on her lap.*] Oh, please, you mustn't be angry with me!

Tell me, is it really true that you didn't love your husband? What made you marry him, then?

MRS. LINDE. My mother was still alive; she was bedridden and helpless. And then I had my two young brothers to look after as well. I didn't think I would be justified in refusing him.

NORA. No, I dare say you are right. I suppose he was fairly wealthy then?

MRS. LINDE. He was quite well off, I believe. But the business was shaky. When he died, it went all to pieces, and there just wasn't anything left.

NORA. What then?

MRS. LINDE. Well, I had to fend for myself, opening a little shop, running a little school, anything I could turn my hand to. These last three years have been one long relentless drudge. But now it's finished, Nora. My poor dear mother doesn't need me any more, she's passed away. Nor the boys either; they're at work now, they can look after themselves.

NORA. What a relief you must find it. . . .

MRS. LINDE. No, Nora! Just unutterably empty. Nobody to live for any more. [*Stands up restlessly.*] That's why I couldn't stand it any longer being cut off up there. Surely it must be a bit easier here to find something to occupy your mind. If only I could manage to find a steady job of some kind, in an office perhaps. . . .

NORA. But, Kristine, that's terribly exhausting; and you look so worn out even before you start. The best thing for you would be a little holiday at some quiet little resort.

MRS. LINDE [*crosses to the window*]. I haven't any father I can fall back on for the money, Nora.

NORA [*rises*]. Oh, please, you mustn't be angry with me!

MRS. LINDE [*goes to her*]. My dear Nora, you mustn't be angry with me either. That's the worst thing about people in my position, they become so bitter. One has nobody to work for, yet one has to be on the look-out all the time. Life has to go on, and one starts thinking only of oneself. Believe it or not, when you told me the good news about your step up, I was pleased not so much for your sake as for mine.

NORA. How do you mean? Ah, I see. You think Torvald might be able to do something for you.

MRS. LINDE. Yes, that's exactly what I thought.

NORA. And so he shall, Kristine. Just leave things to me. I'll bring it up so cleverly . . . I'll think up something to put him in a good mood. Oh, I do so much want to help you.

MRS. LINDE. It is awfully kind of you, Nora, offering to do all this for me, particularly in your case, where you haven't known much trouble or hardship in your own life.

NORA. When I . . . ? I haven't known much . . . ?

MRS. LINDE [*smiling*]. Well, good heavens, a little bit of sewing to do and a few things like that. What a child you are, Nora!

NORA [*tosses her head and walks across the room*]. I wouldn't be too sure of that, if I were you.

MRS. LINDE. Oh?

NORA. You're just like the rest of them. You all think I'm useless when it comes to anything really serious. . . .

MRS. LINDE. Come, come. . . .

NORA. You think I've never had anything much to contend with in this hard world.

MRS. LINDE. Nora dear, you've only just been telling me all the things you've had to put up with.

NORA. Pooh! They were just trivialities! [*Softly.*] I haven't told you about the really big thing.

MRS. LINDE. What big thing? What do you mean?

NORA. I know you rather tend to look down on me, Kristine. But you shouldn't, you know. You are proud of having worked so hard and so long for your mother.

MRS. LINDE. I'm sure I don't look down on anybody. But it's true what you say: I am both proud and happy when I think of how I was able to make Mother's life a little easier towards the end.

NORA. And you are proud when you think of what you have done for your brothers, too.

MRS. LINDE. I think I have every right to be.

NORA. I think so too. But now I'm going to tell you something, Kristine. I too have something to be proud and happy about.

MRS. LINDE. I don't doubt that. But what is it you mean?

NORA. Not so loud. Imagine if Torvald were to hear! He must never on any account . . . nobody must know about it, Kristine, nobody but you.

MRS. LINDE. But what is it?

NORA. Come over here. [*She pulls her down on the sofa beside her.*] Yes, Kristine, I too have something to be proud and happy about. I was the one who saved Torvald's life.

MRS. LINDE. Saved . . . ? How . . . ?

NORA. I told you about our trip to Italy. Torvald would never have recovered but for that. . . .

MRS. LINDE. Well? Your father gave you what money was necessary. . . .

NORA [*smiles*]. That's what Torvald thinks, and everybody else. But . . .

MRS. LINDE. But . . . ?

NORA. Daddy never gave us a penny. I was the one who raised the money.

MRS. LINDE. You? All that money?

NORA. Twelve hundred dollars. Four thousand eight hundred crowns. What do you say to that!

MRS. LINDE. But, Nora, how was it possible? Had you won a sweepstake or something?

NORA [*contemptuously*]. A sweepstake? Pooh! There would have been nothing to it then.

MRS. LINDE. Where did you get it from, then?

NORA [*hums and smiles secretively*]. H'm, tra-la-la!

MRS. LINDE. Because what you couldn't do was borrow it.

NORA. Oh? Why not?

MRS. LINDE. Well, a wife can't borrow without her husband's consent.

NORA [*tossing her head*]. Ah, but when it happens to be a wife with a bit of a sense for business . . . a wife who knows her way about things, then. . . .

MRS. LINDE. But, Nora, I just don't understand. . . .

NORA. You don't have to. I haven't said I did borrow the money. I might have got it some other way. [*Throws herself back on the sofa.*] I might even have got it from some admirer. Anyone as reasonably attractive as I am. . . .

MRS. LINDE. Don't be so silly!

NORA. Now you must be dying of curiosity, Kristine.

MRS. LINDE. Listen to me now, Nora dear—you haven't done anything rash, have you?

NORA [*sitting up again*]. Is it rash to save your husband's life?

MRS. LINDE. I think it was rash to do anything without telling him. . . .

NORA. But the whole point was that he mustn't know anything. Good heavens, can't you see! He wasn't even supposed to know how desperately ill he was. It was me the doctors came and told his life was in danger, that the only way to save him was to go South for a while. Do you think I didn't try talking him into it first? I began dropping hints about how nice it would be if I could be taken on a little trip abroad, like other young wives. I wept, I pleaded. I told him he ought to show some consideration for my condition, and let me have a bit of my own way. And then I suggested he might take out a loan. But at that he nearly lost his temper, Kristine. He said I was being frivolous, that it was his duty as a husband not to give in to all these whims and fancies of mine—as I do believe he called them. All right, I thought, somehow you've got to be saved. And it was then I found a way. . . .

MRS. LINDE. Did your husband never find out from your father that the money hadn't come from him?

NORA. No, never. It was just about the time Daddy died. I'd intended letting him into the secret and asking him not to give me away. But when he was so ill . . . I'm sorry to say it never became necessary.

MRS. LINDE. And you never confided in your husband?

NORA. Good heavens, how could you ever imagine such a thing! When he's so strict about such matters! Besides, Torvald is a man with a good deal of pride—it would be terribly embarrassing and humiliating for him if he thought he owed anything to me. It would spoil everything between us; this happy home of ours would never be the same again.

MRS. LINDE. Are you never going to tell him?

NORA [*reflectively, half-smiling*]. Oh yes, some day perhaps . . . in many years time, when I'm no longer as pretty as I am now. You mustn't laugh! What I mean of course is when Torvald isn't quite so much in love with me as he is now, when he's lost interest in watching me dance, or get dressed up, or recite. Then it might be a good thing to have something in reserve. . . . [*Breaks off.*] What nonsense! That day will never come. Well, what have you got to say to my big secret, Kristine? Still think I'm not much good for anything? One thing, though, it's meant a lot of worry for me, I can tell you. It hasn't always been easy to meet my obligations when the time came. You know in business there is something called quarterly interest, and other things called instalments, and these are always terribly difficult things to cope with. So what I've had to do is save a little here and there, you see, wherever I could. I couldn't really save anything out of the housekeeping, because Torvald has to live in decent style. I couldn't let the children go about badly dressed either—I felt any money I got for them had to go on them alone. Such sweet little things!

MRS. LINDE. Poor Nora! So it had to come out of your own allowance?

NORA. Of course. After all, I was the one it concerned most. Whenever Torvald gave me money for new clothes and such-like, I never spent more than half. And always I bought the simplest and cheapest things. It's a blessing most things look well on me, so Torvald never noticed anything. But sometimes I did feel it was a bit hard, Kristine, because it is nice to be well dressed, isn't it?

MRS. LINDE. Yes, I suppose it is.

NORA. I have had some other sources of income, of course. Last winter I was lucky enough to get quite a bit of copying to do. So I shut myself up every night and sat and wrote through to the small hours of the morning. Oh, sometimes I was so tired, so tired. But it was tremendous fun all the same, sitting there working and earning money like that. It was almost like being a man.

MRS. LINDE. And how much have you been able to pay off like this?

NORA. Well, I can't tell exactly. It's not easy to know where you are with transactions of this kind, you understand. All I know is I've paid off just as much as I could scrape together. Many's the time I was at my wit's end. [*Smiles.*] Then I used to sit here and pretend that some rich old gentleman had fallen in love with me. . . .

MRS. LINDE. What! What gentleman?

NORA. Oh, rubbish! . . . and that now he had died, and when they opened his will, there in big letters were the words: 'My entire fortune is to be paid over, immediately and in cash, to charming Mrs. Nora Helmer.'

MRS. LINDE. But my dear Nora—who *is* this man?

NORA. Good heavens, don't you understand? There never was any old gentleman; it was just something I used to sit here pretending, time and time again, when I didn't know where to turn next for money. But it doesn't make very much difference; as far as I'm concerned, the old boy can do what he likes, I'm tired of him; I can't be bothered any more with him or his will. Because now all my worries are over. [*Jumping up.*] Oh God, what a glorious thought, Kristine! No more worries! Just think of being without a care in the world . . . being able to romp with the children, and making the house nice and attractive, and having things just as Torvald likes to have them! And then spring will soon be here, and blue skies. And maybe we can go away somewhere. I might even see something of the sea again. Oh yes! When you're happy, life is a wonderful thing!

[*The door-bell is heard in the hall.*]

MRS. LINDE [*gets up*]. There's the bell. Perhaps I'd better go.

NORA. No, do stay, please. I don't suppose it's for me; it's probably somebody for Torvald. . . .

MAID [*in the doorway*]. Excuse me, ma'am, but there's a gentleman here wants to see Mr. Helmer, and I didn't quite know . . . because the Doctor is in there. . . .

NORA. Who is the gentleman?

KROGSTAD [*in the doorway*]. It's me, Mrs. Helmer.

[MRS. LINDE *starts, then turns away to the window.*]

NORA [*tense, takes a step towards him and speaks in a low voice*]. You? What is it? What do you want to talk to my husband about?

KROGSTAD. Bank matters . . . in a manner of speaking. I work at the bank, and I hear your husband is to be the new manager. . . .

NORA. So it's . . .

KROGSTAD. Just routine business matters, Mrs. Helmer. Absolutely nothing else.

NORA. Well then, please go into his study.

[*She nods impassively and shuts the hall door behind him; then she walks across and sees to the stove.*]

MRS. LINDE. Nora . . . who was that man?

NORA. His name is Krogstad.

MRS. LINDE. So it really was him.

NORA. Do you know the man?

MRS. LINDE. I used to know him . . . a good many years ago. He was a solicitor's clerk in our district for a while.

NORA. Yes, so he was.

MRS. LINDE. How he's changed!

NORA. His marriage wasn't a very happy one, I believe.

MRS. LINDE. He's a widower now, isn't he?

NORA. With a lot of children. There, it'll burn better now.

[*She closes the stove door and moves the rocking chair a little to one side.*]

MRS. LINDE. He does a certain amount of business on the side, they say?

NORA. Oh? Yes, it's always possible. I just don't know. . . . But let's not think about business . . . it's all so dull.

[DR. RANK *comes in from* HELMER'S *study*.]

DR. RANK [*still in the doorway*]. No, no, Torvald, I won't intrude. I'll just look in on your wife for a moment. [*Shuts the door and notices* MRS. LINDE.] Oh, I beg your pardon. I'm afraid I'm intruding here as well.

NORA. No, not at all! [*Introduces them.*] Dr. Rank . . . Mrs. Linde.

RANK. Ah! A name I've often heard mentioned in this house. I believe I came past you on the stairs as I came in.

MRS. LINDE. I have to take things slowly going upstairs. I find it rather a trial.

RANK. Ah, some little disability somewhere, eh?

MRS. LINDE. Just a bit run down, I think, actually.

RANK. Is that all? Then I suppose you've come to town for a good rest —doing the rounds of the parties?

MRS. LINDE. I have come to look for work.

RANK. Is that supposed to be some kind of sovereign remedy for being run down?

MRS. LINDE. One must live, Doctor.

RANK. Yes, it's generally thought to be necessary.

NORA. Come, come, Dr. Rank. You are quite as keen to live as anybody.

RANK. Quite keen, yes. Miserable as I am, I'm quite ready to let things drag on as long as possible. All my patients are the same. Even those with a moral affliction are no different. As a matter of fact, there's a bad case of that kind in talking with Helmer at this very moment. . . .

MRS. LINDE [*softly*]. Ah!

NORA. Whom do you mean?

RANK. A person called Krogstad—nobody you would know. He's rotten to the core. But even he began talking about having to *live*, as though it were something terribly important.

NORA. Oh? And what did he want to talk to Torvald about?

RANK. I honestly don't know. All I heard was something about the Bank.

NORA. I didn't know that Krog . . . that this Mr. Krogstad had anything to do with the Bank.

RANK. Oh yes, he's got some kind of job down there. [*To* MRS. LINDE.] I wonder if you've got people in your part of the country too who go rushing round sniffing out cases of moral corruption, and then installing the individuals concerned in nice, well-paid jobs where they can keep them under observation. Sound, decent people have to be content to stay out in the cold.

MRS. LINDE. Yet surely it's the sick who most need to be brought in.

RANK [*shrugs his shoulders*]. Well, there we have it. It's that attitude that's turning society into a clinic.

[NORA, *lost in her own thoughts, breaks into smothered laughter and claps her hands.*]

RANK. Why are you laughing at that? Do you know in fact what society is?

NORA. What do I care about your silly old society? I was laughing about something quite different . . . something frightfully funny. Tell me, Dr. Rank, are all the people who work at the Bank dependent on Torvald now?

RANK. Is *that* what you find so frightfully funny?

NORA [*smiles and hums*]. Never you mind! Never you mind! [*Walks about the room.*] Yes, it really is terribly amusing to think that we . . . that Torvald now has power over so many people. [*She takes the bag out of her pocket.*] Dr. Rank, what about a little macaroon?

RANK. Look at this, eh? Macaroons. I thought they were forbidden here.

NORA. Yes, but these are some Kristine gave me.

MRS. LINDE. What? I . . . ?

NORA. Now, now, you needn't be alarmed. You weren't to know that Torvald had forbidden them. He's worried in case they ruin my teeth, you know. Still . . . what's it matter once in a while! Don't you think so, Dr. Rank? Here! [*She pops a macaroon into his mouth.*] And you too, Kristine. And I shall have one as well; just a little one . . . or two at the most. [*She walks about the room again.*] Really I am so happy. There's just one little thing I'd love to do now.

RANK. What's that?

NORA. Something I'd love to say in front of Torvald.

RANK. Then why can't you?

NORA. No, I daren't. It's not very nice.

MRS. LINDE. Not very nice?

RANK. Well, in that case it might not be wise. But to us, I don't see why. . . . What is this you would love to say in front of Helmer?

NORA. I would simply love to say: 'Damn'.

RANK. Are you mad!

MRS. LINDE. Good gracious, Nora. . . !

RANK. Say it! Here he is!

NORA [*hiding the bag of macaroons*]. Sh! Sh!

[*HELMER comes out of his room, his overcoat over his arm and his hat in his hand.*]

NORA [*going over to him*]. Well, Torvald dear, did you get rid of him?

HELMER. Yes, he's just gone.

NORA. Let me introduce you. This is Kristine, who has just arrived in town. . . .

HELMER. Kristine. . . ? You must forgive me, but I don't think I know. . .

NORA. Mrs. Linde, Torvald dear. Kristine Linde.

HELMER. Ah, indeed. A school-friend of my wife's, presumably.

MRS. LINDE. Yes, we were girls together.

NORA. Fancy, Torvald, she's come all this long way just to have a word with you.

HELMER. How is that?

MRS. LINDE. Well, it wasn't really. . . .

NORA. The thing is, Kristine is terribly clever at office work, and she's frightfully keen on finding a job with some efficient man, so that she can learn even more. . . .

HELMER. Very sensible, Mrs. Linde.

NORA. And then when she heard you'd been made Bank Manager— there was a bit in the paper about it—she set off at once. Torvald please! You *will* try and do something for Kristine, won't you? For my sake?

HELMER. Well, that's not altogether impossible. You are a widow, I presume?

MRS. LINDE. Yes.

HELMER. And you've had some experience in business?

MRS. LINDE. A fair amount.

HELMER. Well, it's quite probable I can find you a job, I think. . . .

NORA [*clapping her hands*]. There, you see!

HELMER. You have come at a fortunate moment, Mrs. Linde. . . .

MRS. LINDE. Oh, how can I ever thank you. . . ?

HELMER. Not a bit. [*He puts on his overcoat.*] But for the present I must ask you to excuse me. . . .

RANK. Wait. I'm coming with you.

[*He fetches his fur coat from the hall and warms it at the stove.*]

NORA. Don't be long, Torvald dear.

HELMER. Not more than an hour, that's all.

NORA. Are you leaving too, Kristine?

MRS. LINDE [*putting on her things*]. Yes, I must go and see if I can't find myself a room.

HELMER. Perhaps we can all walk down the road together.

NORA [*helping her*]. What a nuisance we are so limited for space here. I'm afraid it just isn't possible. . . .

MRS. LINDE. Oh, you mustn't dream of it! Goodbye, Nora dear, and thanks for everything.

NORA. Goodbye for the present. But . . . you'll be coming back this evening, of course. And you too, Dr. Rank? What's that? If you are up to it? Of course you'll be up to it. Just wrap yourself up well.

[*They go out, talking, into the hall; children's voices can be heard on the stairs.*]

NORA. Here they are! Here they are! [*She runs to the front door and opens it.* ANNE MARIE, *the nursemaid, enters with the children.*] Come in! Come in! [*She bends down and kisses them.*] Ah! my sweet little darlings. . . . You see them, Kristine? Aren't they lovely!

RANK. Don't stand here chattering in this draught!

HELMER. Come along, Mrs. Linde. The place now becomes unbearable for anybody except mothers.

[DR. RANK, HELMER *and* MRS. LINDE *go down the stairs: the* NURSEMAID *comes into the room with the children, then* NORA, *shutting the door behind her.*]

NORA. How fresh and bright you look! My, what red cheeks you've got! Like apples and roses. [*During the following, the children keep chattering away to her.*] Have you had a nice time? That's splendid. And you gave Emmy and Bob a ride on your sledge? Did you now! Both together! Fancy that! There's a clever boy, Ivar. Oh, let me take her a little while, Anne Marie. There's my sweet little baby-doll! [*She takes the youngest of the children from the nursemaid and dances with her.*] All right, Mummy will dance with Bobby too. What? You've been throwing snowballs? Oh, I wish I'd been there. No, don't bother, Anne Marie, I'll help them off with their things. No, please, let me—I like doing it. You go on in, you look frozen. You'll find some hot coffee on the stove. [*The nursemaid goes into the room, left.* NORA *takes off the children's coats and hats and throws them down anywhere, while the children all talk at once.*] Really! A great big dog came running after you? But he didn't bite. No, the doggies wouldn't bite my pretty little dollies. You mustn't touch the parcels, Ivar! What are they? Wouldn't you like to know! No, no, that's nasty. Now? Shall we play something? What shall we play? Hide and seek? Yes, let's play hide and seek. Bob can hide first. Me first? All right, let me hide first.

[*She and the children play, laughing and shrieking, in this room and in the adjacent room on the right. Finally* NORA *hides under the table; the children come rushing in to look for her but cannot find her; they hear her stifled laughter, rush to the table, lift up the tablecloth and find her. Tremendous shouts of delight. She creeps out and pretends to frighten them. More shouts. Meanwhile there has been a knock at the front door, which nobody has heard. The door half opens, and* KROGSTAD *can be seen. He waits a little; the game continues.*]

KROGSTAD. I beg your pardon, Mrs. Helmer. . . .

NORA [*turns with a stifled cry and half jumps up*]. Ah! What do you want?

KROGSTAD. Excuse me. The front door was standing open. Somebody must have forgotten to shut it. . . .

NORA [*standing up*]. My husband isn't at home, Mr. Krogstad.

KROGSTAD. I know.

NORA. Well . . . what are you doing here?

KROGSTAD. I want a word with you.

NORA. With . . . ? [*Quietly, to the children.*] Go to Anne Marie. What? No, the strange man won't do anything to Mummy. When he's gone we'll have another game. [*She leads the children into the room, left, and shuts the door after them; tense and uneasy.*] You want to speak to me?

KROGSTAD. Yes, I do.

NORA. Today? But it isn't the first of the month yet. . . .

KROGSTAD. No, it's Christmas Eve. It depends entirely on you what sort of Christmas you have.

NORA. What do you want? Today I can't possibly . . .

KROGSTAD. Let's not talk about that for the moment. It's something else. You've got a moment to spare?

NORA. Yes, I suppose so, though . . .

KROGSTAD. Good. I was sitting in Olsen's café, and I saw your husband go down the road. . .

NORA. Did you?

KROGSTAD. . . . with a lady.

NORA. Well?

KROGSTAD. May I be so bold as to ask whether that lady was a Mrs. Linde?

NORA. Yes.

KROGSTAD. Just arrived in town?

NORA. Yes, today.

KROGSTAD. And she's a good friend of yours?

NORA. Yes, she is. But I can't see . . .

KROGSTAD. I also knew her once.

NORA. I know.

KROGSTAD. Oh? So you know all about it. I thought as much. Well, I want to ask you straight: is Mrs. Linde getting a job in the Bank?

NORA. How dare you cross-examine me like this, Mr. Krogstad? You, one of my husband's subordinates? But since you've asked me, I'll tell you. Yes, Mrs. Linde *has* got a job. And I'm the one who got it for her, Mr. Krogstad. Now you know.

KROGSTAD. So my guess was right.

NORA [*walking up and down*]. Oh, I think I can say that some of us have a little influence now and again. Just because one happens to be a woman, that doesn't mean. . . . People in subordinate positions, ought to take care they don't offend anybody . . . who . . . hm . . .

KROGSTAD. . . . has influence?

NORA. Exactly.

KROGSTAD [*changing his tone*]. Mrs. Helmer, will you have the goodness to use your influence on my behalf?

NORA. What? What do you mean?

KROGSTAD. Will you be so good as to see that I keep my modest little job at the Bank?

NORA. What do you mean? Who wants to take it away from you?

KROGSTAD. Oh, you needn't try and pretend to me you don't know. I can quite see that this friend of yours isn't particularly anxious to bump up against me. And I can also see now whom I can thank for being given the sack.

NORA. But I assure you. . . .

KROGSTAD. All right, all right. But to come to the point: there's still time. And I advise you to use your influence to stop it.

NORA. But, Mr. Krogstad, I *have* no influence.

KROGSTAD. Haven't you? I thought just now you said yourself . . .

NORA. I didn't mean it that way, of course. Me? What makes you think I've got any influence of that kind over my husband?

KROGSTAD. I know your husband from our student days. I don't suppose he is any more steadfast than other married men.

NORA. You speak disrespectfully of my husband like that and I'll show you the door.

KROGSTAD. So the lady's got courage.

NORA. I'm not frightened of you any more. After New Year I'll soon be finished with the whole business.

KROGSTAD [*controlling himself*]. Listen to me, Mrs. Helmer. If necessary I shall fight for my little job in the Bank as if I were fighting for my life.

NORA. So it seems.

KROGSTAD. It's not just for the money, that's the last thing I care about. There's something else . . . well, I might as well out with it. You see it's like this. You know as well as anybody that some years ago I got myself mixed up in a bit of trouble.

NORA. I believe I've heard something of the sort.

KROGSTAD. It never got as far as the courts; but immediately it was as if all paths were barred to me. So I started going in for the sort of business you know about. I had to do something, and I think I can say I haven't been one of the worst. But now I have to get out of it. My sons are growing up; for their sake I must try and win back what respectability I can. That job in the Bank was like the first step on the ladder for me. And now your husband wants to kick me off the ladder again, back into the mud.

NORA. But in God's name, Mr. Krogstad, it's quite beyond my power to help you.

KROGSTAD. That's because you haven't the will to help me. But I have ways of making you.

NORA. You wouldn't go and tell my husband I owe you money?

KROGSTAD. Suppose I did tell him?

NORA. It would be a rotten shame. [*Half choking with tears.*] That secret is all my pride and joy—why should he have to hear about it in this nasty, horrid way . . . hear about it from *you*. You would make things horribly unpleasant for me. . . .

KROGSTAD. Merely unpleasant?

NORA [*vehemently*]. Go on, do it then! It'll be all the worse for you. Because then my husband will see for himself what a bad man you are, and then you certainly won't be able to keep your job.

KROGSTAD. I asked whether it was only a bit of domestic unpleasantness you were afraid of?

NORA. If my husband gets to know about it, he'll pay off what's owing at once. And then we'd have nothing more to do with you.

KROGSTAD [*taking a pace towards her*]. Listen, Mrs. Helmer, either you haven't a very good memory, or else you don't understand much about business. I'd better make the position a little bit clearer for you.

NORA. How do you mean?

KROGSTAD. When your husband was ill, you came to me for the loan of twelve hundred dollars.

NORA. I didn't know of anybody else.

KROGSTAD. I promised to find you the money. . . .

NORA. And you did find it.

KROGSTAD. I promised to find you the money on certain conditions. At the time you were so concerned about your husband's illness, and so anxious to get the money for going away with, that I don't think you paid very much attention to all the incidentals. So there is perhaps some point in reminding you of them. Well, I promised to find you the money against an IOU which I drew up for you.

NORA. Yes, and which I signed.

KROGSTAD. Very good. But below that I added a few lines, by which your father was to stand security. This your father was to sign.

NORA. Was to . . . ? He did sign it.

KROGSTAD. I had left the date blank. The idea was that your father was to add the date himself when he signed it. Remember?

NORA. Yes, I think. . . .

KROGSTAD. I then gave you the IOU to post to your father. Wasn't that so?

NORA. Yes.

KROGSTAD. Which of course you did at once. Because only about five or six days later you brought it back to me with your father's signature. I then paid out the money.

NORA. Well? Haven't I paid the instalments regularly?

KROGSTAD. Yes, fairly. But . . . coming back to what we were talking about . . . that was a pretty bad period you were going through then, Mrs. Helmer.

NORA. Yes, it was.

KROGSTAD. Your father was seriously ill, I believe.

NORA. He was very near the end.

KROGSTAD. And died shortly afterwards?

NORA. Yes.

KROGSTAD. Tell me, Mrs. Helmer, do you happen to remember which day your father died? The exact date, I mean.

NORA. Daddy died on 29 September.

KROGSTAD. Quite correct. I made some inquiries. Which brings up a rather curious point [*takes out a paper*] which I simply cannot explain.

NORA. Curious . . . ? I don't know . . .

KROGSTAD. The curious thing is, Mrs. Helmer, that your father signed this document three days after his death.

NORA. What? I don't understand. . . .

KROGSTAD. Your father died on 29 September. But look here. Your father has dated his signature 2 October. Isn't that rather curious, Mrs. Helmer? [NORA *remains silent.*] It's also remarkable that the words '2 October' and the year are not in your father's handwriting, but in a handwriting I rather think I recognize. Well, perhaps that could be explained. Your father might have forgotten to date his signature, and then somebody else might have made a guess at the date later, before the fact of your father's death was known. There is nothing wrong in that. What really matters is the signature. And *that* is of course genuine, Mrs. Helmer? It really was your father who wrote his name here?

NORA [*after a moment's silence, throws her head back and looks at him defiantly*]. No, it wasn't. It was me who signed father's name.

KROGSTAD. Listen to me. I suppose you realize that that is a very dangerous confession?

NORA. Why? You'll soon have all your money back.

KROGSTAD. Let me ask you a question: why didn't you send that document to your father?

NORA. It was impossible. Daddy was ill. If I'd asked him for his signature, I'd have had to tell him what the money was for. Don't you see, when he was as ill as that I couldn't go and tell him that my husband's life was in danger. It was simply impossible.

KROGSTAD. It would have been better for you if you had abandoned the whole trip.

NORA. No, that was impossible. This was the thing that was to save my husband's life. I couldn't give it up.

KROGSTAD. But did it never strike you that this was fraudulent. . . ?

NORA. That wouldn't have meant anything to me. Why should I worry about you? I couldn't stand you, not when you insisted on going through with all those cold-blooded formalities, knowing all the time what a critical state my husband was in.

KROGSTAD. Mrs. Helmer, it's quite clear you still haven't the faintest idea what it is you've committed. But let me tell you, my own offence was no more and no worse than that, and it ruined my entire reputation.

NORA. You? Are you trying to tell me that you once risked everything to save your wife's life?

KROGSTAD. The law takes no account of motives.

NORA. Then they must be very bad laws.

KROGSTAD. Bad or not, if I produce this document in court, you'll be condemned according to them.

NORA. I don't believe it. Isn't a daughter entitled to try and save her father from worry and anxiety on his deathbed? Isn't a wife entitled to save her husband's life? I might not know very much about the law, but I feel sure of one thing: it must say somewhere that things like this are allowed. You mean to say you don't know that—you, when it's your job? You must be a rotten lawyer, Mr. Krogstad.

KROGSTAD. That may be. But when it comes to business transactions— like the sort between us two—perhaps you'll admit I know something about *them*? Good. Now you must please yourself. But I tell you this: if I'm pitched out a second time, you are going to keep me company.

[*He bows and goes out through the hall.*]

NORA [*stands thoughtfully for a moment, then tosses her head*]. Rubbish! He's just trying to scare me. I'm not such a fool as all that. [*Begins gathering up the children's clothes; after a moment she stops.*] Yet . . . ? No, it's impossible! I did it for love, didn't I?

THE CHILDREN [*in the doorway, left*]. Mummy, the gentleman's just gone out of the gate.

NORA. Yes, I know. But you mustn't say anything to anybody about that gentleman. You hear? Not even to Daddy!

THE CHILDREN. All right, Mummy. Are you going to play again?

NORA. No, not just now.

THE CHILDREN. But Mummy, you promised!

NORA. Yes, but I can't just now. Off you go now, I have a lot to do. Off you go, my darlings. [*She herds them carefully into the other room and shuts the door behind them. She sits down on the sofa, picks up her embroidery and works a few stitches, but soon stops.*] No! [*She flings her work down, stands up, goes to the hall door and calls out.*] Helene! Fetch the tree in for me, please. [*She walks across to the table, left, and opens the drawer; again pauses.*] No, really, it's quite impossible!

MAID [*with the Christmas tree*]. Where shall I put it, ma'am?

NORA. On the floor there, in the middle.

MAID. Anything else you want me to bring?

NORA. No, thank you. I've got what I want.

[*The maid has put the tree down and goes out.*]

NORA [*busy decorating the tree*]. Candles here . . . and flowers here.— Revolting man! It's all nonsense! There's nothing to worry about. We'll have a lovely Christmas tree. And I'll do anything you want me to, Torvald; I'll sing for you, dance for you. . . .

[HELMER, *with a bundle of documents under his arm, comes in by the hall door.*]

NORA. Ah, back again already?

HELMER. Yes. Anybody been?

NORA. Here? No.

HELMER. That's funny. I just saw Krogstad leave the house.

NORA. Oh? O yes, that's right. Krogstad was here a minute.

HELMER. Nora, I can tell by your face he's been asking you to put a good word in for him.

NORA. Yes.

HELMER. And you were to pretend it was your own idea? You were to keep quiet about his having been here. He asked you to do that as well, didn't he?

NORA. Yes, Torvald. But . . .

HELMER. Nora, Nora, what possessed you to do a thing like that? Talking to a person like him, making him promises? And then on top of everything, to tell me a lie!

NORA. A lie. . . ?

HELMER. Didn't you say that nobody had been here? [*Wagging his finger at her.*] Never again must my little song-bird do a thing like that! Little song-birds must keep their pretty little beaks out of mischief; no chirruping out of tune! [*Puts his arm round her waist.*] Isn't that the way we want things to be? Yes, of course it is. [*Lets her go.*] So let's say no more about it. [*Sits down by the stove.*] Ah, nice and cosy here!

[*He glances through his papers.*]

NORA [*busy with the Christmas tree, after a short pause*]. Torvald!

HELMAR. Yes.

NORA. I'm so looking forward to the fancy dress ball at the Stenborgs on Boxing Day.

HELMER. And I'm terribly curious to see what sort of surprise you've got for me.

NORA. Oh, it's too silly.

HELMER. Oh?

NORA. I just can't think of anything suitable. Everything seems so absurd, so pointless.

HELMER. Has my little Nora come to *that* conclusion?

NORA [*behind his chair, her arms on the chairback*]. Are you very busy, Torvald?

HELMER. Oh. . . .

NORA. What are all those papers?

HELMER. Bank matters.

NORA. Already?

HELMER. I have persuaded the retiring manager to give me authority to make any changes in organization or personnel I think necessary. I have to work on it over the Christmas week. I want everything straight by the New Year.

NORA. So that was why that poor Krogstad. . . .

HELMER. Hm!

NORA [*still leaning against the back of the chair, running her fingers through his hair*]. If you hadn't been so busy, Torvald, I'd have asked you to do me an awfully big favour.

HELMER. Let me hear it. What's it to be?

NORA. Nobody's got such good taste as you. And the thing is I do so want to look my best at the fancy dress ball. Torvald, couldn't you give me some advice and tell me what you think I ought to go as, and how I should arrange my costume?

HELMER. Aha! So my impulsive little woman is asking for somebody to come to her rescue, eh?

NORA. Please, Torvald, I never get anywhere without your help.

HELMER. Very well, I'll think about it. We'll find something.

NORA. That's sweet of you. [*She goes across to the tree again; pause.*] How pretty these red flowers look.—Tell me, was it really something terribly wrong this man Krogstad did?

HELMER. Forgery. Have you any idea what that means?

NORA. Perhaps circumstances left him no choice?

HELMER. Maybe. Or perhaps, like so many others, he just didn't think. I am not so heartless that I would necessarily want to condemn a man for a single mistake like that.

NORA. Oh no, Torvald, of course not!

HELMER. Many a man might be able to redeem himself, if he honestly confessed his guilt and took his punishment.

NORA. Punishment?

HELMER. But that wasn't the way Krogstad chose. He dodged what was due to him by a cunning trick. And that's what has been the cause of his corruption. ·

NORA. Do you think it would . . . ?

HELMER. Just think how a man with a thing like that on his conscience will always be having to lie and cheat and dissemble; he can never drop the mask, not even with his own wife and children. And the children—*that's* the most terrible part of it, Nora.

NORA. Why?

HELMER. A fog of lies like that in a household, and it spreads disease and infection to every part of it. Every breath the children take in that kind of house is reeking with evil germs.

NORA [*closer behind him*]. Are you sure of that?

HELMER. My dear Nora, as a lawyer I know what I'm talking about. Practically all juvenile delinquents come from homes where the mother is dishonest.

NORA. Why mothers particularly?

HELMER. It's generally traceable to the mothers, but of course fathers can have the same influence. Every lawyer knows that only too well. And yet there's Krogstad been poisoning his own children for years with lies and deceit. That's the reason I call him morally depraved. [*Holds out his hands to her.*] That's why my sweet little Nora must promise me not to try putting in any more good words for him. Shake hands on it. Well? What's this? Give me your hand. There now! That's settled. I assure you I would have found it impossible to work with him. I quite literally feel physically sick in the presence of such people.

NORA [*draws her hand away and walks over to the other side of the Christmas tree*]. How hot it is in here! And I still have such a lot to do.

HELMER [*stands up and collects his papers together*]. Yes, I'd better think of getting some of this read before dinner. I must also think about your costume. And I might even be able to lay my hands on something to wrap in gold paper and hang on the Christmas tree. [*He lays his hand on her head.*] My precious little singing bird.

[*He goes into his study and shuts the door behind him.*]

NORA [*quietly, after a pause*]. Nonsense! It can't be. It's impossible. It *must* be impossible.

MAID [*in the doorway, left*]. The children keep asking so nicely if they can come in and see Mummy.

NORA. No, no, don't let them in! You stay with them, Anne Marie.

MAID. Very well, ma'am.

[*She shuts the door.*]

NORA [*pale with terror*]. Corrupt my children. . . ! Poison my home? [*Short pause; she throws back her head.*] It's not true! It could never, never be true!

ACT TWO

The same room. In the corner beside the piano stands the Christmas tree, stripped, bedraggled and with its candles burnt out. Nora's outdoor things lie on the sofa. NORA, *alone there, walks about restlessly; at last she stops by the sofa and picks up her coat.*

NORA [*putting her coat down again*]. Somebody's coming! [*Crosses to the door, listens.*] No, it's nobody. Nobody will come today, of course, Christmas Day—nor tomorrow, either. But perhaps. . . . [*She opens the door and looks out.*] No, nothing in the letter box; quite empty. [*Comes forward.*] Oh, nonsense! He didn't mean it seriously. Things like that *can't* happen. It's impossible. Why, I have three small children.

[THE NURSEMAID *comes from the room, left, carrying a big cardboard box.*]

NURSEMAID. I finally found it, the box with the fancy dress costumes.

NORA. Thank you. Put it on the table, please.

NURSEMAID [*does this*]. But I'm afraid they are in an awful mess.

NORA. Oh, if only I could rip them up into a thousand pieces!

NURSEMAID. Good heavens, they can be mended all right, with a bit of patience.

NORA. Yes, I'll go over and get Mrs. Linde to help me.

NURSEMAID. Out again? In this terrible weather? You'll catch your death of cold, Ma'am.

NORA. Oh, worse things might happen.—How are the children?

NURSEMAID. Playing with their Christmas presents, poor little things, but . . .

NORA. Do they keep asking for me?

NURSEMAID. They are so used to being with their Mummy.

NORA. Yes, Anne Marie, from now on I can't be with them as often as I was before.

NURSEMAID. Ah well, children get used to anything in time.

NORA. Do you think so? Do you think they would forget their Mummy if she went away for good?

NURSEMAID. Good gracious—for good?

NORA. Tell me, Anne Marie—I've often wondered—how on earth could you bear to hand your child over to strangers?

NURSEMAID. Well, there was nothing else for it when I had to come and nurse my little Nora.

NORA. Yes but . . . how could you *bring* yourself to do it?

NURSEMAID. When I had the chance of such a good place? When a poor girl's been in trouble she must make the best of things. Because *he* didn't help, the rotter.

NORA. But your daughter will have forgotten you.

NURSEMAID. Oh no, she hasn't. She wrote to me when she got confirmed, and again when she got married.

NORA [*putting her arms round her neck*]. Dear old Anne Marie, you were a good mother to me when I was little.

NURSEMAID. My poor little Nora never had any other mother but me.

NORA. And if my little ones only had you, I know you would. . . . Oh, what am I talking about! [*She opens the box.*] Go in to them. I must . . . Tomorrow I'll let you see how pretty I am going to look.

NURSEMAID. Ah, there'll be nobody at the ball as pretty as my Nora.

[*She goes into the room, left.*]

NORA [*begins unpacking the box, but soon throws it down*]. Oh, if only I dare go out. If only I could be sure nobody would come. And that nothing would happen in the meantime here at home. Rubbish— nobody's going to come. I mustn't think about it. Brush this muff. Pretty gloves, pretty gloves! I'll put it right out of my mind. One, two, three, four, five, six. . . . [*Screams.*] Ah, they are coming. . . . [*She starts towards the door, but stops irresolute.* MRS. LINDE *comes from the hall, where she has taken off her things.*] Oh, it's you, Kristine. There's nobody else out there, is there? I'm so glad you've come.

MRS. LINDE. I heard you'd been over looking for me.

NORA. Yes, I was just passing. There's something you must help me with. Come and sit beside me on the sofa here. You see, the Stenborgs are having a fancy dress party upstairs tomorrow evening, and now Torvald wants me to go as a Neapolitan fisher lass and dance the tarantella. I learned it in Capri, you know.

MRS. LINDE. Well, well! So you are going to do a party piece?

NORA. Torvald says I should. Look, here's the costume, Torvald had it made for me down there. But it's got all torn and I simply don't know. . . .

MRS. LINDE. We'll soon have that put right. It's only the trimming come away here and there. Got a needle and thread? Ah, here's what we are after.

NORA. It's awfully kind of you.

MRS. LINDE. So you are going to be all dressed up tomorrow, Nora? Tell you what—I'll pop over for a minute to see you in all your finery. But I'm quite forgetting to thank you for the pleasant time we had last night.

NORA [*gets up and walks across the room*]. Somehow I didn't think yesterday was as nice as things generally are.—You should have come to town a little earlier, Kristine.—Yes, Torvald certainly knows how to make things pleasant about the place.

MRS. LINDE. You too, I should say. You are not your father's daughter for nothing. But tell me, is Dr. Rank always as depressed as he was last night?

NORA. No, last night it was rather obvious. He's got something seriously wrong with him, you know. Tuberculosis of the spine, poor fellow. His father was a horrible man, who used to have mistresses and things like that. That's why the son was always ailing, right from being a child.

MRS. LINDE [*lowering her sewing*]. But my dear Nora, how do you come to know about things like that?

NORA [*walking about the room*]. Huh! When you've got three children, you get these visits from . . . women who have had a certain amount of medical training. And you hear all sorts of things from them.

MRS. LINDE [*begins sewing again; short silence*]. Does Dr. Rank call in every day?

NORA. Every single day. He was Torvald's best friend as a boy, and he's a good friend of *mine*, too. Dr. Rank is almost like one of the family.

MRS. LINDE. But tell me—is he really genuine? What I mean is: doesn't he sometimes rather turn on the charm?

NORA. No, on the contrary. What makes you think that?

MRS. LINDE. When you introduced me yesterday, he claimed he'd often heard my name in this house. But afterwards I noticed your husband hadn't the faintest idea who I was. Then how is it that Dr. Rank should. . . .

NORA. Oh yes, it was quite right what he said, Kristine. You see Torvald is so terribly in love with me that he says he wants me all to himself. When we were first married, it even used to make him sort of jealous if I only as much as mentioned any of my old friends from back home. So of course I stopped doing it. But I often talk to Dr. Rank about such things. He likes hearing about them.

MRS. LINDE. Listen, Nora! In lots of ways you are still a child. Now, I'm a good deal older than you, and a bit more experienced. I'll tell you something: I think you ought to give up all this business with Dr. Rank.

NORA. Give up what business?

MRS. LINDE. The whole thing, I should say. Weren't you saying yesterday something about a rich admirer who was to provide you with money. . . .

NORA. One who's never existed, I regret to say. But what of it?

MRS. LINDE. Has Dr. Rank money?

NORA. Yes, he has.

MRS. LINDE. And no dependents?

NORA. No, nobody. But . . . ?

MRS. LINDE. And he comes to the house every day?

NORA. Yes, I told you.

MRS. LINDE. But how can a man of his position want to pester you like this?

NORA. I simply don't understand.

MRS. LINDE. Don't pretend, Nora. Do you think I don't see now who you borrowed the twelve hundred from?

NORA. Are you out of your mind? Do you really think that? A friend of ours who comes here every day? The whole situation would have been absolutely intolerable.

MRS. LINDE. It *really* isn't him?

NORA. No, I give you my word. It would never have occurred to me for one moment. . . . Anyway, he didn't have the money to lend then. He didn't inherit it till later.

MRS. LINDE. Just as well for you, I'd say, my dear Nora.

NORA. No, it would never have occurred to me to ask Dr. Rank. . . . All the same I'm pretty certain if I were to ask him. . . .

MRS. LINDE. But of course you won't.

NORA. No, of course not. I can't ever imagine it being necessary. But I'm quite certain if ever I were to mention it to Dr. Rank. . . .

MRS. LINDE. Behind your husband's back?

NORA. I have to get myself out of that other business. That's also behind his back. I *must* get myself out of that.

MRS. LINDE. Yes, that's what I said yesterday. But . . .

NORA [*walking up and down*]. A man's better at coping with these things than a woman. . . .

MRS. LINDE. Your own husband, yes.

NORA. Nonsense! [*Stops.*] When you've paid everything you owe, you do get your IOU back again, don't you?

MRS. LINDE. Of course.

NORA. And you can tear it up into a thousand pieces and burn it—the nasty, filthy thing!

MRS. LINDE [*looking fixedly at her, puts down her sewing and slowly rises*]. Nora, you are hiding something from me.

NORA. Is it so obvious?

MRS. LINDE. Something has happened to you since yesterday morning. Nora, what is it?

NORA [*going towards her*]. Kristine! [*Listens.*] Hush! There's Torvald back. Look, you go and sit in there beside the children for the time being. Torvald can't stand the sight of mending lying about. Get Anne Marie to help you.

MRS. LINDE [*gathering a lot of the things together*]. All right, but I'm not leaving until we have thrashed this thing out.

[*She goes into the room, left; at the same time* HELMER *comes in from the hall.*]

NORA [*goes to meet him*]. I've been longing for you to be back, Torvald, dear.

HELMER. Was that the dressmaker. . . ?

NORA. No, it was Kristine; she's helping me with my costume. I think it's going to look very nice. . .

HELMER. Wasn't that a good idea of mine, now?

NORA. Wonderful! But wasn't it also nice of me to let you have your way?

HELMER [*taking her under the chin*]. Nice of you—because you let your husband have his way? All right, you little rogue, I know you didn't mean it that way. But I don't want to disturb you. You'll be wanting to try the costume on, I suppose.

NORA. And I dare say you've got work to do?

HELMER. Yes. [*Shows her a bundle of papers.*] Look at this. I've been down at the Bank. . . .

[*He turns to go into his study.*]

NORA. Torvald!

HELMER [*stopping*]. Yes.

NORA. If a little squirrel were to ask ever so nicely . . . ?

HELMER. Well?

NORA. Would you do something for it?

HELMER. Naturally I would first have to know what it is.

NORA. Please, if only you would let it have its way, and do what it wants, it'd scamper about and do all sorts of marvellous tricks.

HELMER. What is it?

NORA. And the pretty little sky-lark would sing all day long. . . .

HELMER. Huh! It does that anyway.

NORA. I'd pretend I was an elfin child and dance a moonlight dance for you, Torvald.

HELMER. Nora—I hope it's not that business you started on this morning?

NORA [*coming closer*]. Yes, it is, Torvald. I implore you!

HELMER. You have the nerve to bring that up again?

NORA. Yes, yes, you *must* listen to me. You must let Krogstad keep his job at the Bank.

HELMER. My dear Nora, I'm giving his job to Mrs. Linde.

NORA. Yes, it's awfully sweet of you. But couldn't you get rid of somebody else in the office instead of Krogstad?

HELMER. This really is the most incredible obstinacy! Just because you go and make some thoughtless promise to put in a good word for him, you expect me . . .

NORA. It's not that, Torvald. It's for your own sake. That man writes in all the nastiest papers, you told me that yourself. He can do you no end of harm. He terrifies me to death. . . .

HELMER. Aha, now I see. It's your memories of what happened before that are frightening you.

NORA. What do you mean?

HELMER. It's your father you are thinking of.

NORA. Yes . . . yes, that's right. You remember all the nasty insinuations those wicked people put in the papers about Daddy? I honestly
think they would have had him dismissed if the Ministry hadn't
sent you down to investigate, and you hadn't been so kind and
helpful.

HELMER. My dear little Nora, there is a considerable difference between
your father and me. Your father's professional conduct was not
entirely above suspicion. Mine is. And I hope it's going to stay that
way as long as I hold this position.

NORA. But nobody knows what some of these evil people are capable
of. Things could be so nice and pleasant for us here, in the peace
and quiet of our home—you and me and the children, Torvald!
That's why I implore you. . . .

HELMER. The more you plead for him, the more impossible you make
it for me to keep him on. It's already known down at the Bank
that I am going to give Krogstad his notice. If it ever got around
that the new manager had been talked over by his wife. . . .

NORA. What of it?

HELMER. Oh, nothing! As long as the little woman gets her own
stubborn way. . . ! Do you want me to make myself a laughing
stock in the office? . . . Give people the idea that I am susceptible to
any kind of outside pressure? You can imagine how soon I'd feel
the consequences of that! Anyway, there's one other consideration
that makes it impossible to have Krogstad in the Bank as long as
I am manager.

NORA. What's that?

HELMER. At a pinch I might have overlooked his past lapses. . . .

NORA. Of course you could, Torvald!

HELMER. And I'm told he's not bad at his job, either. But we knew each
other rather well when we were younger. It was one of those rather
rash friendships that prove embarrassing in later life. There's no
reason why you shouldn't know we were once on terms of some

familiarity. And he, in his tactless way, makes no attempt to hide the fact, particularly when other people are present. On the contrary, he thinks he has every right to treat me as an equal, with his 'Torvald this' and 'Torvald that' every time he opens his mouth. I find it extremely irritating, I can tell you. He would make my position at the Bank absolutely intolerable.

NORA. Torvald, surely you aren't serious?

HELMER. Oh? Why not?

NORA. Well, it's all so petty.

HELMER. What's that you say? Petty? Do you think I'm petty?

NORA. No, not at all, Torvald dear! And that's why . . .

HELMER. Doesn't make any difference! . . . You call my motives petty; so I must be petty too. Petty! Indeed! Well, we'll put a stop to that, once and for all. [*He opens the hall door and calls.*] Helene!

NORA. What are you going to do?

HELMER [*searching among his papers*]. Settle things. [THE MAID *comes in.*] See this letter? I want you to take it down at once. Get hold of a messenger and get him to deliver it. Quickly. The address is on the outside. There's the money.

MAID. Very good, sir.

[*She goes with the letter.*]

HELMER [*putting his papers together*]. There now, my stubborn little miss.

NORA [*breathless*]. Torvald . . . what was that letter?

HELMER. Krogstad's notice.

NORA. Get it back, Torvald! There's still time! Oh, Torvald, get it back! Please for my sake, for your sake, for the sake of the children! Listen, Torvald, please! You don't realize what it can do to us.

HELMER. Too late.

NORA. Yes, too late.

HELMER. My dear Nora, I forgive you this anxiety of yours, although it is actually a bit of an insult. Oh, but it is, I tell you! It's hardly flattering to suppose that anything this miserable pen-pusher wrote could frighten *me*! But I forgive you all the same, because it is rather a sweet way of showing how much you love me. [*He takes her in his arms.*] This is how things must be, my own darling Nora. When it comes to the point, I've enough strength and enough courage, believe me, for whatever happens. You'll find I'm man enough to take everything on myself.

NORA [*terrified*]. What do you mean?

HELMER. Everything, I said. . . .

NORA [*in command of herself*]. That is something you shall never, never do.

HELMER. All right, then we'll share it, Nora—as man and wife. That's what we'll do. [*Caressing her.*] Does that make you happy now? There, there, don't look at me with those eyes, like a little frightened dove. The whole thing is sheer imagination.—Why don't you run through the tarantella and try out the tambourine? I'll go into my study and shut both the doors, then I won't hear anything. You can make all the noise you want. [*Turns in the doorway.*] And when Rank comes, tell him where he can find me.

[*He nods to her, goes with his papers into his room, and shuts the door behind him.*]

NORA [*wild-eyed with terror, stands as though transfixed*]. He's quite capable of doing it! He would do it! No matter what, he'd do it.— No, never in this world! Anything but that! Help? Some way out. . . ? [*The door-bell rings in the hall.*] Dr. Rank. . . ! Anything but that, *anything*! [*She brushes her hands over her face, pulls herself together and opens the door into the hall.* DR. RANK *is standing outside hanging up his fur coat. During what follows it begins to grow dark.*] Hello, Dr. Rank. I recognized your ring. Do you mind not going in to Torvald just yet, I think he's busy.

RANK. And you?

[DR. RANK *comes into the room and she closes the door behind him.*]

NORA. Oh, you know very well I've always got time for you.

RANK. Thank you. A privilege I shall take advantage of as long as I am able.

NORA. What do you mean—as long as you are able?

RANK. Does that frighten you?

NORA. Well, it's just that it sounds so strange. Is anything likely to happen?

RANK. Only what I have long expected. But I didn't think it would come quite so soon.

NORA [*catching at his arm*]. What have you found out? Dr. Rank, you must tell me!

RANK. I'm slowly sinking. There's nothing to be done about it.

NORA [*with a sigh of relief*]. Oh, it's *you* you're . . . ?

RANK. Who else? No point in deceiving oneself. I am the most wretched of all my patients, Mrs. Helmer. These last few days I've made a careful analysis of my internal economy. Bankrupt! Within a month I shall probably be lying rotting up there in the churchyard.

NORA. Come now, what a ghastly thing to say!

RANK. The whole damned thing is ghastly. But the worst thing is all the ghastliness that has to be gone through first. I only have one more test to make; and when that's done I'll know pretty well when the final disintegration will start. There's something I want to ask you. Helmer is a sensitive soul; he loathes anything that's ugly. I don't want him visiting me. . . .

NORA. But Dr. Rank. . . .

RANK. On no account must he. I won't have it. I'll lock the door on him.—As soon as I'm absolutely certain of the worst, I'll send you my visiting card with a black cross on it. You'll know then the final horrible disintegration has begun.

NORA. Really, you are being quite absurd today. And here was I hoping you would be in a thoroughly good mood.

RANK. With death staring me in the face? Why should I suffer for another man's sins? What justice is there in that? Somewhere, somehow, every single family must be suffering some such cruel retribution. . . .

NORA [*stopping up her ears*]. Rubbish! Do cheer up!

RANK. Yes, really the whole thing's nothing but a huge joke. My poor innocent spine must do penance for my father's gay subaltern life.

NORA [*by the table, left*]. Wasn't he rather partial to asparagus and *pâté de foie gras*?

RANK. Yes, he was. And truffles.

NORA. Truffles, yes. And oysters, too, I believe?

RANK. Yes, oysters, oysters, of course.

NORA. And all the port and champagne that goes with them. It does seem a pity all these delicious things should attack the spine.

RANK. Especially when they attack a poor spine that never had any fun out of them.

NORA. Yes, that is an awful pity.

RANK [*looks at her sharply*]. Hm. . . .

NORA [*after a pause*]. Why did you smile?

RANK. No, it was you who laughed.

NORA. No, it was you who smiled, Dr. Rank!

RANK [*getting up*]. You are a bigger rascal than I thought you were.

NORA. I feel full of mischief today.

RANK. So it seems.

NORA [*putting her hands on his shoulders*]. Dear, dear Dr. Rank, you mustn't go and die on Torvald and me.

RANK. You wouldn't miss me for long. When you are gone, you are soon forgotten.

NORA [*looking at him anxiously*]. Do you think so?

RANK. People make new contacts, then . . .

NORA. Who make new contacts?

RANK. Both you and Helmer will, when I'm gone. You yourself are already well on the way, it seems to me. What was this Mrs. Linde doing here last night?

NORA. Surely you aren't jealous of poor Kristine?

RANK. Yes, I am. She'll be my successor in this house. When I'm done for, I can see this woman. . . .

NORA. Hush! Don't talk so loud, she's in there.

RANK. Today as well? There you are, you see!

NORA. Just to do some sewing on my dress. Good Lord, how absurd you are! [*She sits down on the sofa.*] Now Dr. Rank, cheer up. You'll see tomorrow how nicely I can dance. And you can pretend I'm doing it just for you—and for Torvald as well, of course. [*She takes various things out of the box.*] Come here, Dr. Rank. I want to show you something.

RANK [*sits*]. What is it?

NORA. Look!

RANK. Silk stockings.

NORA. Flesh-coloured! Aren't they lovely! Of course, it's dark here now, but tomorrow. . . . No, no, no, you can only look at the feet. Oh well, you might as well see a bit higher up, too.

RANK. Hm. . . .

NORA. Why are you looking so critical? Don't you think they'll fit?

RANK. I couldn't possibly offer any informed opinion about that.

NORA [*looks at him for a moment*]. Shame on you. [*Hits him lightly across the ear with the stockings.*] Take that! [*Folds them up again.*]

RANK. And what other delights am I to be allowed to see?

NORA. Not another thing. You are too naughty. [*She hums a little and searches among her things.*]

RANK [*after a short pause*]. Sitting here so intimately like this with you, I can't imagine . . . I simply cannot conceive what would have become of me if I had never come to this house.

NORA [*smiles*]. Yes, I rather think you do enjoy coming here.

RANK [*in a low voice, looking fixedly ahead*]. And the thought of having to leave it all . . .

NORA. Nonsense. You aren't leaving.

RANK [*in the same tone*]. . . . without being able to leave behind even the slightest token of gratitude, hardly a fleeting regret even . . . nothing but an empty place to be filled by the first person that comes along.

NORA. Supposing I were to ask you to . . . ? No . . .

RANK. What?

NORA. . . . to show me the extent of your friendship . . .

RANK. Yes?

NORA. I mean . . . to do me a tremendous favour. . . .

RANK. Would you really, for once, give me that pleasure?

NORA. You have no idea what it is.

RANK. All right, tell me.

NORA. No, really I can't, Dr. Rank. It's altogether too much to ask . . . because I need your advice and help as well. . . .

RANK. The more the better. I cannot imagine what you have in mind. But tell me anyway. You do trust me, don't you?

NORA. Yes, I trust you more than anybody I know. You are my best and my most faithful friend. I know that. So I will tell you. Well then, Dr. Rank, there is something you must help me to prevent. You know how deeply, how passionately Torvald is in love with me. He would never hesitate for a moment to sacrifice his life for my sake.

RANK [*bending towards her*]. Nora . . . do you think he's the only one who . . . ?

NORA [*stiffening slightly*]. Who . . . ?

RANK. Who wouldn't gladly give his life for your sake.

NORA [*sadly*]. Oh!

RANK. I swore to myself you would know before I went. I'll never have a better opportunity. Well, Nora! Now you know. And now you know too that you can confide in me as in nobody else.

NORA [*rises and speaks evenly and calmly*]. Let me past.

RANK [*makes way for her, but remains seated*]. Nora. . . .

NORA [*in the hall doorway*]. Helene, bring the lamp in, please. [*Walks over to the stove.*] Oh, my dear Dr. Rank, that really was rather horrid of you.

RANK [*getting up*]. That I have loved you every bit as much as anybody? Is *that* horrid?

NORA. No, but that you had to go and tell me. When it was all so unnecessary. . . .

RANK. What do you mean? Did you know. . . ?

[THE MAID *comes in with the lamp, puts it on the table, and goes out again.*]

RANK. Nora . . . Mrs. Helmer . . . I'm asking you if you knew?

NORA. How can I tell whether I did or didn't. I simply can't tell you. . . . Oh, how could you be so clumsy, Dr. Rank! When everything was so nice.

RANK. Anyway, you know now that I'm at your service, body and soul. So you can speak out.

NORA [*looking at him*]. After this?

RANK. I beg you to tell me what it is.

NORA. I can tell you nothing now.

RANK. You must. You can't torment me like this. Give me a chance— I'll do anything that's humanly possible.

NORA. You can do nothing for me now. Actually, I don't really need any help. It's all just my imagination, really it is. Of course! [*She sits down in the rocking-chair, looks at him and smiles.*] I must say, you are a nice one, Dr. Rank! Don't you feel ashamed of yourself, now the lamp's been brought in?

RANK. No, not exactly. But perhaps I ought to go—for good?

NORA. No, you mustn't do that. You must keep coming just as you've always done. You know very well Torvald would miss you terribly.

RANK. And *you*?

NORA. I always think it's tremendous fun having you.

RANK. That's exactly what gave me wrong ideas. I just can't puzzle you out. I often used to feel you'd just as soon be with me as with Helmer.

NORA. Well, you see, there are those people you love and those people you'd almost rather *be* with.

RANK. Yes, there's something in that.

NORA. When I was a girl at home, I loved Daddy best, of course. But I also thought it great fun if I could slip into the maids' room. For one thing they never preached at me. And they always talked about such exciting things.

RANK. Aha! So it's their role I've taken over!

NORA [*jumps up and crosses to him*]. Oh, my dear, kind Dr. Rank, I didn't mean that at all. But you can see how it's a bit with Torvald as it was with Daddy. . . .

[THE MAID *comes in from the hall.*]

MAID. Please, ma'am. . . !

[*She whispers and hands her a card.*]

NORA [*glances at the card*]. Ah!

[*She puts it in her pocket.*]

RANK. Anything wrong?

NORA. No, no, not at all. It's just . . . it's my new costume. . . .

RANK. How is that? There's your costume in there.

NORA. That one, yes. But this is another one. I've ordered it. Torvald mustn't hear about it. . . .

RANK. Ah, so that's the big secret, is it!

NORA. Yes, that's right. Just go in and see him, will you? He's in the study. Keep him occupied for the time being. . . .

RANK. Don't worry. He shan't escape me.

[*He goes into Helmer's study.*]

NORA [*to the maid*]. Is he waiting in the kitchen?

MAID. Yes, he came up the back stairs. . . .

NORA. But didn't you tell him somebody was here?

MAID. Yes, but it was no good.

NORA. Won't he go?

MAID. No, he won't till he's seen you.

NORA. Let him in, then. But quietly. Helene, you mustn't tell anybody about this. It's a surprise for my husband.

MAID. I understand, ma'am. . . .

[*She goes out.*]

NORA. Here it comes! What I've been dreading! No, no, it can't happen, it *can't* happen.

[*She walks over and bolts Helmer's door. The maid opens the hall door for* KROGSTAD *and shuts it again behind him. He is wearing a fur coat, over-shoes, and a fur cap.*]

NORA [*goes towards him*]. Keep your voice down, my husband is at home.

KROGSTAD. What if he is?

NORA. What do you want with me?

KROGSTAD. To find out something.

NORA. Hurry, then. What is it?

KROGSTAD. You know I've been given notice.

NORA. I couldn't prevent it, Mr. Krogstad, I did my utmost for you, but it was no use.

KROGSTAD. Has your husband so little affection for you? He knows what I can do to you, yet he dares. . . .

NORA. You don't imagine he knows about it!

KROGSTAD. No, I didn't imagine he did. It didn't seem a bit like my good friend Torvald Helmer to show that much courage. . . .

NORA. Mr. Krogstad, I must ask you to show some respect for my husband.

KROGSTAD. Oh, sure! All due respect! But since you are so anxious to keep this business quiet, Mrs. Helmer, I take it you now have a rather clearer idea of just what it is you've done, than you had yesterday.

NORA. Clearer than *you* could ever have given me.

KROGSTAD. Yes, being as I am such a rotten lawyer. . . .

NORA. What do you want with me?

KROGSTAD. I just wanted to see how things stood, Mrs. Helmer. I've been thinking about you all day. Even a mere money-lender, a hack journalist, a—well, even somebody like me has a bit of what you might call feeling.

NORA. Show it then. Think of my little children.

KROGSTAD. Did you or your husband think of mine? But what does it matter now? There was just one thing I wanted to say: you needn't take this business too seriously. I shan't start any proceedings, for the present.

NORA. Ah, I knew you wouldn't.

KROGSTAD. The whole thing can be arranged quite amicably. Nobody need know. Just the three of us.

NORA. My husband must never know.

KROGSTAD. How can you prevent it? Can you pay off the balance?

NORA. No, not immediately.

KROGSTAD. Perhaps you've some way of getting hold of the money in the next few days.

NORA. None I want to make use of.

KROGSTAD. Well, it wouldn't have been very much help to you if you had. Even if you stood there with the cash in your hand and to spare, you still wouldn't get your IOU back from me now.

NORA. What are you going to do with it?

KROGSTAD. Just keep it—have it in my possession. Nobody who isn't implicated need know about it. So if you are thinking of trying any desperate remedies . . .

NORA. Which I am. . . .

KROGSTAD. . . . if you happen to be thinking of running away . . .

NORA. Which I am!

KROGSTAD. . . . or anything worse . . .

NORA. How did you know?

KROGSTAD. . . . forget it!

NORA. How did you know I was thinking of *that*?

KROGSTAD. Most of us think of *that*, to begin with. I did, too; but I didn't have the courage. . . .

NORA [*tonelessly*]. I haven't either.

KROGSTAD [*relieved*]. So you haven't the courage either, eh?

NORA. No, I haven't! I haven't!

KROGSTAD. It would also be very stupid. There'd only be the first domestic storm to get over. . . . I've got a letter to your husband in my pocket here. . . .

NORA. And it's all in there?

KROGSTAD. In as tactful a way as possible.

NORA [*quickly*]. He must never read that letter. Tear it up. I'll find the money somehow.

KROGSTAD. Excuse me, Mrs. Helmer, but I've just told you. . . .

NORA. I'm not talking about the money I owe you. I want to know how much you are demanding from my husband, and I'll get the money.

KROGSTAD. I want no money from your husband.

NORA. What do you want?

KROGSTAD. I'll tell you. I want to get on my feet again, Mrs. Helmer; I want to get to the top. And your husband is going to help me. For the last eighteen months I've gone straight; all that time it's been hard going; I was content to work my way up, step by step. Now I'm being kicked out, and I won't stand for being taken back again as an act of charity. I'm going to get to the top, I tell you. I'm going back into that Bank—with a better job. Your husband is going to create a new vacancy, just for me. . . .

NORA. He'll never do that!

KROGSTAD. He will do it. I know him. He'll do it without so much as a whimper. And once I'm in there with him, you'll see what's what. In less than a year I'll be his right-hand man. It'll be Nils Krogstad, not Torvald Helmer, who'll be running that Bank.

NORA. You'll never live to see that day!

KROGSTAD. You mean you . . . ?

NORA. Now I have the courage.

KROGSTAD. You can't frighten me! A precious pampered little thing like you. . . .

NORA. I'll show you! I'll show you!

KROGSTAD. Under the ice, maybe? Down in the cold, black water? Then being washed up in the spring, bloated, hairless, unrecognizable. . . .

NORA. You can't frighten me.

KROGSTAD. You can't frighten me, either. People don't do that sort of thing, Mrs. Helmer. There wouldn't be any point to it, anyway, I'd still have him right in my pocket.

NORA. Afterwards? When I'm no longer . . .

KROGSTAD. Aren't you forgetting that your reputation would then be entirely in my hands? [NORA *stands looking at him, speechless.*] Well, I've warned you. Don't do anything silly. When Helmer gets my letter, I expect to hear from him. And don't forget: it's him who is forcing me off the straight and narrow again, your own husband! That's something I'll never forgive him for. Goodbye, Mrs. Helmer.

[*He goes out through the hall.* NORA *crosses to the door, opens it slightly, and listens.*]

NORA. He's going. He hasn't left the letter. No, no, that would be impossible! [*Opens the door further and further.*] What's he doing? He's stopped outside. He's not going down the stairs. Has he changed his mind? Is he . . . ? [*A letter falls into the letter-box. Then* KROGSTAD'S *footsteps are heard receding as he walks downstairs.* NORA *gives a stifled cry, runs across the room to the sofa table; pause.*] In the letter-box! [*She creeps stealthily across to the hall door.*] There it is! Torvald, Torvald! It's hopeless now!

MRS. LINDE [*comes into the room, left, carrying the costume*]. There, I think that's everything. Shall we try it on?

NORA [*in a low, hoarse voice*]. Kristine, come here.

MRS. LINDE [*throws the dress down on the sofa*]. What's wrong with you? You look upset.

NORA. Come here. Do you see that letter? *There*, look! Through the glass in the letter-box.

MRS. LINDE. Yes, yes, I can see it.

NORA. It's a letter from Krogstad.

MRS. LINDE. Nora! It was Krogstad who lent you the money!

NORA. Yes. And now Torvald will get to know everything.

MRS. LINDE. Believe me, Nora, it's best for you both.

NORA. But there's more to it than that. I forged a signature. . . .

MRS. LINDE. Heavens above!

NORA. Listen, I want to tell you something, Kristine, so you can be my witness.

MRS. LINDE. What do you mean 'witness'? What do you want me to . . . ?

NORA. If I should go mad . . . which might easily happen . . .

MRS. LINDE. Nora!

NORA. Or if anything happened to me . . . which meant I couldn't be here. . . .

MRS. LINDE. Nora, Nora! Are you out of your mind?

NORA. And if somebody else wanted to take it all upon himself, the whole blame, you understand. . . .

MRS. LINDE. Yes, yes. But what makes you think . . . ?

NORA. Then you must testify that it isn't true, Kristine. I'm not out of my mind; I'm quite sane now. And I tell you this: nobody else knew anything, I alone was responsible for the whole thing. Remember that!

MRS. LINDE. I will. But I don't understand a word of it.

NORA. Why should you? You see something miraculous is going to happen.

MRS. LINDE. Something miraculous?

NORA. Yes, a miracle. But something so terrible as well, Kristine— oh, it must *never* happen, not for anything.

MRS. LINDE. I'm going straight over to talk to Krogstad.

NORA. Don't go. He'll only do you harm.

MRS. LINDE. There was a time when he would have done anything for me.

NORA. Him!

MRS. LINDE. Where does he live?

NORA. How do I know. . . ? Wait a minute. [*She feels in her pocket.*] Here's his card. But the letter, the letter. . . !

HELMER [*from his study, knocking on the door*]. Nora!

NORA [*cries out in terror*]. What's that? What do you want?

HELMER. Don't be frightened. We're not coming in. You've locked the door. Are you trying on?

NORA. Yes, yes, I'm trying on. It looks so nice on me, Torvald.

MRS. LINDE [*who has read the card*]. He lives just round the corner.

NORA. It's no use. It's hopeless. The letter is there in the box.

MRS. LINDE. Your husband keeps the key?

NORA. Always.

MRS. LINDE. Krogstad must ask for his letter back unread, he must find some sort of excuse. . . .

NORA. But this is just the time that Torvald generally . . .

MRS. LINDE. Put him off! Go in and keep him busy. I'll be back as soon as I can.

[*She goes out hastily by the hall door.* NORA *walks over to Helmer's door, opens it and peeps in.*]

NORA. Torvald!

HELMER [*in the study*]. Well, can a man get into his own living-room again now? Come along, Rank, now we'll see . . . [*In the doorway.*] But what's this?

NORA. What, Torvald dear?

HELMER. Rank led me to expect some kind of marvellous transformation.

RANK [*in the doorway*]. That's what I thought too, but I must have been mistaken.

NORA. I'm not showing myself off to anybody before tomorrow.

HELMER. Nora dear, you look tired. You haven't been practising too hard?

NORA. No, I haven't practised at all yet.

HELMER. You'll have to, though.

NORA. Yes, I certainly must, Torvald. But I just can't get anywhere without your help: I've completely forgotten it.

HELMER. We'll soon polish it up.

NORA. Yes, do help me, Torvald. Promise? I'm so nervous. All those people. . . . You must devote yourself exclusively to me this evening. Pens away! Forget all about the office! Promise me, Torvald dear!

HELMER. I promise. This evening I am wholly and entirely at your service . . . helpless little thing that you are. Oh, but while I remember, I'll just look first . . .

[*He goes towards the hall door.*]

NORA. What do you want out there?

HELMER. Just want to see if there are any letters.

NORA. No, don't, Torvald!

HELMER. Why not?

NORA. Torvald, *please*! There aren't any.

HELMER. Just let me see.

[*He starts to go.* NORA, *at the piano, plays the opening bars of the tarantella.*]

HELMER [*at the door, stops*]. Aha!

NORA. I shan't be able to dance tomorrow if I don't rehearse it with you.

HELMER [*walks to her*]. Are you really so nervous, Nora dear?

NORA. Terribly nervous. Let me run through it now. There's still time before supper. Come and sit here and play for me, Torvald dear. Tell me what to do, keep me right—as you always do.

HELMER. Certainly, with pleasure, if that's what you want.

[*He sits at the piano.* NORA *snatches the tambourine out of the box, and also a long gaily-coloured shawl which she drapes round herself, then with a bound she leaps forward.*]

NORA [*shouts*]. Now play for me! Now I'll dance!

[HELMER *plays and* NORA *dances;* DR. RANK *stands at the piano behind Helmer and looks on.*]

HELMER [*playing*]. Not so fast! Not so fast!

NORA. I can't help it.

HELMER. Not so wild, Nora!

NORA. This is how it has to be.

HELMER [*stops*]. No, no, that won't do at all.

NORA [*laughs and swings the tambourine*]. Didn't I tell you?

RANK. Let me play for her.

HELMER[*gets up*]. Yes, do. Then I'll be better able to tell her what to do.

[RANK *sits down at the piano and plays.* NORA *dances more and more wildly.* HELMER *stands by the stove giving her repeated directions as she dances; she does not seem to hear them. Her hair comes undone and falls about her shoulders; she pays no attention and goes on dancing.* MRS. LINDE *enters.*]

MRS. LINDE [*standing as though spellbound in the doorway*]. Ah. . . !

NORA [*dancing*]. See what fun we are having, Kristine.

HELMER. But my dear darling Nora, you are dancing as though your life depended on it.

NORA. It does.

HELMER. Stop, Rank! This is sheer madness. Stop, I say.

[RANK *stops playing and* NORA *comes to a sudden halt.*]

HELMER [*crosses to her*]. I would never have believed it. You have forgotten everything I ever taught you.

NORA [*throwing away the tambourine*]. There you are, you see.

HELMER. Well, some more instruction is certainly needed there.

NORA. Yes, you see how necessary it is. You must go on coaching me right up to the last minute. Promise me, Torvald?

HELMER. You can rely on me.

NORA. You mustn't think about anything else but me until after tomorrow . . . mustn't open any letters . . . mustn't touch the letter-box.

HELMER. Ah, you are still frightened of what that man might . . .

NORA. Yes, yes, I am.

HELMER. I can see from your face there's already a letter there from him.

NORA. I don't know. I think so. But you mustn't read anything like that now. We don't want anything horrid coming between us until all this is over.

RANK [*softly to* HELMER]. I shouldn't cross her.

HELMER [*puts his arm round her*]. The child must have her way. But tomorrow night, when your dance is done. . . .

NORA. Then you are free.

MAID [*in the doorway, right*]. Dinner is served, madam.

NORA. We'll have champagne, Helene.

MAID. Very good, madam.

[*She goes.*]

HELMER. Aha! It's to be quite a banquet, eh?

NORA. With champagne flowing until dawn. [*Shouts.*] And some macaroons, Helene . . . lots of them, for once in a while.

HELMER [*seizing her hands*]. Now, now, not so wild and excitable! Let me see you being my own little singing bird again.

NORA. Oh yes, I will. And if you'll just go in . . . you, too, Dr. Rank. Kristine, you must help me to do my hair.

RANK [*softly, as they leave*]. There isn't anything . . . anything as it were, impending, is there?

HELMER. No, not at all, my dear fellow. It's nothing but these childish fears I was telling you about.

[*They go out to the right.*]

NORA. Well?

MRS. LINDE. He's left town.

NORA. I saw it in your face.

MRS. LINDE. He's coming back tomorrow evening. I left a note for him.

NORA. You shouldn't have done that. You must let things take their course. Because really it's a case for rejoicing, waiting like this for the miracle.

MRS. LINDE. What is it you are waiting for?

NORA. Oh, you wouldn't understand. Go and join the other two. I'll be there in a minute.

[MRS. LINDE *goes into the dining-room.* NORA *stands for a moment as though to collect herself, then looks at her watch.*]

NORA. Five. Seven hours to midnight. Then twenty-four hours till the next midnight. Then the tarantella will be over. Twenty-four and seven? Thirty-one hours to live.

HELMER [*in the doorway, right*]. What's happened to our little sky-lark?

NORA [*running towards him with open arms*]. Here she is!

ACT THREE

The same room. The round table has been moved to the centre of the room, and the chairs placed round it. A lamp is burning on the table. The door to the hall stands open. Dance music can be heard coming from the floor above. MRS. LINDE *is sitting by the table, idly turning over the pages of a book; she tries to read, but does not seem able to concentrate. Once or twice she listens, tensely, for a sound at the front door.*

MRS. LINDE [*looking at her watch*]. Still not here. There isn't much time left. I only hope he hasn't . . . [*She listens again.*] Ah, there he is. [*She goes out into the hall, and cautiously opens the front door. Soft footsteps can be heard on the stairs. She whispers.*] Come in. There's nobody here.

KROGSTAD [*in the doorway*]. I found a note from you at home. What does it all mean?

MRS. LINDE. I *had* to talk to you.

KROGSTAD. Oh? And did it have to be here, in this house?

MRS. LINDE. It wasn't possible over at my place, it hasn't a separate entrance. Come in. We are quite alone. The maid's asleep and the Helmers are at a party upstairs.

KROGSTAD [*comes into the room*]. Well, well! So the Helmers are out dancing tonight! Really?

MRS. LINDE. Yes, why not?

KROGSTAD. Why not indeed!

MRS. LINDE. Well then, Nils. Let's talk.

KROGSTAD. Have we two anything more to talk about?

MRS. LINDE. We have a great deal to talk about.

KROGSTAD. I shouldn't have thought so.

MRS. LINDE. That's because you never really understood me.

KROGSTAD. What else was there to understand, apart from the old, old story? A heartless woman throws a man over the moment something more profitable offers itself.

MRS. LINDE. Do you really think I'm so heartless? Do you think I found it easy to break it off.

KROGSTAD. Didn't you?

MRS. LINDE. You didn't really believe that?

KROGSTAD. If that wasn't the case, why did you write to me as you did?

MRS. LINDE. There was nothing else I could do. If I had to make the break, I felt in duty bound to destroy any feeling that you had for me.

KROGSTAD [*clenching his hands*]. So that's how it was. And all that . . . was for money!

MRS. LINDE. You mustn't forget I had a helpless mother and two young brothers. We couldn't wait for you, Nils. At that time you hadn't much immediate prospect of anything.

KROGSTAD. That may be. But you had no right to throw me over for somebody else.

MRS. LINDE. Well, I don't know. Many's the time I've asked myself whether I was justified.

KROGSTAD [*more quietly*]. When I lost you, it was just as if the ground had slipped away from under my feet. Look at me now: a broken man clinging to the wreck of his life.

MRS. LINDE. Help might be near.

KROGSTAD. It was near. Then you came along and got in the way.

MRS. LINDE. Quite without knowing, Nils. I only heard today it's you I'm supposed to be replacing at the Bank.

KROGSTAD. If you say so, I believe you. But now you do know, aren't you going to withdraw?

MRS. LINDE. No, that wouldn't benefit you in the slightest.

KROGSTAD. Benefit, benefit. . . . ! I would do it just the same.

MRS. LINDE. I have learned to go carefully. Life and hard, bitter necessity have taught me that.

KROGSTAD. And life has taught me not to believe in pretty speeches.

MRS. LINDE. Then life has taught you a very sensible thing. But deeds are something you surely must believe in?

KROGSTAD. How do you mean?

MRS. LINDE. You said you were like a broken man clinging to the wreck of his life.

KROGSTAD. And I said it with good reason.

MRS. LINDE. And I am like a broken woman clinging to the wreck of her life. Nobody to care about, and nobody to care for.

KROGSTAD. It was your own choice.

MRS. LINDE. At the time there was no other choice.

KROGSTAD. Well, what of it?

MRS. LINDE. Nils, what about us two castaways joining forces.

KROGSTAD. What's that you say?

MRS. LINDE. Two of us on *one* wreck surely stand a better chance than each on his own.

KROGSTAD. Kristine!

MRS. LINDE. Why do you suppose I came to town?

KROGSTAD. You mean, you thought of me?

MRS. LINDE. Without work I couldn't live. All my life I have worked, for as long as I can remember; that has always been my one great joy. But now I'm completely alone in the world, and feeling horribly empty and forlorn. There's no pleasure in working only for yourself. Nils, give me somebody and something to work for.

KROGSTAD. I don't believe all this. It's only a woman's hysteria, wanting to be all magnanimous and self-sacrificing.

MRS. LINDE. Have you ever known me hysterical before?

KROGSTAD. Would you really do this? Tell me—do you know all about my past?

MRS. LINDE. Yes.

KROGSTAD. And you know what people think about me?

MRS. LINDE. Just now you hinted you thought you might have been a different person with me.

KROGSTAD. I'm convinced I would.

MRS. LINDE. Couldn't it still happen?

KROGSTAD. Kristine! You know what you are saying, don't you? Yes, you do. I can see you do. Have you really the courage. . . ?

MRS. LINDE. I need someone to mother, and your children need a mother. We two need each other. Nils, I have faith in what, deep down, you are. With you I can face anything.

KROGSTAD [*seizing her hands*]. Thank you, thank you, Kristine. And I'll soon have everybody looking up to me, or I'll know the reason why. Ah, but I was forgetting. . . .

MRS. LINDE. Hush! The tarantella! You must go!

KROGSTAD. Why? What is it?

MRS. LINDE. You hear that dance upstairs? When it's finished they'll be coming.

KROGSTAD. Yes, I'll go. It's too late to do anything. Of course, you know nothing about what steps I've taken against the Helmers.

MRS. LINDE. Yes, Nils, I do know.

KROGSTAD. Yet you still want to go on. . . .

MRS. LINDE. I know how far a man like you can be driven by despair.

KROGSTAD. Oh, if only I could undo what I've done!

MRS. LINDE. You still can. Your letter is still there in the box.

KROGSTAD. Are you sure?

MRS. LINDE. Quite sure. But . . .

KROGSTAD [*regards her searchingly*]. Is that how things are? You want to save your friend at any price? Tell me straight. Is that it?

MRS. LINDE. When you've sold yourself *once* for other people's sake, you don't do it again.

KROGSTAD. I shall demand my letter back.

MRS. LINDE. No, no.

KROGSTAD. Of course I will, I'll wait here till Helmer comes. I'll tell him he has to give me my letter back . . . that it's only about my notice . . . that he mustn't read it. . . .

MRS. LINDE. No, Nils, don't ask for it back.

KROGSTAD. But wasn't that the very reason you got me here?

MRS. LINDE. Yes, that was my first terrified reaction. But that was yesterday, and it's quite incredible the things I've witnessed in this house in the last twenty-four hours. Helmer must know everything. This unhappy secret must come out. Those two must have the whole thing out between them. All this secrecy and deception, it just can't go on.

KROGSTAD. Well, if you want to risk it. . . . But one thing I can do, and I'll do it at once. . . .

MRS. LINDE [*listening*]. Hurry! Go, go! The dance has stopped. We aren't safe a moment longer.

KROGSTAD. I'll wait for you downstairs.

MRS. LINDE. Yes, do. You must see me home.

KROGSTAD. I've never been so incredibly happy before.

[*He goes out by the front door. The door out into the hall remains standing open.*]

MRS. LINDE [*tidies the room a little and gets her hat and coat ready*]. How things change! How things change! Somebody to work for . . . to live for. A home to bring happiness into. Just let me get down to it. . . . I wish they'd come. . . . [*Listens.*] Ah, there they are. . . . Get my things.

[*She takes her coat and hat. The voices of* HELMER *and* NORA *are heard outside. A key is turned and* HELMER *pushes* NORA *almost forcibly into the hall. She is dressed in the Italian costume, with a big black shawl over it. He is in evening dress, and over it a black cloak, open.*]

NORA [*still in the doorway, reluctantly*]. No, no, not in here! I want to go back up again. I don't want to leave so early.

HELMER. But my dearest Nora . . .

NORA. Oh, please, Torvald, I beg you. . . . *Please*, just for another hour.

HELMER. Not another minute, Nora my sweet. You remember what we agreed. There now, come along in. You'll catch cold standing there.

[*He leads her, in spite of her resistance, gently but firmly into the room.*]

MRS. LINDE. Good evening.

NORA. Kristine!

HELMER. Why, Mrs. Linde. You here so late?

MRS. LINDE. Yes. You must forgive me but I did so want to see Nora all dressed up.

NORA. Have you been sitting here waiting for me?

MRS. LINDE. Yes, I'm afraid I wasn't in time to catch you before you went upstairs. And I felt I couldn't leave again without seeing you.

HELMER [*removing* NORA's *shawl*]. Well take a good look at her. I think I can say she's worth looking at. Isn't she lovely, Mrs. Linde?

MRS. LINDE. Yes, I must say. . . .

HELMER. Isn't she quite extraordinarily lovely? That's what everybody at the party thought, too. But she's dreadfully stubborn . . . the sweet little thing! And what shall we do about that? Would you believe it, I nearly had to use force to get her away.

NORA. Oh Torvald, you'll be sorry you didn't let me stay, even for half an hour.

HELMER. You hear that, Mrs. Linde? She dances her tarantella, there's wild applause—which was well deserved, although the performance was perhaps rather realistic . . . I mean, rather more so than was strictly necessary from the artistic point of view. But anyway! The main thing is she was a success, a tremendous success. Was I supposed to let her stay after that? Spoil the effect? No thank you! I took my lovely little Capri girl—my capricious little Capri girl, I might say—by the arm, whisked her once round the room, a curtsey all round, and then—as they say in novels—the beautiful vision vanished. An exit should always be effective, Mrs. Linde. But I just can't get Nora to see that. Phew! It's warm in here. [*He throws his cloak over a chair and opens the door to his study.*] What? It's dark. Oh yes, of course. Excuse me. . . .

[*He goes in and lights a few candles.*]

NORA [*quickly, in a breathless whisper*]. Well?

MRS. LINDE [*softly*]. I've spoken to him.

NORA. And . . . ?

MRS. LINDE. Nora . . . you must tell your husband everything.

NORA [*tonelessly*]. I knew it.

MRS. LINDE. You've got nothing to fear from Krogstad. But you must speak.

NORA. I won't.

MRS. LINDE. Then the letter will.

NORA. Thank you, Kristine. Now I know what's to be done. Hush . . . !

HELMER [*comes in again*]. Well, Mrs. Linde, have you finished admiring her?

MRS. LINDE. Yes. And now I must say good night.

HELMER. Oh, already? Is this yours, this knitting?

MRS. LINDE [*takes it*]. Yes, thank you. I nearly forgot it.

HELMER. So you knit, eh?

MRS. LINDE. Yes.

HELMER. You should embroider instead, you know.

MRS. LINDE. Oh? Why?

HELMER. So much prettier. Watch! You hold the embroidery like this in the left hand, and then you take the needle in the right hand, like this, and you describe a long, graceful curve. Isn't that right?

MRS. LINDE. Yes, I suppose so. . . .

HELMER. Whereas knitting on the other hand just can't help being ugly. Look! Arms pressed into the sides, the knitting needles going up and down—there's something Chinese about it. . . . Ah, that was marvellous champagne they served tonight.

MRS. LINDE. Well, good night, Nora! And stop being so stubborn.

HELMER. Well said, Mrs. Linde!

MRS. LINDE. Good night, Mr. Helmer.

HELMER [*accompanying her to the door*]. Good night, good night! You'll get home all right, I hope? I'd be only too pleased to . . . But you haven't far to walk. Good night, good night! [*She goes; he shuts the door behind her and comes in again.*] There we are, got rid of her at last. She's a frightful bore, that woman.

NORA. Aren't you very tired, Torvald?

HELMER. Not in the least.

NORA. Not sleepy?

HELMER. Not at all. On the contrary, I feel extremely lively. What about you? Yes, you look quite tired and sleepy.

NORA. Yes, I'm very tired. I just want to fall straight off to sleep.

HELMER. There you are, you see! Wasn't I right in thinking we shouldn't stay any longer.

NORA. Oh, everything you do is right.

HELMER [*kissing her forehead*]. There's my little sky-lark talking common sense. Did you notice how gay Rank was this evening?

NORA. Oh, was he? I didn't get a chance to talk to him.

HELMER. I hardly did either. But it's a long time since I saw him in such a good mood. [*Looks at* NORA *for a moment or two, then comes nearer her.*] Ah, it's wonderful to be back in our own home again, and quite alone with you. How irresistibly lovely you are, Nora!

NORA. Don't look at me like that, Torvald!

HELMER. Can't I look at my most treasured possession? At all this loveliness that's mine and mine alone, completely and utterly mine.

NORA [*walks round to the other side of the table*]. You mustn't talk to me like that tonight.

HELMER [*following her*]. You still have the tarantella in your blood, I see. And that makes you even more desirable. Listen! The guests are beginning to leave now. [*Softly.*] Nora . . . soon the whole house will be silent.

NORA. I should hope so.

HELMER. Of course you do, don't you, Nora my darling? You know, whenever I'm out at a party with you . . . do you know why I never talk to you very much, why I always stand away from you and only steal a quick glance at you now and then . . . do you know why I do that? It's because I'm pretending we are secretly in love, secretly engaged and nobody suspects there is anything between us.

NORA. Yes, yes. I know your thoughts are always with me, of course.

HELMER. And when it's time to go, and I lay your shawl round those shapely, young shoulders, round the exquisite curve of your neck . . . I pretend that you are my young bride, that we are just leaving our wedding, that I am taking you to our new home for the first time . . to be alone with you for the first time . . . quite alone with your young and trembling loveliness! All evening I've been longing for you, and nothing else. And as I watched you darting and swaying in the tarantella, my blood was on fire . . . I couldn't bear it any longer . . . and that's why I brought you down here with me so early. . . .

NORA. Go away, Torvald! Please leave me alone. I won't have it.

HELMER. What's this? It's just your little game isn't it, my little Nora. Won't! Won't! Am I not your husband. . . ?

[*There is a knock on the front door.*]

NORA [*startled*]. Listen . . . !

HELMER [*going towards the hall*]. Who's there?

RANK [*outside*]. It's me. Can I come in for a minute?

HELMER [*in a low voice, annoyed*]. Oh, what does he want now? [*Aloud.*] Wait a moment. [*He walks across and opens the door.*] How nice of you to look in on your way out.

RANK. I fancied I heard your voice and I thought I would just look in.

[*He takes a quick glance round.*] Ah yes, this dear, familiar old place! How cosy and comfortable you've got things here, you two.

HELMER. You seemed to be having a pretty good time upstairs yourself.

RANK. Capital! Why shouldn't I? Why not make the most of things in this world? At least as much as one can, and for as long as one can. The wine was excellent. . . .

HELMER. Especially the champagne.

RANK. You noticed that too, did you? It's incredible the amount I was able to put away.

NORA. Torvald also drank a lot of champagne this evening.

RANK. Oh?

NORA. Yes, and that always makes him quite merry.

RANK. Well, why shouldn't a man allow himself a jolly evening after a day well spent?

HELMER. Well spent? I'm afraid I can't exactly claim that.

RANK [*clapping him on the shoulder*]. But I can, you see!

NORA. Dr. Rank, am I right in thinking you carried out a certain laboratory test today?

RANK. Exactly.

HELMER. Look at our little Nora talking about laboratory tests!

NORA. And may I congratulate you on the result?

RANK. You may indeed.

NORA. So it was good?

RANK. The best possible, for both doctor and patient—certainty!

NORA [*quickly and searchingly*]. Certainty?

RANK. Absolute certainty. So why shouldn't I allow myself a jolly evening after that?

NORA. Quite right, Dr. Rank.

HELMER. I quite agree. As long as you don't suffer for it in the morning.

RANK. Well, you never get anything for nothing in this life.

NORA. Dr. Rank . . . you are very fond of masquerades, aren't you?

RANK. Yes, when there are plenty of amusing disguises. . . .

NORA. Tell me, what shall we two go as next time?

HELMER. There's frivolity for you . . . thinking about the next time already!

RANK. We two? I'll tell you. You must go as Lady Luck. . . .

HELMER. Yes, but how do you find a costume to suggest *that*?

RANK. Your wife could simply go in her everyday clothes. . . .

HELMER. That was nicely said. But don't you know what you would be?

RANK. Yes, my dear friend, I know exactly what I shall be.

HELMER. Well?

RANK. At the next masquerade, I shall be invisible.

HELMER. That's a funny idea!

RANK. There's a big black cloak . . . haven't you heard of the cloak of invisibility? That comes right down over you, and then nobody can see you.

HELMER [*suppressing a smile*]. Of course, that's right.

RANK. But I'm clean forgetting what I came for. Helmer, give me a cigar, one of the dark Havanas.

HELMER. With the greatest of pleasure.

[*He offers his case.*]

RANK [*takes one and cuts the end off*]. Thanks.

NORA [*strikes a match*]. Let me give you a light.

RANK. Thank you. [*She holds out the match and he lights his cigar.*] And now, goodbye!

HELMER. Goodbye, goodbye, my dear fellow!

NORA. Sleep well, Dr. Rank.

RANK. Thank you for that wish.

NORA. Wish me the same.

RANK. You? All right, if you want me to. . . . Sleep well. And thanks for the light.

[*He nods to them both, and goes.*]

HELMER [*subdued*]. He's had a lot to drink.

NORA [*absently*]. Very likely.

[HELMER *takes a bunch of keys out of his pocket and goes out into the hall.*]

NORA. Torvald . . . what do you want there?

HELMER. I must empty the letter-box, it's quite full. There'll be no room for the papers in the morning. . . .

NORA. Are you going to work tonight?

HELMER. You know very well I'm not. Hello, what's this? Somebody's been at the lock.

NORA. At the lock?

HELMER. Yes, I'm sure of it. Why should that be? I'd hardly have thought the maids . . . ? Here's a broken hair-pin. Nora, it's one of yours. . . .

NORA [*quickly*]. It must have been the children. . . .

HELMER. Then you'd better tell them not to. Ah . . . there . . . I've managed to get it open. [*He takes the things out and shouts into the kitchen.*] Helene! . . . Helene, put the light out in the hall. [*He comes into the room again with the letters in his hand and shuts the hall door.*] Look how it all mounts up. [*Runs through them.*] What's this?

NORA. The letter! Oh no, Torvald, no!

HELMER. Two visiting cards . . . from Dr. Rank.

NORA. From Dr. Rank?

HELMER [*looking at them*]. Dr. Rank, Medical Practitioner. They were on top. He must have put them in as he left.

NORA. Is there anything on them?

HELMER. There's a black cross above his name. Look. What an uncanny idea. It's just as if he were announcing his own death.

NORA. He is.

HELMER. What? What do you know about it? Has he said anything to you?

NORA. Yes. He said when these cards came, he would have taken his last leave of us. He was going to shut himself up and die.

HELMER. Poor fellow! Of course I knew we couldn't keep him with us very long. But so soon. . . . And hiding himself away like a wounded animal.

NORA. When it has to happen, it's best that it should happen without words. Don't you think so, Torvald?

HELMER [*walking up and down*]. He had grown so close to us. I don't think I can imagine him gone. His suffering and his loneliness seemed almost to provide a background of dark cloud to the sunshine of our lives. Well, perhaps it's all for the best. For him at any rate. [*Pauses.*] And maybe for us as well, Nora. Now there's just the two of us. [*Puts his arms round her.*] Oh, my darling wife, I can't hold you close enough. You know, Nora . . . many's the time I wish you were threatened by some terrible danger so I could risk everything, body and soul, for your sake.

NORA [*tears herself free and says firmly and decisively*]. Now you must read your letters, Torvald.

HELMER. No, no, not tonight. I want to be with you, my darling wife.

NORA. Knowing all the time your friend is dying. . . ?

HELMER. You are right. It's been a shock to both of us. This ugly thing has come between us . . . thoughts of death and decay. We must try to free ourselves from it. Until then . . . we shall go our separate ways.

NORA [*her arms round his neck*]. Torvald . . . good night! Good night!

HELMER [*kisses her forehead*]. Goodnight, my little singing bird. Sleep well, Nora, I'll just read through my letters.

[*He takes the letters into his room and shuts the door behind him.*]

NORA [*gropes around her, wild-eyed, seizes Helmer's cloak, wraps it round herself, and whispers quickly, hoarsely, spasmodically*]. Never see him again. Never, never, never. [*Throws her shawl over her head.*] And never see the children again either. Never, never. Oh, that black icy water. Oh, that bottomless . . . ! If only it were all over! He's got it now. Now he's reading it. Oh no, no! Not yet! Torvald, goodbye . . . and my children. . . .

[*She rushes out in the direction of the hall; at the same moment* HELMER *flings open his door and stands there with an open letter in his hand.*]

HELMER. Nora!

NORA [*shrieks*]. Ah!

HELMER. What is this? Do you know what is in this letter?

NORA. Yes, I know. Let me go! Let me out!

HELMER [*holds her back*]. Where are you going?

NORA [*trying to tear herself free*]. You mustn't try to save me, Torvald!

HELMER [*reels back*]. True! Is it true what he writes? How dreadful! No, no, it can't possibly be true.

NORA. It *is* true. I loved you more than anything else in the world.

HELMER. Don't come to me with a lot of paltry excuses!

NORA [*taking a step towards him*]. Torvald. . . !

HELMER. Miserable woman . . . what is this you have done?

NORA. Let me go. I won't have you taking the blame for me. You mustn't take it on yourself.

HELMER. Stop play-acting! [*Locks the front door.*] You are staying here to give an account of yourself. Do you understand what you have done? Answer me! Do you understand?

NORA [*looking fixedly at him, her face hardening*]. Yes, now I'm really beginning to understand.

HELMER [*walking up and down*]. Oh, what a terrible awakening this is. All these eight years . . . this woman who was my pride and joy . . . a hypocrite, a liar, worse than that, a criminal! Oh, how utterly squalid it all is! Ugh! Ugh! [NORA *remains silent and looks fixedly at him.*] I should have realized something like this would happen. I should have seen it coming. All your father's irresponsible ways. . . . Quiet! All your father's irresponsible ways are coming out in you. No religion, no morals, no sense of duty. . . . Oh, this is my punishment for turning a blind eye to him. It was for your sake I did it, and this is what I get for it.

NORA. Yes, this.

HELMER. Now you have ruined my entire happiness, jeopardized my whole future. It's terrible to think of. Here I am, at the mercy of a thoroughly unscrupulous person; he can do whatever he likes with me, demand anything be wants, order me about just as he chooses . . . and I daren't even whimper. I'm done for, a miserable failure, and it's all the fault of a feather-brained woman!

NORA. When I've left this world behind, you will be free.

HELMER. Oh, stop pretending! Your father was just the same, always ready with fine phrases. What good would it do me if you left this world behind, as you put it? Not the slightest bit of good. He can still let it all come out, if he likes; and if he does, people might even suspect me of being an accomplice in these criminal acts of yours. They might even think I was the one behind it all, that it was I who pushed you into it! And it's you I have to thank for this . . . and when I've taken such good care of you, all our married life. Now do you understand what you have done to me?

NORA [*coldly and calmly*]. Yes.

HELMER. I just can't understand it, it's so incredible. But we must see about putting things right. Take that shawl off. Take it off, I tell you! I must see if I can't find some way or other of appeasing him. The thing must be hushed up at all costs. And as far as you and I are concerned, things must appear to go on exactly as before. But only in the eyes of the world, of course. In other words you'll go on living here; that's understood. But you will not be allowed to bring up the children, I can't trust you with them. . . . Oh, that I should have to say this to the woman I loved so dearly, the woman I still. . . . Well, that must be all over and done with. From now on, there can be no question of happiness. All we can do is save the bits and pieces from the wreck, preserve appearances. . . . [*The front door-bell rings.* HELMER *gives a start.*] What's that? So late? How terrible, supposing. . . . If he should . . . ? Hide, Nora! Say you are not well.

[NORA *stands motionless.* HELMER *walks across and opens the door into the hall.*]

MAID [*half dressed, in the hall*]. It's a note for Mrs. Helmer.

HELMER. Give it to me. [*He snatches the note and shuts the door.*] Yes, it's from him. You can't have it. I want to read it myself.

NORA. You read it then.

HELMER [*by the lamp*]. I hardly dare. Perhaps this is the end, for both of us. Well, I *must* know. [*He opens the note hurriedly, reads a few lines, looks at another enclosed sheet, and gives a cry of joy.*] Nora! [NORA *looks at him inquiringly.*] Nora! I must read it again. Yes, yes, it's true! I am saved! Nora, I am saved!

NORA. And me?

HELMER. You too, of course, we are both saved, you as well as me. Look, he's sent your IOU back. He sends his regrets and apologies for what he has done. . . . His luck has changed. . . . Oh, what does it matter what he says. We are saved, Nora! Nobody can do anything to you now. Oh, Nora, Nora . . . but let's get rid of this disgusting thing first. Let me see. . . . [*He glances at the IOU.*] No, I don't want to see it. I don't want it to be anything but a dream. [*He tears up the IOU and both letters, throws all the pieces into the stove and watches them burn.*] Well, that's the end of that. He said in his note you'd known since Christmas Eve. . . . You must have had three terrible days of it, Nora.

NORA. These three days haven't been easy.

HELMER. The agonies you must have gone through! When the only way out seemed to be. . . . No, let's forget the whole ghastly thing. We can rejoice and say: It's all over! It's all over! Listen to me, Nora! You don't seem to understand: it's all over! Why this grim look on your face? Oh, poor little Nora, of course I understand. You can't bring yourself to believe I've forgiven you. But I have, Nora, I swear it. I forgive you everything. I know you did what you did because you loved me.

NORA. That's true.

HELMER. You loved me as a wife should love her husband. It was simply that you didn't have the experience to judge what was the best way of going about things. But do you think I love you any the less for that; just because you don't know how to act on your own responsibility? No, no, you just lean on me, I shall give you all the advice and guidance you need. I wouldn't be a proper man if I didn't find a woman doubly attractive for being so obviously helpless. You mustn't dwell on the harsh things I said in that first moment of horror, when I thought everything was going to come crashing down about my ears. I have forgiven you, Nora, I swear it! I have forgiven you!

NORA. Thank you for your forgiveness.

[*She goes out through the door, right.*]

HELMER. No, don't go! [*He looks through the doorway.*] What are you doing in the spare room?

NORA. Taking off this fancy dress.

HELMER [*standing at the open door*], Yes, do. You try and get some rest, and set your mind at peace again, my frightened little song-bird. Have a good long sleep; you know you are safe and sound under my wing. [*Walks up and down near the door.*] What a nice, cosy little home we have here, Nora! Here you can find refuge. Here I shall hold you like a hunted dove I have rescued unscathed from the cruel talons of the hawk, and calm your poor beating heart. And that will come, gradually, Nora, believe me. Tomorrow you'll see everything quite differently. Soon everything will be just as it was before. You won't need me to keep on telling you I've forgiven you; you'll feel convinced of it in your own heart. You don't really imagine me ever thinking of turning you out, or even of reproaching you? Oh, a real man isn't made that way, you know, Nora. For a man, there's something indescribably moving and very satisfying in knowing that he has forgiven his wife—forgiven her, completely and genuinely, from the depths of his heart. It's as though it made her his property in a double sense: he has, as it were, given her a new life, and she becomes in a way both his wife and at the same time his child. That is how you will seem to me after today, helpless, perplexed little thing that you are. Don't you worry your pretty little head about anything, Nora. Just you be frank with me, and I'll take all the decisions for you. . . . What's this? Not in bed? You've changed your things?

NORA [*in her everyday dress*]. Yes, Torvald, I've changed.

HELMER. What for? It's late.

NORA. I shan't sleep tonight.

HELMER. But my dear Nora. . . .

NORA [*looks at her watch*]. It's not so terribly late. Sit down, Torvald. We two have a lot to talk about.

[*She sits down at one side of the table.*]

HELMER. Nora, what is all this? Why so grim?

NORA. Sit down. It'll take some time. I have a lot to say to you.

HELMER [*sits down at the table opposite her*]. You frighten me, Nora. I don't understand you.

NORA. Exactly. You don't understand me. And I have never understood you, either—until tonight. No, don't interrupt. I just want you to listen to what I have to say. We are going to have things out, Torvald.

HELMER. What do you mean?

NORA. Isn't there anything that strikes you about the way we two are sitting here?

HELMER. What's that?

NORA. We have now been married eight years. Hasn't it struck you this is the first time you and I, man and wife, have had a serious talk together?

HELMER. Depends what you mean by 'serious'.

NORA. Eight whole years—no, more, ever since we first knew each other—and never have we exchanged one serious word about serious things.

HELMER. What did you want me to do? Get you involved in worries that you couldn't possibly help me to bear?

NORA. I'm not talking about worries. I say we've never once sat down together and seriously tried to get to the bottom of anything.

HELMER. But, my dear Nora, would that have been a thing for you?

NORA. That's just it. You have never understood me . . . I've been greatly wronged, Torvald. First by my father, and then by you.

HELMER. What! Us two! The two people who loved you more than anybody?

NORA [*shakes her head*]. You two never loved me. You only thought now nice it was to be in love with me.

HELMER. But, Nora, what's this you are saying?

NORA. It's right, you know, Torvald. At home, Daddy used to tell me what he thought, then I thought the same. And if I thought differently, I kept quiet about it, because he wouldn't have liked it. He used to call me his baby doll, and he played with me as I used to play with my dolls. Then I came to live in your house. . . .

HELMER. What way is that to talk about our marriage?

NORA [*imperturbably*]. What I mean is: I passed out of Daddy's hands into yours. You arranged everything to your tastes, and I acquired the same tastes. Or I pretended to . . . I don't really know . . . I think it was a bit of both, sometimes one thing and sometimes the other. When I look back, it seems to me I have been living here like a beggar, from hand to mouth. I lived by doing tricks for you, Torvald. But that's the way you wanted it. You and Daddy did me a great wrong. It's your fault that I've never made anything of my life.

HELMER. Nora, how unreasonable . . . how ungrateful you are! Haven't you been happy here?

NORA. No, never. I thought I was, but I wasn't really.

HELMER. Not . . . not happy!

NORA. No, just gay. And you've always been so kind to me. But our house has never been anything but a play-room. I have been your doll wife, just as at home I was Daddy's doll child. And the children in turn have been my dolls. I thought it was fun when you came and played with me, just as they thought it was fun when I went and played with them. That's been our marriage, Torvald.

HELMER. There is some truth in what you say, exaggerated and hysterical though it is. But from now on it will be different. Play-time is over; now comes the time for lessons.

NORA. Whose lessons? Mine or the children's?

HELMER. Both yours and the children's, my dear Nora.

NORA. Ah, Torvald, you are not the man to teach me to be a good wife for you.

HELMER. How can you say that?

NORA. And what sort of qualifications have I to teach the children?

HELMER. Nora!

NORA. Didn't you say yourself, a minute or two ago, that you couldn't trust me with that job.

HELMER. In the heat of the moment! You shouldn't pay any attention to that.

NORA. On the contrary, you were quite right. I'm not up to it. There's another problem needs solving first. I must take steps to educate myself. You are not the man to help me there. That's something I must do on my own. That's why I'm leaving you.

HELMER [*jumps up*]. What did you say?

NORA. If I'm ever to reach any understanding of myself and the things around me, I must learn to stand alone. That's why I can't stay here with you any longer.

HELMER. Nora! Nora!

NORA. I'm leaving here at once. I dare say Kristine will put me up for tonight. . . .

HELMER. You are out of your mind! I won't let you! I forbid you!

NORA. It's no use forbidding me anything now. I'm taking with me my own personal belongings. I don't want anything of yours, either now or later.

HELMER. This is madness!

NORA. Tomorrow I'm going home—to what used to be my home, I mean. It will be easier for me to find something to do there.

HELMER. Oh, you blind, inexperienced . . .

NORA. I must set about *getting* experience, Torvald.

HELMER. And leave your home, your husband and your children? Don't you care what people will say?

NORA. That's no concern of mine. All I know is that this is necessary for *me*.

HELMER. This is outrageous! You are betraying your most sacred duty.

NORA. And what do you consider to be my most sacred duty?

HELMER. Does it take me to tell you that? Isn't it your duty to your husband and your children?

NORA. I have another duty equally sacred.

HELMER. You have not. What duty might *that* be?

NORA. My duty to myself.

HELMER. First and foremost, you are a wife and mother.

NORA. That I don't believe any more. I believe that first and foremost I am an individual, just as much as you are—or at least I'm going to try to be. I know most people agree with you, Torvald, and that's also what it says in books. But I'm not content any more with what most people say, or with what it says in books. I have to think things out for myself, and get things clear.

HELMER. Surely you are clear about your position in your own home? Haven't you an infallible guide in questions like these? Haven't you your religion?

NORA. Oh, Torvald, I don't really know what religion is.

HELMER. What do you say!

NORA. All I know is what Pastor Hansen said when I was confirmed. He said religion was this, that and the other. When I'm away from all this and on my own, I'll go into that, too. I want to find out whether what Pastor Hansen told me was right—or at least whether it's right for *me*.

HELMER. This is incredible talk from a young woman! But if religion cannot keep you on the right path, let me at least stir your conscience. I suppose you do have some moral sense? Or tell me—perhaps you don't?

NORA. Well, Torvald, that's not easy to say. I simply don't know. I'm really very confused about such things. All I know is my ideas about such things are very different from yours. I've also learnt that the law is different from what I thought; but I simply can't get it into my head that that particular law is right. Apparently a woman has no right to spare her old father on his death-bed, or to save her husband's life, even. I just don't believe it.

HELMER. You are talking like a child. You understand nothing about the society you live in.

NORA. No, I don't. But I shall go into that too. I must try to discover who is right, society or me.

HELMER. You are ill, Nora. You are delirious. I'm half inclined to think you are out of your mind.

NORA. Never have I felt so calm and collected as I do tonight.

HELMER. Calm and collected enough to leave your husband and children?

NORA. Yes.

HELMER. Then only one explanation is possible.

NORA. And that is?

HELMER. You don't love me any more.

NORA. Exactly.

HELMER. Nora! Can you say that!

NORA. I'm desperately sorry, Torvald. Because you have always been so kind to me. But I can't help it. I don't love you any more.

HELMER [*struggling to keep his composure*]. Is that also a 'calm and collected' decision you've made?

NORA. Yes, absolutely calm and collected. That's why I don't want to stay here.

HELMER. And can you also account for how I forfeited your love?

NORA. Yes, very easily. It was tonight, when the miracle didn't happen. It was then I realized you weren't the man I thought you were.

HELMER. Explain yourself more clearly. I don't understand.

NORA. For eight years I have been patiently waiting. Because, heavens, I knew miracles didn't happen every day. Then this devastating business started, and I became absolutely convinced the miracle *would* happen. All the time Krogstad's letter lay there, it never so much as crossed my mind that you would ever submit to that man's conditions. I was absolutely convinced you would say to him: Tell the whole wide world if you like. And when that was done . . .

HELMER. Yes, then what? After I had exposed my own wife to dishonour and shame . . . !

NORA. When that was done, I was absolutely convinced you would come forward and take everything on yourself, and say: I am the guilty one.

HELMER. Nora!

NORA. You mean I'd never let you make such a sacrifice for my sake? Of course not. But what would my story have counted for against yours?—That was the miracle I went in hope and dread of. It was to prevent it that I was ready to end my life.

HELMER. I would gladly toil day and night for you, Nora, enduring all manner of sorrow and distress. But nobody sacrifices his *honour* for the one he loves.

NORA. Hundreds and thousands of women have.

HELMER. Oh, you think and talk like a stupid child.

NORA. All right. But you neither think nor talk like the man I would want to share my life with. When you had got over your fright— and you weren't concerned about me but only about what might happen to you—and when all danger was past, you acted as though nothing had happened. I was your little sky-lark again, your little doll, exactly as before; except you would have to protect it twice as carefully as before, now that it had shown itself to be so weak and fragile. [*Rises.*] Torvald, that was the moment I realised that for eight years I'd been living with a stranger, and had borne him three children. . . . Oh, I can't bear to think about it! I could tear myself to shreds.

HELMER [*sadly*]. I see. I see. There is a tremendous gulf dividing us. But, Nora, is there no way we might bridge it?

NORA. As I am now, I am no wife for you.

HELMER. I still have it in me to change.

NORA. Perhaps . . . if you have your doll taken away.

HELMER. And be separated from you! No, no, Nora, the very thought of it is inconceivable.

NORA [*goes into the room, right*]. All the more reason why it must be done.

[*She comes back with her outdoor things and a small travelling bag which she puts on the chair beside the table.*]

HELMER. Nora, Nora, not now! Wait till the morning.

NORA [*putting on her coat*]. I can't spend the night in a strange man's room.

HELMER. Couldn't we go on living here like brother and sister. . . . ?

NORA [*tying on her hat*]. You know very well that wouldn't last. [*She draws the shawl round her.*] Goodbye, Torvald. I don't want to see the children. I know they are in better hands than mine. As I am now, I can never be anything to them.

HELMER. But some day, Nora, some day. . . ?

NORA. How should I know? I've no idea what I might turn out to be.

HELMER. But you are my wife, whatever you are.

NORA. Listen, Torvald, from what I've heard, when a wife leaves her husband's house as I am doing now, he is absolved by law of all responsibility for her. I can at any rate free you from all responsibility. You must not feel in any way bound, any more than I shall. There must be full freedom on both sides. Look, here's your ring back. Give me mine.

HELMER. That too?

NORA. That too.

HELMER. There it is.

NORA. Well, that's the end of that. I'll put the keys down here. The maids know where everything is in the house—better than I do, in fact. Kristine will come in the morning after I've left to pack up the few things I brought with me from home. I want them sent on.

HELMER. The end! Nora, will you never think of me?

NORA. I dare say I'll often think about you and the children and this house.

HELMER. May I write to you, Nora?

NORA. No, never. I won't let you.

HELMER. But surely I can send you . . .

NORA. Nothing, nothing.

HELMER. Can't I help you if ever you need it?

NORA. I said 'no'. I don't accept things from strangers.

HELMER. Nora, can I never be anything more to you than a stranger?

NORA [*takes her bag*]. Ah, Torvald, only by a miracle of miracles. . . .

HELMER. Name it, this miracle of miracles!

NORA. Both you and I would have to change to the point where . . . Oh, Torvald, I don't believe in miracles any more.

HELMER. But I *will* believe. Name it! Change to the point where. . . ?

NORA. Where we could make a real marriage of our lives together. Goodbye!

[*She goes out through the hall door.*]

HELMER [*sinks down on a chair near the door, and covers his face with his hands*]. Nora! Nora! [*He rises and looks round.*] Empty! She's gone! [*With sudden hope.*] The miracle of miracles. . . ?

[*The heavy sound of a door being slammed is heard from below.*]

THE ALTERNATIVE 'GERMAN' ENDING

Under strong pressure, and very reluctantly, Ibsen wrote an alternative ending for the German theatre. Both Maurice in Hamburg and Laube in Vienna pressed for a 'conciliatory' ending, as also did Frau Hedwig Niemann-Raabe who was to play Nora on tour. In the end, Ibsen himself provided the following additional dialogue:

NORA. . . . dass unser Zusammenleben eine Ehe werden könnte. Leb' wohl. [*Will gehen.*]

HELMER. Nun denn gehe! [*Fasst sie am Arm.*] Aber erst sollst Du Deine Kinder zum letzten Mal sehen!

NORA. Lass mich los! Ich will sie nicht sehen! Ich kann es nicht!

HELMER [*zieht sie gegen die Thür links*]. Du sollst sie sehen! [*Öffnet die Thür und sagt leise.*] Siehst Du; dort schlafen sie sorglos und ruhig. Morgen, wenn sie erwachen und rufen nach ihrer Mutter, dann sind sie—mutterlos.

NORA [*bebend*]. Mutterlos. . . !

HELMER. Wie Du es gewesen bist.

NORA. Mutterlos! [*Kämpft innerlich, lässt die Reisetasche fallen und sagt.*] O, ich versündige mich gegen mich selbst, aber ich kann sie nicht verlassen. [*Sinkt halb nieder vor der Thür.*]

HELMER [*freudig, aber leise*]. Nora!

[*Der Vorhang fällt.*]

⟨NORA. . . . Where we could make a real marriage out of our lives together. Goodbye. [*Begins to go.*]

HELMER. Go then! [*Seizes her arm.*] But first you shall see your children for the last time!

NORA. Let me go! I will not see them! I cannot!

HELMER [*draws her over to the door, left*]. You shall see them. [*Opens the door and says softly.*] Look, there they are asleep, peaceful and carefree. Tomorrow, when they wake up and call for their mother, they will be—motherless.

NORA [*trembling*]. Motherless. . . !

HELMER. As you once were.

NORA. Motherless! [*Struggles with herself, lets her travelling bag fall, and says.*] Oh, this is a sin against myself, but I cannot leave them. [*Half sinks down by the door.*]

HELMER [*joyfully, but softly*]. Nora!

[*The curtain falls.*]

For an insight into what eventually persuaded Ibsen to commit this 'barbaric outrage'—as he himself called it—see his letters to a Copenhagen newspaper of 17 Feb. 1880, to Heinrich Laube of 18 Feb. 1880, and to Moritz Prozor of 23 Jan. 1891 (translated below, pp. 454–56).

GHOSTS

[*Gengangere*]

A DOMESTIC DRAMA IN THREE ACTS
(1881)

Translated by James McFarlane

CHARACTERS

MRS. HELENE ALVING, widow of Captain (and Chamberlain) Alving

OSWALD ALVING, her son, an artist

PASTOR MANDERS

JACOB ENGSTRAND, a carpenter

REGINE ENGSTRAND, in service with Mrs. Alving

The action takes place on Mrs. Alving's country estate by one of the large fjords of Western Norway

ACT ONE

A spacious garden room, with one door on the left wall, and two on the right. In the centre of the room stands a round table, with chairs round it; books, periodicals, and newspapers are lying on the table. Downstage, left, is a window, and near it a small sofa with a work-table in front of it. The room is continued at the back of the stage into an open and rather narrower conservatory, the walls of which are extensively glazed. In the right wall of the conservatory is a door that leads out into the garden. Through the glass wall may be glimpsed a gloomy fjord landscape, shrouded in steady rain.

JACOB ENGSTRAND is standing beside the door into the garden. His left leg is somewhat deformed, and he wears a boot with a built-up wooden sole. REGINE, with an empty garden syringe in her hand, is trying to prevent him coming any further.

REGINE [*keeping her voice low*]. What do you want? Stay where you are. You are dripping wet.

ENGSTRAND. It's God's own rain, my child.

REGINE. More like the devil's, you mean.

ENGSTRAND. Lord, the things you say, Regine. [*Takes a few limping steps into the room.*] But what I wanted to tell you was . . .

REGINE. Stop clumping about with that foot, man! The young master's upstairs asleep.

ENGSTRAND. Asleep? At this time of day?

REGINE. That's got nothing to do with you.

ENGSTRAND. I was out having a few drinks last night. . . .

REGINE. That I can well believe.

ENGSTRAND. Well, we are frail creatures, all of us, my child . . .

REGINE. We are that.

ENGSTRAND. . . . and many are the temptations of this world, you know . . . but still, there was I up and at work at half-past five this morning.

REGINE. Yes, yes, but off you go now. I'm not standing for having *rendez-vous's* here with you.

ENGSTRAND. Having what, did you say?

REGINE. I'm not going to have anybody finding you here. So, away you go.

ENGSTRAND [*comes a few steps closer*]. I'm damned if I'm going before I've had a word with you. I'll have that work down at the school-house finished by this afternoon, and I'm taking the night boat home, back to town.

REGINE [*mutters*]. Pleasant journey!

ENGSTRAND. Thank you, my child. You see tomorrow, the Orphanage is being opened, and I expect there'll be a lot of drinking and such like going on. And nobody's going to say about Jacob Engstrand that he can't resist temptation when it comes along.

REGINE. Huh!

ENGSTRAND. There'll be a lot of posh people here tomorrow. And they're expecting Pastor Manders from town as well.

REGINE. He'll be here today.

ENGSTRAND. There you are, you see. Got to be damned careful I don't put my foot in it with him, you know.

REGINE. Aha! So *that's* it!

ENGSTRAND. So what's it?

REGINE [*looks hard at him*]. What are you going to try and talk him into this time?

ENGSTRAND. Sh! Are you crazy? *Me* talk Pastor Manders into anything? Oh no, Pastor Manders has been far too good to me for *that*. But look, what I really wanted to talk to you about was me going back home again tonight.

REGINE. The sooner the better, as far as I'm concerned.

ENGSTRAND. Yes, but I want you to come with me, Regine.

REGINE [*open-mouthed*]. You want me to. . . . What did you say?

ENGSTRAND. I said I want you to come home with me.

REGINE [*scornfully*]. Not likely! You'll never get me coming home with you.

ENGSTRAND. Oh? We'll see about that.

REGINE. Yes, I'll say we will. *Me?* Who's been brought up here by a lady like Mrs. Alving . . . ? Who's been treated like one of the family, almost. . . ? Expect me to go home with you? To a place like that? Puh!

ENGSTRAND. What the devil. . . ? Setting yourself up against your own father, you little bitch?

REGINE [*mutters, without looking at him*]. Often enough you've said I wasn't any concern of yours.

ENGSTRAND. Huh! You are not going to bother your head about *that*. . . ?

REGINE. And what about all the times you've sworn at me and called me a . . . ? *Fi donc!*

ENGSTRAND. I'll be damned if I ever used such filthy language.

REGINE. Oh, I know well enough what language you used.

ENGSTRAND. Well, but only when I'd had a few . . . h'm. Many are the temptations of this world, Regine.

REGINE. Ugh!

ENGSTRAND. Or else when your mother started her nagging. I had to have something to get my own back on her, my girl. Always so stuck-up, she was. [*Mimics.*] 'Let me go, Engstrand. Let me be. I was three years in service at Rosenvold, with Chamberlain Alving, I was.' [*Laughs.*] My God! She couldn't ever forget that the captain was made a chamberlain while she was in service there.

REGINE. Poor mother! You drove her to her death the way you tormented her.

ENGSTRAND [*shrugs*]. Oh, that's right! Blame me for everything.

REGINE [*turns away, under her breath*]. Ugh! And then that leg!

ENGSTRAND. What's that you say, my girl?

REGINE. *Pied de mouton.*

ENGSTRAND. Is that English?

REGINE. Yes.

ENGSTRAND. Ah, you've learned quite a lot out here, and that might come in very handy now, Regine.

REGINE [*after a short silence*]. And what did you want with me in town?

ENGSTRAND. How can you ask what a father wants with his only child? I'm a lonely, deserted widower, aren't I?

REGINE. Oh, don't come that fiddle-faddle with me. What do you want me there for?

ENGSTRAND. Well, the thing is I've been thinking of going in for something new.

REGINE [*sneers*]. How many times haven't I heard *that* one before! But you always made a mess of it.

ENGSTRAND. Yes, but just you watch me this time, Regine! Damn me if . . .

REGINE [*stamps her foot*]. Stop that swearing!

ENGSTRAND. Sh! sh! You are right enough there, my girl! I just wanted to say this: I've saved quite a bit of money out of this Orphanage job.

REGINE. Have you? How nice for you.

ENGSTRAND. Because what can you spend your money on, stuck out here in the country?

REGINE. What about it?

ENGSTRAND. Well, you see, I'd thought of putting the money into something worthwhile. A sort of hotel for seamen. . . .

REGINE. Ugh!

ENGSTRAND. A real classy hotel, I mean . . . not one of them cheap dumps for deckhands. By God, no! It'd be for captains and mates and . . . and real classy people, you know.

REGINE. And I'd have to . . . ?

ENGSTRAND. To lend a hand, that's right. Just help to look after the place, if you know what I mean. You wouldn't have such a hell of a lot to do, my girl. You could do pretty well what you liked.

REGINE. Oh, really!

ENGSTRAND. There has to be some women about the place, that's clear. Because we'd want a bit of fun in the evenings, singing and dancing and that sort of thing. These are seafaring men, you've got to remember, roaming the high seas. [*Comes closer.*] Now don't be such a fool as to stand in your own way, Regine. What can you do with yourself out here? Is it going to be any use to you, all this education the lady's lavished on you? You'll be looking after the children in the new Orphanage, they tell me. What sort of thing is that for a girl like you, eh? Are you all that keen on working yourself to death for the sake of a lot of dirty little brats?

REGINE. No, if things worked out as *I* wanted them to. . . . Well, it could happen. It could happen!

ENGSTRAND. What could happen?

REGINE. Never you mind. . . . Have you managed to put a lot of money by?

ENGSTRAND. What with one thing and another, it might be about seven or eight hundred crowns.

REGINE. Not bad.

ENGSTRAND. Enough to make a start with, my girl.

REGINE. You didn't think of giving me any of it?

ENGSTRAND. No, I'm damned if I did.

REGINE. Don't even think of sending me a bit of stuff for a dress?

ENGSTRAND. Come back to town with me, and you can have plenty of dresses.

REGINE. Puh, I can manage that on my own if I want.

ENGSTRAND. Ah, but it's better with a father's hand to guide you, Regine. I can get a nice little house that's going in Little Harbour Road. They're not asking a big deposit; and it could be a kind of Sailors' Home, see?

REGINE. But I don't *want* to come with *you*! I don't want anything to do with you. Now get away!

ENGSTRAND. I bet you damn well wouldn't stay very long with me, my girl. Not much chance of that. Not if you played your cards properly. Pretty little piece you've turned into, this last year or two. . . .

REGINE. Well. . . ?

ENGSTRAND. It wouldn't be long before some ship's officer would turn up . . . maybe even a captain. . . .

REGINE. I wouldn't marry anybody like that. Sailors have no *savoir vivre*.

ENGSTRAND. What's that they haven't got?

REGINE. I know what sailors are, let me tell you. No use marrying *them*.

ENGSTRAND. You don't have to marry them. It can still be worth your while. [*More confidentially.*] That Englishman, now . . . the one with the yacht . . . he paid three hundred dollars . . . and she wasn't any prettier than you.

REGINE [*going towards him*]. Get out!

ENGSTRAND [*retreating*]. Now, now, you wouldn't hit me, would you!

REGINE. Wouldn't I! You say one word about Mother, and I'll let you have it. Get out, I say! [*Drives him towards the door into the garden.*] And don't go slamming any doors. Young Mr. Alving. . .

ENGSTRAND. He's asleep, I know. You seem very concerned about this young Mr. Alving. [*Softly.*] Aha! It wouldn't be *him* . . . eh?

REGINE. Out, and quick about it! You're barmy, man! No, not that way. There's Pastor Manders coming. Down the back stairs.

ENGSTRAND [*towards the right*]. All right, I'm going. But you just have a talk with *him*, coming in there. *He's* the man to tell you what a child owes its father. Because after all I am your father, you know. I can prove it from the Parish Register.

[*He goes out through the other door which* REGINE *opens for him, and closes again after him.* REGINE *hastily looks at herself in the mirror, dabs herself with her handkerchief and straightens her collar; then she busies herself with the flowers.* PASTOR MANDERS, *in topcoat, carrying an umbrella and with a small satchel slung over his shoulder, enters the conservatory from the garden.*]

MANDERS. Good morning, Miss Engstrand.

REGINE [*turning round in glad surprise*]. Why it's Pastor Manders! Good morning, Pastor. Is the steamer in already?

MANDERS. Just arrived. [*He comes into the room.*] Miserable rainy weather we've been having lately.

REGINE [*following him*]. A blessing for the farmers, though, Pastor.

MANDERS. Ah, you are quite right. We townsfolk so rarely think of that. [*He begins to take off his topcoat.*]

REGINE. Oh, please let me help you. There! Goodness, how wet it is. I'll just hang it up in the hall. And your umbrella . . . I'll leave it up somewhere, so it can be drying.

[*She takes the things out through the second door, right.* PASTOR MANDERS *takes his satchel and lays it along with his hat on a chair. Meanwhile* REGINE *returns.*]

MANDERS. Ah, it's good to get indoors. And how are things out here? All right, I hope.

REGINE. Yes, thank you.

MANDERS. But pretty busy, I imagine, getting ready for tomorrow?

REGINE. Oh yes, there's plenty to do.

MANDERS. And Mrs. Alving is at home, I trust?

REGINE. Yes, of course. She's just upstairs seeing to some cocoa for Mr. Oswald.

MANDERS. Ah yes . . . I heard down at the quay that Oswald is supposed to have arrived.

REGINE. Yes, he came the day before yesterday. We hadn't been expecting him till today.

MANDERS. Fit and well, I hope?

REGINE. Yes, thank you, quite well. But horribly tired after his journey. He did the whole trip from Paris in one. . . . I mean he travelled all the way without a break. I think he's having a little sleep now, so perhaps we'd better talk just a little bit quieter.

MANDERS. Sh! We'll be very quiet.

REGINE [*moving an armchair into place beside the table*]. Do sit down, Pastor Manders, and make yourself comfortable. [*He sits down; she places a footstool under his feet.*] There now! Nice and comfortable?

MANDERS. Splendid, thank you. [*Looks at her.*] You know, Miss Engstrand, I do believe you've grown since I saw you last.

REGINE. Do you think so, Pastor? Mrs. Alving says I've also filled out.

MANDERS. Filled out? Oh, yes, a little perhaps . . . quite nicely.

[*Short pause.*]

REGINE. Should I go and tell Mrs. Alving?

MANDERS. Thank you, but there's no hurry, my dear. . . . Tell me, Regine, how is your father getting on out here?

REGINE. Fairly well, thank you, Pastor.

MANDERS. He looked in to see me last time he was in town.

REGINE. Did he? He's always glad to have a talk with you, Pastor.

MANDERS. And you run across and see him pretty regularly, I suppose?

REGINE. Me? Oh yes, I do, whenever I have a moment. . . .

MANDERS. Your father is not a particularly strong character, Miss Engstrand. He sorely needs a guiding hand.

REGINE. Oh yes, that's very likely.

MANDERS. He needs somebody near and dear to him to turn to, some-body whose judgement he respects. He admitted that himself quite frankly the last time he came to see me.

REGINE. Yes, he mentioned something of the kind to me too. But I don't know that Mrs. Alving would want to let me go . . . especially now we've got the new Orphanage to run. And then again, I would hate to leave Mrs. Alving, because she's always been so kind to me.

MANDERS. But a daughter's duty, my good girl. . . . Of course we'd have to get the consent of your mistress first.

REGINE. But I'm not sure it's quite the thing for me, at my age, to keep house for a single man.

MANDERS. What! But my dear Miss Engstrand, we happen to be talking about your own father.

REGINE. Yes, that may be, but all the same. . . . Now, if it was in a *good* house with a proper gentleman . . .

MANDERS. But my dear Regine. . . .

REGINE. . . . Somebody I could feel affection and respect for, and be a sort of daughter to . . .

MANDERS. Yes, but my dear, good child . . .

REGINE. Then I should be quite happy to go back to town. It's awfully lonely out here . . . and you know well enough yourself, Pastor, what it's like to be alone in the world. And I think I can honestly say I'm both willing and able. You don't know of any place like that for me, Pastor, do you?

MANDERS. Who, me? No, to be quite honest, I don't.

REGINE. But dear, dear Pastor Manders . . . you will think of me, won't you, if ever . . .

MANDERS [*gets up*]. Yes, that I will, Miss Engstrand.

REGINE. Because if I . . .

MANDERS. Would you be so kind as to fetch Mrs. Alving?

REGINE. I'll see to it at once, Pastor.

[REGINE *goes out, left.* PASTOR MANDERS *walks up and down the room a few times, stands at the back of the room for a moment with his hands clasped behind his back, looking out at the garden. Then he again comes back near the table, picks up a book and looks at the title page; he gives a start and looks at several more.*]

MANDERS. H'm! Indeed!

[MRS. ALVING *enters through the door, left. She is followed by* REGINE *who immediately goes off again, right.*]

MRS. ALVING [*holds out her hand*]. Welcome, Pastor.

MANDERS. Good morning, Mrs. Alving. Here I am, just as I promised.

MRS. ALVING. Punctual, as ever.

MANDERS. But it wasn't easy getting away, believe me. All these blessed committees and things I've been put on. . . .

MRS. ALVING. All the nicer of you to come so promptly. Now we can get our business settled before dinner. But where's your suitcase?

MANDERS [*hurriedly*]. I left my things down at the store. I'll stay there tonight.

MRS. ALVING [*suppressing a smile*]. Can't you be persuaded even yet to stay the night in my house?

MANDERS. No, no, Mrs. Alving, thanks all the same. I'll stay down there again as usual. It's so handy for catching the boat.

MRS. ALVING. Well, have it your own way. All the same, I really do think a couple of old things like us. . . .

MANDERS. Dear me, you will have your little joke, won't you? Well, of course you must be feeling extremely pleased with yourself today. First the celebrations tomorrow, and then having Oswald at home.

MRS. ALVING. Yes, just fancy! Isn't it marvellous! It's more than two years since he was last home. Now he's promised to stay with me the whole winter.

MANDERS. Has he now? There's a nice dutiful son for you. Because I imagine the attractions of living in Rome or Paris are altogether different.

MRS. ALVING. Yes, but you see here at home he has his mother. Ah, my dear, darling boy . . . he still has a soft spot for his mother!

MANDERS. I must say it would be a sad thing if leaving home and taking up Art and all that interfered with his natural feelings.

MRS. ALVING. Ah, it's right what you say. But there isn't any danger of that with him, no really there isn't. It will be fun to see if you recognize him again. He'll be coming down later. He's just upstairs having a little rest on the sofa. But do sit down, my dear Pastor.

MANDERS. Thank you. You are sure it's quite convenient. . . ?

MRS. ALVING. Yes, of course it is.

[*She sits down at the table.*]

MANDERS. Good. Let's see then. . . . [*He goes over to the chair on which his satchel is lying, takes a sheaf of papers out of it, sits down at the opposite side of the table and looks for a clear space to put his papers down.*] First of all we have . . . [*Breaking off.*] Tell me, Mrs. Alving, how did *these* books get *here*?

MRS. ALVING. These books? They are books *I* am reading.

MANDERS. You read that sort of thing?

MRS. ALVING. Of course I do.

MANDERS. Do you think reading that sort of thing makes you feel any better, or any happier?

MRS. ALVING. I feel, as it were, more confident.

MANDERS. Strange. How?

MRS. ALVING. Well, I find it seems to explain and confirm a lot of the things I had been thinking myself. That's the strange thing, Pastor Manders . . . there's really nothing new in these books; there's nothing there but what most people think and believe already. It's just that most people either haven't really considered these things, or won't admit them.

MANDERS. Good God! Do you seriously believe that most people . . . ?

MRS. ALVING. Yes, I do.

MANDERS. Yes, but surely not in this country? Not here?

MRS. ALVING. Oh yes, here too.

MANDERS. Well, I must say. . . !

MRS. ALVING. Anyway, what is it in fact you've got against these books?

MANDERS. Got against them? You don't think I waste my time examining publications of that kind, surely?

MRS. ALVING. Which means you know absolutely nothing about what you are condemning?

MANDERS. I have read sufficient about these publications to disapprove of them.

MRS. ALVING. Yes, but your own personal opinion. . . .

MANDERS. My dear lady, there are many occasions in life when one must rely on others. That's the way of the world, and things are best that way. How else would society manage?

MRS. ALVING. Well, you may be right.

MANDERS. Not that I want to deny, of course, that these books can have a considerable fascination. Nor can I blame you for wanting to get to know something about the new trends of thought which, so they tell me, are current in the great world outside—that world in which you have allowed your son so much rein for so long. But . . .

MRS. ALVING. But . . . ?

MANDERS [*lowering his voice*]. But one doesn't talk about it, Mrs. Alving. One doesn't have to account to all and sundry for what one reads and thinks in the privacy of one's own room.

MRS. ALVING. No, of course not. I quite agree.

MANDERS. Think for a moment of the responsibilities you have towards this Orphanage. You decided to found it at a time when your opinions and beliefs were very different from what they are now—as far as *I* can judge, anyway.

MRS. ALVING. Yes, yes, I quite admit that. But about the Orphanage. . . .

MANDERS. That's right, we were going to discuss the Orphanage. Still . . . caution, dear lady! Now let's get down to business. [*Opens an envelope and takes some papers out.*] You see these?

MRS. ALVING. The deeds?

MANDERS. Complete, and in order. It wasn't easy getting them ready in time, believe me. I had to bring a certain amount of pressure to bear. The authorities are painfully conscientious when it comes to drawing up agreements. But anyway, here they are. [*He turns over the papers.*] Here is the deed of conveyance for the site known as Solvik, being part of the Rosenvold estate, together with the buildings newly erected thereon, the school, the school house and the chapel. And here is the authorization for the bequest and for the regulations of the institution. Would you like to see.... [*Reads.*] Regulations for the Captain Alving Memorial Home.

MRS. ALVING [*looks long at the paper*]. So there it is.

MANDERS. I chose 'Captain' rather than 'Chamberlain' for the name. 'Captain' looks less ostentatious.

MRS. ALVING. Yes, just as you think best.

MANDERS. And in this Bank Book you have details of the capital sum, the interest on which is to cover the running expenses of the Orphanage.

MRS. ALVING. Thank you. But it would be a great convenience if you would please hold on to them.

MANDERS. With pleasure. I think we'll leave the money in the bank for the time being. The interest isn't very attractive, it's true—four per cent. at six months' notice. If in time we could find some good mortgage investment . . . a first mortgage it would have to be, of course, and absolutely sound . . . then we could discuss the thing again in more detail.

MRS. ALVING. Yes, yes, dear Pastor Manders, you know best about these things.

MANDERS. Anyway, I'll keep my eyes open. . . . But there's just one other thing I've been meaning to ask you several times.

MRS. ALVING. And what is that?

MANDERS. Are the Orphanage buildings to be insured or not?

MRS. ALVING. Yes, of course they must be insured.

MANDERS. Ah, but wait a moment Mrs. Alving. Let's examine this matter more closely.

MRS. ALVING. I keep everything insured—the buildings, the contents, the crops and the stock.

MANDERS. Naturally. On your own property. I do the same . . . of course. But this is quite a different thing, you see. The Orphanage is, as it were, to be dedicated to a higher purpose.

MRS. ALVING. Yes, but . . .

MANDERS. As for me personally, I don't honestly see anything objectionable in covering ourselves against all possible contingencies...

MRS. ALVING. Nor do I.

MANDERS. ... but what about the people round here, how would they react? That's something you know better than I.

MRS. ALVING. H'm, people's reactions. ...

MANDERS. Would there be any considerable body of responsible opinion—really responsible opinion—that might take exception to it?

MRS. ALVING. Well, what actually is it you mean by responsible opinion?

MANDERS. I'm thinking principally of men in independent and influential positions of the kind that makes it difficult not to attach a certain importance to their opinions.

MRS. ALVING. Oh, there are plenty here of the kind that might very easily take exception if ...

MANDERS. Well, there you are! In town we have plenty of that kind. You've only got to think of all those who support my colleague! It would be so terribly easy to interpret things as meaning that neither you nor I had a proper faith in Divine Providence.

MRS. ALVING. But as far as you are concerned, my dear Pastor, you know perfectly well yourself. ...

MANDERS. Yes, I know, I know ... my conscience is clear, that's true enough. But all the same, we might not be able to stop people from seriously misrepresenting us. And that in turn might well have an inhibiting effect on the activities of the Orphanage.

MRS. ALVING. Well, if *that* were to be the case ...

MANDERS. Nor can I altogether disregard the difficult ... I might well call it painful position, I might conceivably find myself in. All the influential people in town have been talking about this Orphanage. It's partly intended to benefit the town, of course, and people are hoping it will help considerably towards reducing the burden on the rates. But since I have acted as your adviser and looked after the business side of things, I rather fear the more zealous ones would turn on *me* in the first place. . . .

MRS. ALVING. Yes, that risk you mustn't run.

MANDERS. To say nothing of the attacks that would undoubtedly be made on me in certain papers and periodicals. . . .

MRS. ALVING. You've said enough, my dear Pastor Manders. That settles it.

MANDERS. So you don't want any insurance?

MRS. ALVING. No, we'll let it go.

MANDERS [*leaning back in his chair*]. But if there did happen to be an accident? You never know . . . would you be able to make good the damage?

MRS. ALVING. No, I can tell you straight, I wouldn't.

MANDERS. Well, you know, Mrs. Alving . . . this is really a grave responsibility we are taking upon ourselves.

MRS. ALVING. But *can* we do anything else, do you think?

MANDERS. No, that's just it. In fact, we *can't*. We mustn't run the risk of giving people the wrong impression; and mustn't at any cost give offence to the general public.

MRS. ALVING. You mustn't anyway, a clergyman.

MANDERS. And really I think we may assume that an institution of this kind will have luck on its side . . . indeed that it will enjoy a very special measure of protection.

MRS. ALVING. Let us hope so, Pastor Manders.

MANDERS. So we leave things as they are?

MRS. ALVING. Yes, certainly.

MANDERS. Good. Just as you wish. [*Notes down.*] Well, then—no insurance.

MRS. ALVING. Incidentally, it's odd you should happen to mention this today . . .

MANDERS. I had often thought of asking you about it. . . .

MRS. ALVING. . . . because yesterday we nearly had a fire down there.

MANDERS. What!

MRS. ALVING. Well, it wasn't anything very much. Some shavings caught fire in the carpenter's shop.

MANDERS. Where Engstrand works?

MRS. ALVING. Yes. They say he's sometimes rather careless with matches.

MANDERS. He has a lot on his mind, that man . . . all sorts of worries. From what I hear, he's trying very hard to turn over a new leaf, thank God.

MRS. ALVING. Oh? Who told you that?

MANDERS. He told me so himself. He's a good workman, too.

MRS. ALVING. Oh yes, when he's sober.

MANDERS. Ah, it's sad, that failing of his! He says he's very often driven to it because of his bad leg. The last time he was in town, I really felt very touched. He came and thanked me so sincerely for getting him this work here, so he could be beside Regine.

MRS. ALVING. He doesn't see much of her.

MANDERS. Oh yes. He has a word with her every day, he told me so himself.

MRS. ALVING. Oh well, it could be.

MANDERS. He feels he needs somebody to stand by him when temptation comes along. *That's* what is so likeable about Jacob Engstrand— the fact that he comes along so helplessly, so full of self-reproach, to confess his failings. The last time he looked in to see me. . . . Look, Mrs. Alving, suppose he desperately needed Regine back home with him again . . .

MRS. ALVING [*rises quickly*]. Regine!

MANDERS. . . . *You* mustn't try to prevent it.

MRS. ALVING. I will. I most certainly will try to prevent it. Anyway . . . Regine is going to work in the Orphanage.

MANDERS. But remember, he *is* her father. . . .

MRS. ALVING. Oh, I know best what sort of a father he's been to her. No, she's not going back to him if I can help it.

MANDERS [*rises*]. But dear Mrs. Alving, you mustn't get so worked-up about it. It's sad the way you misjudge poor Engstrand. It's almost as though you were terrified. . . .

MRS. ALVING [*calmer*]. That's as may be. I have taken Regine into my house and in my house she shall remain. [*Listens.*] Sh! my dear Pastor Manders, I don't want to hear any more about it. [*Her face lights up with joy.*] Listen! There's Oswald coming downstairs. Let's think about *him* now.

[OSWALD ALVING *enters by the door, left; he has on a light overcoat, carries his hat in his hand, and is smoking a large Meerschaum pipe.*]

OSWALD [*remains standing in the doorway*]. Oh, I beg your pardon . . . I thought you were in the study. [*Comes forward.*] Good morning, Pastor.

MANDERS [*staring*]. Ah . . . ! Astounding . . . !

MRS. ALVING. Well, what have you got to say about him *now*, Pastor Manders.

MANDERS. I say . . . I say . . . But is it really . . . ?

OSWALD. Yes, it really is the Prodigal Son, Pastor.

MANDERS. But my dear young friend. . . .

OSWALD. Well, the exile returned, then.

MRS. ALVING. Oswald is thinking of the time when you were so very much against the idea of his becoming an artist.

MANDERS. Some decisions often seem to mortal view unwise at the time, but later. . . . [*Shakes his hand.*] Welcome, welcome! Really, my dear Oswald . . . I can call you Oswald, can't I?

OSWALD. What else would you call me?

MANDERS. Good. What I wanted to say, my dear Oswald, was *this*—you mustn't think I want to condemn out of hand all artists and their ways. I assume there are many who can still preserve some integrity of soul even in their circumstances.

OSWALD. We must hope so.

MRS. ALVING [*beaming with pleasure*]. I know one who has preserved his integrity, both of soul and of body. Just look at him, Pastor Manders.

OSWALD [*pacing up and down*]. Mother dear, please. . . !

MANDERS. Oh, indubitably . . . nobody will deny that. And already you've begun to make a name for yourself. There have often been things in the paper about you, and extremely favourable too. Well that is . . . I believe things seem to have fallen off a bit of late.

OSWALD [*near the conservatory*]. I haven't been doing much painting lately.

MRS. ALVING. Even an artist must rest now and again.

MANDERS. I can well imagine that. Then he gathers strength in preparation for something big.

OSWALD. Yes. . . . Mother, how soon will dinner be ready?

MRS. ALVING. In just half an hour. He's got a good appetite, thank God.

MANDERS. And a taste for tobacco, too.

OSWALD. I found Father's pipe in the little room upstairs, and . . .

MANDERS. Aha! So that was it!

MRS. ALVING. What?

MANDERS. When Oswald was standing there in the door, with that pipe in his mouth, he looked the very spit and image of his father.

OSWALD. Really?

MRS. ALVING. How can you say that! Oswald takes after me.

MANDERS. Yes, but there's something about the corners of the mouth, something about the lips, that reminds one exactly of Alving . . . at least when he is smoking.

MRS. ALVING. Not at all. Oswald is much more like a clergyman about the mouth, I would say.

MANDERS. Yes, yes, quite a lot of my colleagues have a similar expression.

MRS. ALVING. But put that pipe away now, my dear boy. I don't want smoke in here.

OSWALD [*does so*]. Certainly. I just wanted to try it. Because I smoked it once before, as a child.

MRS. ALVING. You?

OSWALD. Yes. I was quite small at the time. And I remember I went up to Father's room one evening when he was feeling rather pleased with himself.

MRS. ALVING. You can't remember anything of those years.

OSWALD. I can. I distinctly remember he sat me on his knee and gave me the pipe to smoke. 'Smoke, lad,' he said, 'go on, lad, smoke!' And I smoked as hard as I could, till I felt I was going quite pale and great beads of sweat stood out on my forehead. Then he roared with laughter. . . .

MANDERS. Most extraordinary!

MRS. ALVING. My dear Pastor, it's only something Oswald has dreamt.

OSWALD. No, Mother, I certainly didn't dream it. Because—don't you remember—you came in and carried me off to the nursery. Then I was sick, and I saw you were crying. . . . Did Father often play tricks like that?

MANDERS. When he was young, he was always full of the joys of living. . . .

OSWALD. And still managed to accomplish such a lot in life. So much that was good and useful, though he wasn't very old when he died.

MANDERS. Yes, you certainly bear the name of a fine, enterprising man, my dear Oswald Alving. I trust it will be an incentive to you. . . .

OSWALD. Yes, it ought to be.

MANDERS. It was nice of you to come home for these celebrations in his honour.

OSWALD. That's the least I could do for Father.

MRS. ALVING. The really nice thing is that he is letting me keep him here a while.

MANDERS. You are going to be at home over the winter, I hear.

OSWALD. I'm going to be at home indefinitely, Pastor. . . . Ah, it *is* nice to be home again.

MRS. ALVING [*beaming*]. Yes, isn't it, Oswald?

MANDERS [*looking sympathetically at him*]. You left home at a very early age, my dear Oswald.

OSWALD. I did. Sometimes I wonder whether it wasn't *too* early.

MRS. ALVING. Not at all. It's a good thing for a bright lad. Especially when he's an only child. You don't want him staying at home with his mother and father getting spoilt.

MANDERS. That's a very moot point, Mrs. Alving. A child's proper place is and must be the home.

OSWALD. I rather think I agree with the pastor there.

MANDERS. Look at your own son. There's no reason why we shouldn't talk about it in front of him. What has been the result in his case? There he is—twenty-six, twenty-seven years old, and never had an opportunity of knowing what a proper home is like.

OSWALD. I beg your pardon, Pastor . . . you are quite wrong there.

MANDERS. Oh? I thought you had been moving more or less exclusively in artistic circles.

OSWALD. I have.

MANDERS. And mostly among the younger artists.

OSWALD. Yes.

MANDERS. But I thought most of those people couldn't afford to set up a home and start a family.

OSWALD. Plenty of them can't afford to get married, Pastor Manders.

MANDERS. Yes. That's what I am saying.

OSWALD. Yet they can still have a home. And some of them *do*. And very proper and very comfortable homes they are.

[MRS. ALVING *follows with close attention, and nods but says nothing.*]

MANDERS. But I'm not talking about bachelor establishments. By 'home' I mean a place for a family, where a man lives with his wife and children.

OSWALD. Yes, or with his children and his children's mother.

MANDERS [*startled, clasps his hands*]. Good heavens!

OSWALD. Well?

MANDERS. Live with his children's mother!

OSWALD. Well, would you rather he abandoned his children's mother?

MANDERS. So it's illicit relationships you are talking about. These so-called sham marriages!

OSWALD. I have never noticed anything particularly sham about these people's lives together.

MANDERS. But how is it possible for any young man or woman with . . . with the slightest sense of decency to consent to live in that fashion . . . openly, for all the world to see!

OSWALD. But what are they to do? A poor young artist . . . a poor girl. . . . It costs money to get married. What are they to do?

MANDERS. What are they to do? Yes, Mr. Alving, I'll tell you what they are to do. They should have kept away from each other from the very start—that's what they should have done!

OSWALD. That kind of talk won't get you very far with eager young people in love.

MRS. ALVING. No, that won't get you very far!

MANDERS [*continuing*]. To think the authorities tolerate such things! That this sort of thing goes on openly! [*Facing* MRS. ALVING.] Hadn't I good reason to be so deeply concerned about your son? Moving in circles where blatant immorality is rampant, where it's even become the accepted thing. . . .

OSWALD. I'll tell you something, Pastor Manders. I have been a regular Sunday visitor in some of these unconventional homes. . . .

MANDERS. On Sundays, even!

OSWALD. Yes, surely that's when people should enjoy themselves? But never have I heard one word that could give offence, let alone seen anything that could be called immoral. No, do you know where and when I *have* encountered immorality in artistic circles?

MANDERS. No, thank God!

OSWALD. Well then, permit me to tell you. When some of our model husbands and fathers took themselves a trip to Paris to have a look round on the loose . . . and condescended to drop in on the artists in their modest haunts, that's when I've met it. Then we got to know what was what. These gentlemen were able to tell us about places and things we'd never even dreamt of.

MANDERS. What? Are you insinuating that respectable men from this country would . . . ?

OSWALD. Have you never heard these respectable men when they get home again? Never heard them holding forth about the outrageous immorality that's to be found abroad?

MANDERS. Yes, of course. . . .

MRS. ALVING. I have too.

OSWALD. Well, you can believe every word they say. Some of them are experts. [*Clutching his head.*] Oh, when I think of that glorious, free life out there . . . smeared by this filth.

MRS. ALVING. You mustn't excite yourself, Oswald. It's not good for you.

OSWALD. Yes, you are right, Mother. It's bad for my health. It's this confounded tiredness, you know. Well, I'll take a little walk before dinner. Forgive me, Pastor Manders, I know you can't agree with all this. But I just had to say it.

[*He goes out through the second door, right.*]

MRS. ALVING. My poor boy. . . !

MANDERS. Yes, you may well say so. So this is what he's come to. [MRS. ALVING *looks at him in silence.* MANDERS *walks up and down.*] He called himself the Prodigal Son. Alas . . . it's true! [MRS. ALVING *continues to look at him.*] And what do you say to all this?

MRS. ALVING. I say Oswald was right in every single word he said.

MANDERS [*stops short*]. Right! Right! To have standards like that!

MRS. ALVING. Living here alone, I have come round to the same way of thinking myself, Pastor Manders. But I've never had the courage to say so. All right, now my boy shall speak for me.

MANDERS. Then you are greatly to be pitied, Mrs. Alving. But now I have something very serious to say to you. No longer as your business executor and adviser, nor even as you and your husband's life-long friend do I stand before you now. It is as your priest, standing now as he stood once before at that most critical moment of your life.

MRS. ALVING. And what does my priest have to say to me?

MANDERS. Let me first refresh your memory, Mrs. Alving. The time is well chosen. Tomorrow is the tenth anniversary of your husband's death. Tomorrow a memorial is to be unveiled in his honour. Tomorrow I shall address the assembled company. But today I want to speak to you alone.

MRS. ALVING. Very well, Pastor Manders. Go on!

MANDERS. You remember how, after little more than a year of married life, you stood on the very brink of disaster? How you left house and home. . . . How you ran away from your husband. . . . Yes, Mrs. Alving, ran away, and refused to go back to him, no matter how much he begged and pleaded?

MRS. ALVING. Have you forgotten how utterly miserable I felt that first year?

MANDERS. All this demanding to be happy in life, it's all part of this same wanton idea. What right have people to happiness? No, we have our duty to do, Mrs. Alving! And your duty was to stand by the man you had chosen, and to whom you were bound by sacred ties.

MRS. ALVING. You know very well what sort of life my husband was living in those days, the excesses he committed.

MANDERS. I know quite well the rumours that were going about. And I would be the last person to condone his conduct as a young man, assuming these rumours told the truth. But it is not a wife's place to sit in judgement on her husband. Your duty should have been to bear with humility that cross which a higher power had judged proper for you. But instead you have the effrontery to cast away the cross, you abandon the man whose stumbling steps you should have guided, you go and risk your own good name, and . . . very nearly jeopardize other people's reputations into the bargain.

MRS. ALVING. Other people's? *One* other person's, you mean?

MANDERS. It was extremely inconsiderate of you to seek refuge with *me*.

MRS. ALVING. With our priest? With our close friend?

MANDERS. Precisely for that reason. . . . Yes, you should thank God I possessed the necessary strength of mind . . . that I managed to dissuade you from your hysterical intentions, and that it was granted to me to lead you back into the path of duty, and home to your lawful husband.

MRS. ALVING. Yes, Pastor Manders, that certainly was your doing.

MANDERS. I was only the humble instrument of a higher power. And the fact that I made you return to the path of duty and obedience, hasn't that proved a tremendous blessing to you ever since? Didn't things go just as I had prophesied? Didn't Alving turn his back on his profligate ways, as a decent man should? And didn't he, from then on, live a quite irreproachable and affectionate life with you for the rest of his days? Didn't he become a great benefactor to this district? And didn't he help and encourage you, so much that you eventually came to collaborate with him in all his enterprises? And a very efficient helpmate you were, too. . . . Oh, I know that, Mrs. Alving. Credit where credit is due. . . . But then I come to the next big mistake in your life.

MRS. ALVING. What do you mean?

MANDERS. Just as you once denied your duty as a wife, you have since denied it as a mother.

MRS. ALVING. Ah. . . !

MANDERS. All your life, you've always been quite disastrously selfish and stubborn. In everything you have done, you have tended to be headstrong and undisciplined. Never would you tolerate any kind of restraint. Anything that became an encumbrance to you in your life, you had no scruples or hesitations about throwing it off, as though it were a burden you could dispose of as and when you pleased. It didn't suit you any longer to be a wife, so you left your husband. You found it irksome being a mother, so you put your child out with strangers.

MRS. ALVING. Yes, that's true. I did do that.

MANDERS. With the result that you are now a stranger to him.

MRS. ALVING. No, no, I'm not!

MANDERS. You are! You must be! And what is he like, now you've got him back? Stop and think, Mrs. Alving. You did your husband great wrong—the fact that you are raising this memorial to him shows you recognize that. You should also recognize the wrong you have done your son. There may still be time to lead him back from the paths of iniquity. Turn back yourself, and save what can perhaps still be saved in him. Because, Mrs. Alving [*with raised forefinger*], you are in truth a very guilty mother. . . . I see it as my duty to tell you this.

[*Silence.*]

MRS. ALVING [*slowly, and with control*]. You have had your say, Pastor Manders. And tomorrow you will make a speech in my husband's memory. I shall not speak tomorrow. But now I'm going to talk to you just as you have talked to me.

MANDERS. Of course, you want to make excuses for what you did. . . .

MRS. ALVING. No. I just want to tell you something.

MANDERS. Well?

MRS. ALVING. None of these things you have been saying about my husband and me and our life together after you had led me back to the path of duty, as you put it—absolutely none of these things do you know from first-hand. From that moment on, you—our closest friend, who regularly used to call every day—you never once set foot in our house.

MANDERS. You and your husband moved out of town immediately afterwards.

MRS. ALVING. Yes. And never once while my husband was alive did you come and see us. It was business that finally forced you to come and visit me, when you had to see about the Orphanage.

MANDERS [*in a low, uncertain voice*]. Helene, if this is meant as a reproach, I must ask you to bear in mind . . .

MRS. ALVING. . . . the consideration you owed to your position. Oh, yes! Also that I was a runaway wife. One can never be too careful where such reckless women are concerned.

MANDERS. My dear . . . Mrs. Alving, that is a gross exaggeration. . . .

MRS. ALVING. All right, all right. I just wanted to say *this*: that when you pass judgement on my married life, you are simply taking it for granted that popular opinion is right.

MANDERS. Well? What then?

MRS. ALVING. But now, Pastor Manders, now I'm going to tell you the truth. I swore to myself that one day you should know. You and you alone!

MANDERS. And what is the truth, then?

MRS. ALVING. The truth is this: my husband was just as debauched when he died as he had been all his life.

MANDERS [*fumbling for a chair*]. What did you say?

MRS. ALVING. After nineteen years of marriage, just as debauched—in his pleasures, at any rate—as he was before you married us.

MANDERS. Those youthful indiscretions . . . those irregularities . . . excesses, if you like . . . you call that a debauched life!

MRS. ALVING. That was the expression our doctor used.

MANDERS. I don't understand you.

MRS. ALVING. Nor is it necessary.

MANDERS. I feel quite dazed. Am I to believe that your entire married life ... all those years together with your husband ... were nothing but a façade.

MRS. ALVING. Precisely that. Now you know.

MANDERS. This is something ... I find very hard to accept. I just don't understand. It's beyond me. How was it possible. . . ? How could a thing like that be kept hidden?

MRS. ALVING. That was the endless battle I fought, day after day. When we had Oswald, I rather thought Alving improved a little. But it didn't last long. And then I had to battle twice as hard, fight tooth and nail to prevent anybody from knowing what sort of person my child's father was. And you know, of course, how charming Alving could be. Nobody could believe anything but good of him. He was one of those people whose reputation is proof against anything they may do. But then, Pastor Manders ... something else you must know ... then came the most hideous thing of all.

MANDERS. More hideous than this?

MRS. ALVING. I put up with things, although I knew very well what was going on in secret outside this house. But when it came to scandal within these very walls. . . .

MANDERS. What's that you say! Here!

MRS. ALVING. Yes, here in our own home. In there [*points to the first door right*] in the dining-room, that's where I first got wind of it. I was doing something in there, and the door was standing ajar. Then I heard our maid come in from the garden with some water for the plants over there.

MANDERS. Well. . . ?

MRS. ALVING. Shortly afterwards I heard my husband come in, too. I heard him say something to her in a low voice. And then I heard. . . . [*With a short laugh.*] Oh, I can still hear it, so devastating and yet at the time so ludicrous ... I heard my own maid whisper: 'Let me go, Mr. Alving! Leave me alone!'

MANDERS. How unseemly! How indiscreet of him! But I'm sure it was no more than an indiscretion, Mrs. Alving, please believe me.

MRS. ALVING. I soon knew what to believe. My husband had his way
with the girl. . . . And *that* affair had its consequences, Pastor
Manders.

MANDERS [*as though stunned*]. And all that in this very house! In this
house!

MRS. ALVING. I had to put up with a lot in this house. To keep him at
home in the evenings . . . and at nights . . . I had to join him in secret
drinking orgies up in his room. I had to sit there with him, just the
two of us drinking, and listen to his obscene, stupid remarks, and
then struggling with him to get him dragged into his bed. . . .

MANDERS [*shaken*]. How could you bear it?

MRS. ALVING. I had to bear it for the sake of my little boy. But then
came that final humiliation when my own servant girl . . . Then
I swore to myself that this would have to stop! So I took control in
the house . . . complete control . . . over him and everything else.
Because now I had a weapon against him, you see, and he didn't dare
say anything. That was the time Oswald was sent away. He was
getting on for seven, and beginning to notice things and ask questions, as children do. That was something I couldn't bear. I felt the
child would somehow be poisoned simply by breathing the foul air
of this polluted house. That was why I sent him away. And now
you understand why he was never allowed to set foot in this place
as long as his father was alive. Nobody knows what that cost me.

MANDERS. What a terrible ordeal for you.

MRS. ALVING. I'd never have stood it if it hadn't been for my work.
And I think I can say I have worked! The extensions to the estate,
the improvements, all those useful innovations Alving got the credit
for—do you imagine he was capable of anything like that? *Him*,
sprawling there all day long on the sofa reading an old government
gazette! No. And I will tell you this as well: I was the one who
urged him on when he had his occasional more lucid intervals; and
it was I who was left to run everything when he started kicking
over the traces again, or lapsed into moaning and self-pity.

MANDERS. And this is the man you are raising a memorial to.

MRS. ALVING. Such is the power of a bad conscience.

MANDERS. Bad. . . ? What do you mean?

MRS. ALVING. I was obsessed by the thought that inevitably the truth must come out sometime and be believed. So the Orphanage was meant as it were to kill any rumours, and sweep away any misgivings.

MANDERS. I must say you haven't failed in that respect, Mrs. Alving.

MRS. ALVING. There was also one other reason. I didn't want Oswald, my son, to inherit a single thing from his father.

MANDERS. So it's Alving's money that . . . ?

MRS. ALVING. Yes. The money I have donated, year by year, to this Orphanage adds up exactly—and I've calculated it very carefully—exactly to the amount that made Lieutenant Alving such a good match in his day.

MANDERS. I don't understand. . . .

MRS. ALVING. That was my purchase price . . . I don't want any of that money to pass to Oswald. Anything my son gets is to come from me, and that's that.

[OSWALD ALVING *enters through the second door, right; he has taken off his hat and coat outside.*]

MRS. ALVING [*going towards him*]. Back already? My dear, dear boy!

OSWALD. Yes, what can you do outside in this everlasting rain? But I hear dinner's ready. Splendid!

REGINE [*with a parcel, from the dining-room*]. A parcel's come for you, Mrs. Alving.

[*She hands it to her.*]

MRS. ALVING [*with a glance at* PASTOR MANDERS]. The song sheets for tomorrow, presumably.

MANDERS. H'm. . . .

REGINE. And dinner is served.

MRS. ALVING. Good. We'll be there in a moment. I just want to. . .

[*She begins to open the parcel.*]

REGINE [*to* OSWALD]. Would Mr. Alving like white or red wine?

OSWALD. Both, please, Miss Engstrand.

REGINE. *Bien.* . . . Very good, Mr. Alving.

[*She goes into the dining-room.*]

OSWALD. I may as well help to draw the corks. . . .

[*He also goes into the dining-room; the door swings half open after him.*]

MRS. ALVING [*who has opened the parcel*]. Yes, quite right. Here are the song sheets, Pastor Manders.

MANDERS [*with folded hands*]. How I shall ever have the face to give my speech tomorrow . . . !

MRS. ALVING. Oh, you'll manage it somehow.

MANDERS [*in a low voice, so as not to be heard in the dining-room*]. Yes, we mustn't have any scandal, of course.

MRS. ALVING [*quietly but firmly*]. No. But *then* this long, ghastly farce will be over. After tomorrow I shall feel as though that man had never lived in this house. There'll be nobody else here but my son and his mother.

[*From the dining-room comes the sound of a chair being overturned; simultaneously a voice is heard.*]

REGINE'S VOICE [*in a sharp whisper*]. Oswald! Are you mad? Let me go!

MRS. ALVING [*stiffening with horror*]. Ah. . . !

[*She stares wild-eyed towards the half-open door.* OSWALD *can be heard coughing and humming. A bottle is uncorked.*]

MANDERS [*agitated*]. What on earth was that! What's the matter, Mrs. Alving?

MRS. ALVING [*hoarsely*]. Ghosts! Those two in the conservatory . . . come back to haunt us.

MANDERS. What do you say! Regine. . . ? Is *she* . . . ?

MRS. ALVING. Yes. Come. Not a word. . . !

[*She grips* PASTOR MANDERS *by the arm and walks unsteadily towards the dining-room.*]

ACT TWO

The same room. A heavy mist still lies over the landscape. PASTOR
MANDERS *and* MRS. ALVING *come out of the dining-room.*

MRS. ALVING [*still in the doorway*]. Kind of you to say so, Pastor.
[*Calling into the dining-room.*] Aren't you coming, Oswald?

OSWALD [*within*]. No, thank you. I think I'll go out for a bit.

MRS. ALVING. Yes, do. It's a little clearer now. [*She shuts the dining-
room door, walks over to the hall door, and calls.*] Regine!

REGINE [*outside*]. Yes, Mrs. Alving?

MRS. ALVING. Go and help with the decorations down in the ironing
room.

REGINE. Yes, Mrs. Alving.

[MRS. ALVING *assures herself that* REGINE *is going, then she shuts the
door.*]

MANDERS. I suppose he can't hear anything in there?

MRS. ALVING. Not when the door is shut. Anyway, he's going out.

MANDERS. I'm still quite bewildered. How I managed to swallow a
single bite of that excellent dinner, I don't know.

MRS. ALVING [*controlling her agitation, walking up and down*]. Nor I.
But what's to be done?

MANDERS. Yes, what's to be done? I'm blessed if I know. I'm completely inexperienced in matters of this kind.

MRS. ALVING. I'm convinced nothing disastrous has happened yet.

MANDERS. No, God forbid. But it's a most unfortunate state of affairs,
all the same.

MRS. ALVING. The whole thing's only a passing fancy of Oswald's,
you can be sure.

MANDERS. Well, as I said, I'm not very well up in these things. But I cannot help feeling. . .

MRS. ALVING. Of course, we must get her out of the house. Immediately. That's quite clear. . . .

MANDERS. Naturally.

MRS. ALVING. But where to? We can't very well. . . .

MANDERS. Where to? Home to her father, of course.

MRS. ALVING. To whom did you say?

MANDERS. To her. . . . Ah, but of course Engstrand isn't. . . . Good heavens, Mrs. Alving, this can't be possible? You must be mistaken, surely?

MRS. ALVING. I'm afraid there's no mistake. Johanna had to confess everything to me, and Alving couldn't deny it. There was nothing else we could do but get the thing hushed up.

MANDERS. I suppose there was nothing else for it.

MRS. ALVING. The girl left at once, and she was given quite a fair amount to keep her mouth shut. The rest she managed for herself when she got to town. She took up with Engstrand again and I dare say dropped a few hints about how much money she had, and told him a tale about some foreigner who was supposed to have put in here that summer with his yacht. So she and Engstrand got married, all in a great hurry. Why, you married them yourself.

MANDERS. But what am I to make of . . . ? I distinctly remember Engstrand coming to arrange about the wedding. He was quite abject, and full of remorse about the foolish thing he and the girl had done.

MRS. ALVING. Of course, he had to take the blame on himself.

MANDERS. But the deceit of the man! And to *me*! I would honestly never have believed it of Jacob Engstrand. Well I shall have something to say to him about that, so he can just look out. . . . The immorality of a match of that sort! And all for money. . . ! How much did the girl have?

MRS. ALVING. Three hundred dollars.

MANDERS. Fancy going and getting married to a fallen woman for three hundred miserable dollars!

MRS. ALVING. What do you say about me, then, going and letting myself be married to a fallen man?

MANDERS. But . . . good heavens! What are you talking about? A fallen man!

MRS. ALVING. Do you imagine when I went to the altar with Alving, he was any purer than Johanna was when Engstrand married her?

MANDERS. But these are two utterly different things. . . .

MRS. ALVING. Not so terribly different, in fact. Admittedly there was a big difference in the price . . . three hundred miserable dollars as against a whole fortune.

MANDERS. But how can you compare things so utterly dissimilar. You had taken counsel with your own heart, and with your family.

MRS. ALVING [*not looking at him*]. I thought you realized where my heart, as you put it, had strayed at that time.

MANDERS [*distantly*]. If I had realized anything of the kind, I would not have been a daily guest in your husband's house.

MRS. ALVING. Well, the fact remains I did not, after all, take counsel with myself.

MANDERS. Well, with your nearest relatives, then, as it was your duty to. With your mother and your two aunts.

MRS. ALVING. Yes, that's true. The three of them reckoned it all up for me. It's incredible how nicely worked out they had it all, showing how it would be sheer madness to turn down an offer like that. If only Mother could look in now and see what had become of all the glory.

MANDERS. Nobody can be held responsible for the way things have turned out. But nevertheless one thing is clear: your marriage was arranged in strict accord with law and order.

MRS. ALVING. Oh, all this law and order! I often think *that's* the cause of all the trouble in the world.

MANDERS. Mrs. Alving, that's a very wrong thing to say.

MRS. ALVING. Well, perhaps it is. But I'm not putting up with it any longer, all these ties and restrictions. I can't stand it! I must work myself free.

MANDERS. What do you mean by that?

MRS. ALVING [*drumming on the window frame*]. I should never have kept it a secret, the kind of life Alving led. But at the time I didn't dare do anything else . . . and it was partly for my own sake. What a coward I was!

MANDERS. Coward?

MRS. ALVING. If people had got to know about it, they'd probably have said 'Poor man, no wonder he lets himself go a bit, with a wife who runs off and leaves him.'

MANDERS. There would have been some justification for saying that.

MRS. ALVING [*looking hard at him*]. If I were the sort of person I should be, I would take Oswald on one side and say: 'Listen, my son, your father was an old reprobate. . . .'

MANDERS. Heavens above!

MRS. ALVING. . . . and then I would tell him everything I've told you . . . the whole lot.

MANDERS. I am really rather shocked at you, Mrs. Alving.

MRS. ALVING. Oh, I know! I know! I find the idea shocking myself. [*Walks away from the window.*] What a coward I am!

MANDERS. Do you call it cowardice, to do what is quite plainly your duty? Have you forgotten that a child is supposed to love and honour its father and mother?

MRS. ALVING. Let's not generalize. The question is: is Oswald supposed to love and honour Captain Alving?

MANDERS. Don't you feel your mother's heart prompting you not to shatter your son's ideals?

MRS. ALVING. But what about the truth?

MANDERS. What about his ideals?

MRS. ALVING. Oh, ideals, ideals! If only I weren't such a coward!

MANDERS. Don't despise ideals, Mrs. Alving ... that can bring a cruel reckoning. Especially in Oswald's case. Oswald hasn't so very many ideals, unfortunately. But I saw enough to realize that his father represents a kind of ideal to him.

MRS. ALVING. Yes, you are right.

MANDERS. And it was you yourself who gave him these ideas, and your letters encouraged him in them.

MRS. ALVING. Yes, I was doing my duty, observing the proprieties. That's why I lied to my son, year in and year out. Oh, what a coward ... what a coward I have been!

MANDERS. You have built up a beautiful illusion in your son's mind, Mrs. Alving ... and really, that's something you shouldn't under-estimate.

MRS. ALVING. H'm! Who knows if it is actually such a good thing after all. ... But I won't stand for any funny business with Regine. He's not going to go and mess up that girl's life.

MANDERS. Good Lord, no! That would be terrible!

MRS. ALVING. If I thought he was serious, and that it would make him happy. ...

MANDERS. Well? What then?

MRS. ALVING. But it wouldn't. I'm afraid Regine isn't that kind.

MANDERS. What of it? What do you mean?

MRS. ALVING. If only I weren't such a miserable coward, I'd say to him: marry the girl, or come to some arrangement between yourselves. So long as there's nothing underhand.

MANDERS. Merciful heavens! Legal marriage, even! Of all the fright-ful. ... Of all the unheard-of ... !

MRS. ALVING. Unheard-of, you say? Hand on heart, Pastor Manders, do you think there aren't plenty of couples all over the country who are every bit as closely related?

MANDERS. I simply don't understand you.

MRS. ALVING. Oh yes, you do.

MANDERS. I suppose you are thinking of the possibility that. . . . Yes, I regret to say family life is in fact not always as pure as it ought to be. But with the sort of thing you are hinting at, nobody can ever really tell . . . not with any certainty, at least. Here, on the other hand. . . ! How you, as a mother, could be willing to allow your . . . !

MRS. ALVING. But I'm *not* willing! I couldn't wish it, not for anything. That's precisely what I'm saying.

MANDERS. No, because you are a coward, as you put it. But supposing you weren't a coward. . . ! God in Heaven, what a shocking union!

MRS. ALVING. Well, for that matter we are all descended from unions of that sort, they say. And who was it arranged things like that here on earth, Pastor Manders?

MANDERS. I do not propose to discuss such questions with you, Mrs. Alving. You are far from having the right attitude of mind. But how you dare call it cowardice. . . !

MRS. ALVING. I'll tell you what I mean. The reason I'm so timid and afraid is that I can never get properly rid of the ghosts that haunt me.

MANDERS. What did you call them?

MRS. ALVING. Ghosts. When I heard Regine and Oswald in there, it was just like seeing ghosts. But then I'm inclined to think that we are all ghosts, Pastor Manders, every one of us. It's not just what we inherit from our mothers and fathers that haunts us. It's all kinds of old defunct theories, all sorts of old defunct beliefs, and things like that. It's not that they actually *live* on in us; they are simply lodged there, and we cannot get rid of them. I've only to pick up a newspaper and I seem to see ghosts gliding between the lines. Over the whole country there must be ghosts, as numerous as the sands of the sea. And here we are, all of us, abysmally afraid of the light.

MANDERS. Aha! So there we see the fruits of your reading. And a nice harvest it is, I must say. Oh, these disgusting, free-thinking pamphlets! Revolting!

MRS. ALVING. You are wrong, my dear Pastor. You were the one who goaded me into doing some thinking. And I shall always be grateful to you for that.

MANDERS. *I* did!

MRS. ALVING. Yes, when you forced me to submit to what you called my duty and my obligations. When you praised as right and proper what my whole mind revolted against, as against some loathsome thing. It was then I began to examine the fabric of your teachings. I began picking at one of the knots, but as soon as I'd got that undone, the whole thing came apart at the seams. It was then I realized it was just tacked together.

MANDERS [*softly, moved*]. And that's all that came of what was the hardest struggle of my life?

MRS. ALVING. Call it rather your most pitiful defeat.

MANDERS. It was my life's greatest victory, Helene; victory over myself.

MRS. ALVING. It was a crime against us both.

MANDERS. Was it a crime to say to you: 'Woman, go back to your lawful husband'? When you came to me, demented, shouting: 'Here I am! Take me!'? Was *that* a crime?

MRS. ALVING. Yes, I think so.

MANDERS. We two don't understand each other.

MRS. ALVING. Not any more, at least.

MANDERS. Never once . . . not in my most secret thoughts . . . have I ever regarded you as anything other than another man's wife.

MRS. ALVING. Really?

MANDERS. Helene. . . .

MRS. ALVING. It's so easy to forget one's own past.

MANDERS. Not me. I'm the same as I always was.

MRS. ALVING [*changing her tone*]. Well, well, well, let's not talk any more about the old days. You are now up to the ears in committee work and other undertakings; and here I go battling on with ghosts, both within and without.

MANDERS. The latter kind I can at least help you to put down. After all the dreadful things I've heard from you today, I cannot in all conscience think of permitting a young defenceless girl to remain in your house.

MRS. ALVING. Don't you think the best thing would be if we could see her settled? Decently married, I mean?

MANDERS. Indubitably. I think in her case it's in every way desirable. Regine is now of an age when. . . . Of course, I'm not an expert in these things, but. . . .

MRS. ALVING. Regine matured very early.

MANDERS. Yes she did, didn't she. I seem to remember she was remarkably well developed physically when I was preparing her for confirmation. But she'd better go home for the present, under her father's care. . . . Ah, but of course Engstrand isn't. . . . To think that he, *he* of all people, could conceal the truth from me like that!

[*There is a knock on the hall door.*]

MRS. ALVING. Who can *that* be? Come in!

ENGSTRAND [*in his Sunday suit, in the doorway*]. Begging your pardon, but . . .

MANDERS. Aha! H'm. . . .

MRS. ALVING. It's you, is it, Engstrand?

ENGSTRAND. . . . there was none of the maids around, so I made so bold as to knock.

MRS. ALVING. Oh, very well, come in. Something you want to see me about?

ENGSTRAND [*comes in*]. No, thanks all the same. It was really the pastor I was wanting a word with.

MANDERS [*walking up and down*]. H'm, indeed. You want to talk to me, do you?

ENGSTRAND. Yes, I'd be awfully glad if . . .

MANDERS [*stops in front of him*]. Well? What is it, may I ask?

ENGSTRAND. Well, it's like this, Pastor. We are being paid off now down there . . . and many thanks to you, ma'am . . . and now everything's finished. And I was thinking it would be a good idea if us that's been working so hard together all this time . . . I was thinking we ought perhaps to finish up this evening with a bit of a service.

MANDERS. A service? Down at the Orphanage?

ENGSTRAND. Yes, but if you don't happen to think it's such a good idea, Pastor. . . .

MANDERS. Oh yes, I do, but . . . H'm. . . .

ENGSTRAND. I often used to say a prayer or two myself down there in the evenings. . . .

MRS. ALVING. Did you?

ENGSTRAND. Yes, now and again. Nothing like a bit of uplift, as you might say. But I'm just a simple, ordinary man with no real gift for it, so help me . . . and then it struck me that since Pastor Manders happened to be here. . . .

MANDERS. Look, Engstrand, first I must ask you something. Are you in the right frame of mind for a meeting of this kind? Do you feel your conscience is clear?

ENGSTRAND. God help us, Pastor, there's not much point in talking about consciences.

MANDERS. Oh yes, there is. That's exactly what we *are* going to talk about. Well? What have you got to say?

ENGSTRAND. Ah . . . it can be pretty bad, conscience can, sometimes.

MANDERS. Well, at least you admit it. But now I want you to tell me straight—what's the real story about Regine?

MRS. ALVING [*quickly*]. Pastor Manders!

MANDERS [*reassuringly*]. Please allow me. . . .

ENGSTRAND. About Regine? Lord, you put the wind up me there! [*Looks at* MRS. ALVING.] There's nothing the matter about Regine, is there?

MANDERS. Let's hope not. What I mean is this: what's the position as far as you and Regine are concerned? You are supposed to be her father, aren't you? Well?

ENGSTRAND [*hesitantly*]. Well . . . h'm . . . you know all about that business about me and poor Johanna.

MANDERS. No more prevarication. Your late wife informed Mrs. Alving of the true state of affairs before she left her service.

ENGSTRAND. Well I'll be. . . ! She did, did she?

MANDERS. So we've found you out, Engstrand.

ENGSTRAND. And she swore by all that was holy . . .

MANDERS. Swore?

ENGSTRAND. Well, took her oath, then. Really solemn.

MANDERS. And all these years you've been hiding the truth from me. From *me*, when I've always gone out of my way to show every confidence in you.

ENGSTRAND. Yes, I'm sorry to say I have that.

MANDERS. Have I deserved this of you, Engstrand? Haven't I always been ready to lend you a helping hand in any way, as far as it lay in my power? Answer me! Haven't I?

ENGSTRAND. Many's the time things would have looked pretty black for me if I hadn't had Pastor Manders.

MANDERS. And this is what I get for it. You get me to make false entries in the church register, and then for years afterwards you withhold the information you owed to me and to truth. Your conduct has been quite indefensible, Engstrand. And that's the end as far as we two are concerned.

ENGSTRAND [*with a sigh*]. Well, that's that, I suppose.

MANDERS. Because I can't see what possible excuse you could have?

ENGSTRAND. You didn't expect her to go round making the scandal worse by talking about it, did you? Now, Pastor, you just imagine yourself now in the same predicament as poor Johanna. . . .

MANDERS. Me?

ENGSTRAND. Good Lord, I don't mean exactly the same. What I mean is, suppose you had something you were ashamed of in the eyes of the world, as they say. We men shouldn't judge a poor woman too harshly, Pastor.

MANDERS. But I'm not. It's you I'm accusing.

ENGSTRAND. Could I ask you one little question, Pastor?

MANDERS. All right.

ENGSTRAND. Isn't it right and proper for a man to try and raise the fallen?

MANDERS. Yes, of course.

ENGSTRAND. And isn't a man bound to keep his promise?

MANDERS. Certainly he is. But. . . .

ENGSTRAND. When Johanna got into trouble on account of that Englishman—or maybe it was an American, or a Russian or whatever they're called—well, she came back to town. Poor thing, she'd already turned me down once or twice before; she only had eyes for the good-looking ones, she had; and of course I had this gammy leg of mine. You'll remember, Pastor, how I once screwed up my courage to go into one of them dance-halls where you get seafaring men carrying on all drunk and disorderly, as the saying goes. And just as I was appealing to them to turn over a new leaf . . .

MRS. ALVING [*over beside the window*]. H'm. . . .

MANDERS. I know, Engstrand. The brutes threw you downstairs. You've told me about that incident before. Your injury does you honour.

ENGSTRAND. I'm not the one to brag about it, Pastor. But what I was going to say was that she came along to me and confessed everything, with weeping and wailing and gnashing of teeth. I must say it fair broke my heart to listen to her.

MANDERS. Did it really, Engstrand. What then?

ENGSTRAND. So then I says to her: this American is off roaming the seven seas. And as for you Johanna, I says, you've committed a sin, you're a fallen woman. But Jacob Engstrand, I says, he's a man that stands firm on his own two feet, he is . . . in a manner of speaking, that is, I meant, Pastor.

MANDERS. I quite understand. Go on.

ENGSTRAND. Well, so then I married her properly and set her on her feet again, so as nobody would get to know about her carrying on with foreigners.

MANDERS. All this is very admirable. What I can't approve of is that you could stoop to accepting money. . . .

ENGSTRAND. Money? Me? Not a cent.

MANDERS [*inquiringly to* MRS. ALVING]. But . . . ?

ENGSTRAND. Oh, yes, wait a minute . . . now I remember. Johanna did have a copper or two. But I wouldn't have anything to do with *that*. Puh, that's Mammon, I says, that's the wages of sin. We'll take that filthy gold—or notes, or whatever it was—and we'll chuck it back at that American, I says. But he was already up and away, over the stormy seas.

MANDERS. Was he now, Engstrand, my good fellow?

ENGSTRAND. Yes. So then Johanna and I agreed that the money was to go towards the child's education. And so it did. And I can account for every cent of it.

MANDERS. But this changes things quite considerably.

ENGSTRAND. That's the way things are, Pastor. And I think I can say I've been a good father to Regine . . . as far as my strength would let me . . . because I'm just a poor sinner, I'm afraid.

MANDERS. Come now, my dear Engstrand. . . .

ENGSTRAND. But I think I can say I was a loving husband to poor Johanna, and I brought up the child and provided a home, as the good book says we should. But it would never have occurred to me to go bragging to Pastor Manders and giving myself a pat on the back just because I'd happened to do a good deed for once in a while. No, when anything like that happens to Jacob Engstrand, he keeps his mouth shut about it. I should say it doesn't happen all that often, I'm afraid. And whenever I go along to see Pastor Manders, I've always plenty to do, talking about my mistakes and short-comings. Because as I said just now, and I say it again: my conscience can be in a pretty bad way, sometimes.

MANDERS. Give me your hand, Jacob Engstrand.

ENGSTRAND. Oh Lord, Pastor. . . .

MANDERS. No beating about the bush! [*Grasps his hand.*] There now!

ENGSTRAND. And please, Pastor, I want to ask you very humbly to forgive me. . . .

MANDERS. You? On the contrary. I'm the one who should be asking you. . . .

ENGSTRAND. Oh, Lord, no!

MANDERS. But yes, I insist. And I do so with all my heart. Please forgive me for misjudging you like that. I only wish there were some way I could show my sincere regret, and my good will. . . .

ENGSTRAND. Would you, Pastor?

MANDERS. With the very greatest of pleasure. . . .

ENGSTRAND. Well, in point of fact there is something. With the bit of money I've put aside out of this job, I was thinking of starting a kind of Seamen's Home down in town.

MRS. ALVING. You *what*?

ENGSTRAND. Yes, the idea is to make it into a kind of home from home, as you might say. Many are the temptations open to a sailor when he sets foot ashore. But in this place of mine, I was thinking he could be sort of under a fatherly eye.

MANDERS. What do you say to that, Mrs. Alving!

ENGSTRAND. Heaven knows I haven't a great deal to make a start with. But if only I could be given a bit of a helping hand. . . .

MANDERS. Yes, yes, we must go into that in more detail. But now, you go on ahead and get things ready, and light the candles and brighten up the place a little. And we'll spend an improving hour together there, my dear Engstrand. Because now I do think you are in the right frame of mind.

ENGSTRAND. Yes, I think I am. Goodbye then, Mrs. Alving, and thank you. And take good care of Regine for me. [*He wipes away a tear.*] Poor Johanna's little girl . . . ah, it's a funny thing . . . but it's just as though she were tied fast to my heartstrings. Yes, it really is.

[*He bows and goes out through the hall.*]

MANDERS. Well, what do you say to our man now, Mrs. Alving? That was a very different explanation we got from him, wasn't it?

MRS. ALVING. Yes, it certainly was.

MANDERS. You see now how extremely careful one has to be when passing judgement on one's fellow men. But then what a real joy it is to discover that one has been mistaken. What do *you* say?

MRS. ALVING. I say you are a great big baby, and always will be.

MANDERS. Me?

MRS. ALVING [*places both hands on his shoulders*]. And I say I could almost feel like hugging you.

MANDERS [*drawing back hastily*]. Bless me, no. . . . What an idea!

MRS. ALVING [*with a smile*]. Oh, you needn't be afraid of me.

MANDERS [*beside the table*]. Sometimes you have such an extravagant way of expressing yourself. I'll just collect up these documents first and put them in my case. [*He does this.*] There now. And now, good-bye for the present. Keep your eyes open when Oswald returns. I'll look in on you again later.

[*He takes his hat and goes out through the hall door.* MRS. ALVING *sighs, looks for a moment out of the window, tidies up the room a little and is about to go into the dining-room but stops with a stifled cry in the doorway.*]

MRS. ALVING. Oswald, are you still in the dining-room!

OSWALD [*in the dining-room*]. I'm just finishing my cigar.

MRS. ALVING. I thought you'd gone for a little walk up the road.

OSWALD. In *this* weather?

[*A glass clinks.* MRS. ALVING *lets the door stand open and sits down with her knitting on the sofa by the window.*]

OSWALD. Wasn't that Pastor Manders who just went out?

MRS. ALVING. Yes, he went down to the Orphanage.

OSWALD. H'm.

[*The glass and the decanter clink again.*]

MRS. ALVING [*with a worried look*]. Oswald dear, you ought to go carefully with that liqueur. It's strong.

OSWALD. It keeps out the damp.

MRS. ALVING. Wouldn't you rather come in here beside me?

OSWALD. I can't smoke in there.

MRS. ALVING. You know it's all right to smoke cigars.

OSWALD. All right, I'll come then. Just another little drop. . . . There now.

[*He comes into the room smoking his cigar and shuts the door behind him. There is a short silence.*]

OSWALD. Where's the pastor gone?

MRS. ALVING. I told you, he's gone down to the Orphanage.

OSWALD. Oh yes, that's right.

MRS. ALVING. You shouldn't sit so long at the table, Oswald.

OSWALD [*holding his cigar behind his back*]. But I find it so pleasant, Mother. [*Pats and caresses her.*] Think what it means to me . . . to be home, to sit at my mother's own table, in my mother's room, and enjoy my mother's delicious cooking.

MRS. ALVING. My dear, dear boy!

OSWALD [*somewhat impatiently walks up and down, smoking*]. What else is there for me to do here? I can't get started on anything.

MRS. ALVING. Oh, can't you?

OSWALD. This dull weather? When there isn't a glimpse of the sun all day? [*Walks across the room.*] Oh, this not being able to work. . . !

MRS. ALVING. Perhaps you should have thought twice about coming home.

OSWALD. Oh no, Mother. I had to.

MRS. ALVING. Because I'd ten times rather sacrifice the joy of having you here than see you. . .

OSWALD [*stops beside the table*]. But tell me, Mother . . . does it really make you so very happy to have me home?

MRS. ALVING. Make me happy!

OSWALD [*crumpling a newspaper*]. I shouldn't have thought it made much difference to you whether I was around or not.

MRS. ALVING. Have you the heart to say that to your mother, Oswald?

OSWALD. Yet you managed to get on quite well without me before.

MRS. ALVING. Yes. I got on without you, that's true.

[*Silence. It begins slowly to grow dusk.* OSWALD *walks up and down the room. He has put the cigar down.*]

OSWALD [*stops beside* MRS. ALVING]. Mother, may I sit beside you on the sofa?

MRS. ALVING [*makes room for him*]. Yes, do, my dear.

OSWALD [*sits down*]. There is something I must tell you, Mother.

MRS. ALVING [*tense*]. Well?

OSWALD [*staring into space*]. Because I can't stand it any longer.

MRS. ALVING. Stand what? What is it?

OSWALD [*as before*]. I couldn't bring myself to write to you about it. And since I got home . . .

MRS. ALVING [*gripping his arm*]. Oswald, what is it?

OSWALD. Yesterday and again today, I tried to shake off these thoughts . . . fight myself free. But it's no use.

MRS. ALVING [*rising*]. You must tell me everything, Oswald!

OSWALD [*drags her down on the sofa again*]. Sit still, and I'll try and tell you . . . I've been complaining of feeling tired after my journey, you know. . . .

MRS. ALVING. Yes? Well?

OSWALD. But that's not what is wrong with me. Not ordinary tiredness. . . .

MRS. ALVING [*tries to jump up*]. You aren't ill, Oswald!

OSWALD [*pulling her down again*]. Sit still, Mother. Take it easy. I'm not really ill, either. Not what people generally call being ill. [*He puts his hands to his head.*] Mother, it's my mind that's given way . . . destroyed . . . I'll never be able to work again!

[*Hiding his face in his hands, he buries his head in her lap, sobbing bitterly.*]

MRS. ALVING [*pale and trembling*]. Oswald! Look at me! No, no, it isn't true!

OSWALD [*looks up with despair in his eyes*]. Never to be able to work again! Never . . . never! Like a living death! Mother, can you imagine anything more horrible?

MRS. ALVING. My poor boy! How did this terrible thing happen to you?

OSWALD [*sitting up again*]. Yes, that's just what I can't for the life of me understand. I've never gone in for reckless living. Not in any sense of the word. You must believe me, Mother. I've never done that.

MRS. ALVING. I'm sure you haven't, Oswald.

OSWALD. And yet a thing like this happens to me! This terrible thing!

MRS. ALVING. Oh, but it will get better, my darling. It's simply overwork, believe me.

OSWALD [*dully*]. That's also what I believed at first. But it isn't.

MRS. ALVING. Tell me everything, from beginning to end.

OSWALD. All right, I will.

MRS. ALVING. When did you first notice anything?

OSWALD. Immediately after the last time I was home, when I got back to Paris. I began to get the most violent pains in the head . . . generally here at the back of the head, it seemed. It was just like having an iron band clamped tight round your neck, and up there.

MRS. ALVING. And then?

OSWALD. At first I didn't think it was anything more than the ordinary headache I'd always suffered from, ever since I was a child.

MRS. ALVING. Yes, yes. . . .

OSWALD. But it wasn't. I soon realized that. I couldn't work any more. I wanted to start on a big new picture. But my skill just seemed to desert me, I felt paralysed, I couldn't concentrate, I felt giddy, everything went round and round. Oh, I was in a terrible state! In the end I sent for the doctor . . . and I learned the truth from him.

MRS. ALVING. What do you mean?

OSWALD. He was one of the leading doctors over there. I had to tell him how I felt. And then he started asking me a whole lot of questions that didn't seem to me to have anything at all to do with it. I couldn't understand what the man was getting at. . . .

MRS. ALVING. Well!

OSWALD. At last he said: there's been something worm-eaten about you since birth. He used that very word: 'vermoulu'.

MRS. ALVING [*tense*]. What did he mean by that?

OSWALD. I couldn't understand it either, and I asked him for a more detailed explanation. And then he said, the old cynic . . . [*Clenches his fist.*] Oh. . . !

MRS. ALVING. What did he say?

OSWALD. He said: the sins of the fathers are visited upon the children.

MRS. ALVING [*rising slowly*]. The sins of the fathers . . . !

OSWALD. I very nearly hit him in the face. . . .

MRS. ALVING [*walks across the floor*]. The sins of the fathers. . . .

OSWALD [*smiling sadly*]. Yes, what do you think? Of course, I assured him that was quite out of the question. But do you think he would give way? No, he wouldn't budge. And it wasn't until I'd produced your letters and translated for him all those bits about Father. . . .

MRS. ALVING. What then. . . ?

OSWALD. Well, then he naturally had to admit that he'd been on the wrong track. Then I learnt the truth. The incredible truth! This blissfully happy life I'd been living with my friends, I should never have indulged in it. It had been too much for my strength. So it was my own fault, you see!

MRS. ALVING. Oswald! Oh no, you mustn't think that!

OSWALD. There was no other possible explanation, he said. *That's* the really terrible thing. A hopeless wreck for the rest of my life . . . and all the result of my own thoughtlessness. All the things I wanted to do in life . . . I daren't even think about them again . . . can't think about them. Oh, if only I could live my life over again . . . undo everything I've done!

[*He throws himself face-down on the sofa.* MRS. ALVING *wrings her hands and walks up and down in silent inner conflict.*]

OSWALD [*after a moment, looks up and remains lying propped on his elbow*]. If only it had been something inherited . . . something one couldn't have helped. But this! The shame of it, throwing everything away like that, wantonly, thoughtlessly . . . happiness, health, everything . . . one's future . . . one's whole life . . . !

MRS. ALVING. No, no, my dear, darling boy! This is impossible. [*Bends over him.*] Things are not as desperate as you think.

OSWALD. Oh, you don't know. . . . [*Jumps up.*] And then there's all the worry I'm causing you, Mother. Many's the time I've half hoped you didn't really care very much about me.

MRS. ALVING. Oh, Oswald, my own boy! The one thing I have in all the world. The one thing I care anything at all about.

OSWALD [*seizes both her hands and kisses them*]. Yes, yes, I can see that. When I'm at home, I can see it all right. And that's almost the hardest thing about it for me.—Still, now you know. And let's not talk about it any more today. I can't bear thinking about it for long. [*Walks across the room.*] Get me something to drink, Mother!

MRS. ALVING. Drink? What do you want to drink now?

OSWALD. Oh, anything. You must have some of that cold punch in the house, haven't you?

MRS. ALVING. Yes, but my dear Oswald. . . !

OSWALD. Don't begrudge me that, Mother. Please! I *must* have something to swill all these nagging thoughts down with. [*He goes into the conservatory.*] How . . . how dark it is here! [MRS. ALVING *pulls the bell-rope, right.*] And this incessant rain! Week after week it can go on, for months on end. Never a glimpse of the sun. All the times I've been home, I can't ever remember having once seen the sun.

MRS. ALVING. Oswald . . . you are thinking of leaving me!

OSWALD. H'm. . . . [*Sighs deeply.*] I'm not thinking of anything. I *can't* think of anything! [*In a low voice.*] I've given up thinking.

REGINE [*from the dining-room*]. You rang, ma'am?

MRS. ALVING. Yes, can we have the lamp in, please?

REGINE. At once, ma'am. It's already lit.

[*She goes out.*]

MRS. ALVING [*walks over to* OSWALD]. Oswald, don't keep anything back from me.

OSWALD. I'm not, Mother. [*He walks over to the table.*] I think I've told you plenty.

[REGINE *brings in the lamp and puts it on the table.*]

MRS. ALVING. And, Regine, you might bring us a half-bottle of champagne.

REGINE. Very good, ma'am.

[*She goes out again.*]

OSWALD [*puts his arm round* MRS. ALVING'S *neck.*] That's the style. I knew my mother wouldn't let her son go thirsty.

MRS. ALVING. My poor darling Oswald. How could I possibly refuse you anything now?

OSWALD [*eagerly*]. Is that true, Mother. Do you mean it?

MRS. ALVING. What?

OSWALD. That you couldn't refuse me anything?

MRS. ALVING. But Oswald dear. . .

OSWALD. Hush!

[REGINE *brings in a tray with a half-bottle of champagne and two glasses, which she places on the table.*]

REGINE. Shall I open . . . ?

OSWALD. No, thank you, I'll do it myself.

[REGINE *goes out again.*]

MRS. ALVING [*sits down at the table*]. What was it you thought . . . I couldn't refuse you?

OSWALD [*busy opening the bottle*]. First we'll have a glass . . . or two.

[*The cork pops, he fills one glass and is about to fill the other.*]

MRS. ALVING [*putting her hand over it*]. No, thanks . . . not for me.

OSWALD. All right, for me, then!

[*He empties his glass, re-fills it and empties it again; then he sits down at the table.*]

MRS. ALVING [*expectantly*]. Well?

OSWALD [*without looking at her*]. Tell me . . . I thought you and Pastor Manders were looking strangely . . . h'm . . . subdued, at dinner.

MRS. ALVING. You noticed?

OSWALD. Yes. H'm. . . . [*After a silence.*] Tell me . . . what do you think of Regine?

MRS. ALVING. What do I think of her?

OSWALD. Yes, isn't she marvellous?

MRS. ALVING. Oswald dear, you don't know her as well as I do. . . .

OSWALD. Well?

MRS. ALVING. Unfortunately Regine stayed too long at home. I should have had her here earlier.

OSWALD. Yes, but isn't she marvellous looking, Mother?

[*He fills his glass.*]

MRS. ALVING. Regine has many serious shortcomings. . . .

OSWALD. Well, what's that matter?

[*He drinks again.*]

MRS. ALVING. All the same, I'm fond of her; and I'm responsible for her. I wouldn't for the world want anything to happen to her.

OSWALD [*jumps up*]. Mother, Regine is my only hope!

MRS. ALVING [*rising*]. What do you mean by that?

OSWALD. I can't go on bearing all this agony of mind alone.

MRS. ALVING. Haven't you got your mother to bear it with you?

OSWALD. Yes, that's what I thought. That's why I came home to you. But that way's no use. I can see it's no use. I can't stand living here.

MRS. ALVING. Oswald!

OSWALD. I must live a different life, Mother. That's why I must leave you. I don't want you to have to watch it.

MRS. ALVING. My poor boy! But, Oswald, while you are as ill as this. . . .

OSWALD. If it were only the illness, I'd have been quite ready to stay with you, Mother. Because you are the best friend I have in the world.

MRS. ALVING. Yes, Oswald, I am, aren't I?

OSWALD [*wandering restlessly up and down*]. But it's all the torment, the anguish, the remorse . . . and this great mortal dread. Oh . . . this terrible feeling of dread!

MRS. ALVING [*following him*]. Dread? What feeling of dread? What do you mean?

OSWALD. Oh, you mustn't ask me any more. I don't know. I can't describe it to you. [MRS. ALVING *walks over and pulls the bell-rope, right.*] What do you want?

MRS. ALVING. I want my boy to be happy, that's what I want. He mustn't go on brooding like this. [*To* REGINE *who appears in the doorway.*] More champagne. A whole bottle.

[REGINE *goes.*]

OSWALD. Mother!

MRS. ALVING. Perhaps you think we don't know how to live out here in the country?

OSWALD. Isn't she marvellous looking? What a figure! And as sound as a bell!

MRS. ALVING [*sits down at the table*]. Sit down, Oswald, and let's talk things over quietly.

OSWALD [*sits down*]. You probably don't know, Mother, but I have to make it up to Regine for something I've done to her.

MRS. ALVING. *You've* done?

OSWALD. A bit of thoughtlessness . . . or whatever you like to call it. All very innocent, incidentally. When I was last home . . .

MRS. ALVING. Yes?

OSWALD. . . . she was always asking me about Paris, and I used to tell her something of what went on over there. Then one day I remember I happened to say: 'Wouldn't you like to come over yourself?'

MRS. ALVING. Well?

OSWALD. I saw her blush, and then she said: 'Yes, I wouldn't mind at all.' 'All right,' I said, 'we'll see if it can't be managed' . . . or something like that.

MRS. ALVING. Yes?

OSWALD. Of course I'd forgotten the whole thing. But when I happened to ask her a couple of days ago if she was glad I was going to be at home for so long. . .

MRS. ALVING. Yes?

OSWALD. . . . she gave me a funny look and said: 'But what about my trip to Paris?'

MRS. ALVING. Her trip!

OSWALD. And then she came out with it: she'd taken it all seriously, she'd been thinking about me the whole time, she'd even started learning French. . . .

MRS. ALVING. So that's why. . . .

OSWALD. Mother . . . this girl looked so marvellous standing there, so good-looking and vital . . . I'd never really noticed her very much before. . . . Then when she stood there, ready it seemed to take me in her arms . . .

MRS. ALVING. Oswald!

OSWALD. . . . it was then I realized that she was my salvation. Because she was filled with the joy of life.

MRS. ALVING [*starts*]. Joy of life. . . ? Can there be salvation in *that*?

REGINE [*from the dining-room with a bottle of champagne*]. I'm sorry I took so long, but I had to go down to the cellar. . . .

[*She puts the bottle on the table.*]

OSWALD. And fetch another glass.

REGINE [*looks at him in surprise*]. Mrs. Alving's glass is there, Mr. Alving.

OSWALD. Yes, but fetch one for yourself, Regine. [REGINE *starts, and casts a swift timid glance at* MRS. ALVING.] Well?

REGINE [*softly and hesitantly*]. If Mrs. Alving doesn't object. . . .

MRS. ALVING. Fetch the glass, Regine.

[REGINE *goes out to the dining-room.*]

OSWALD [*watching her*]. Have you noticed the way she walks? So firm, so unafraid.

MRS. ALVING. This is impossible, Oswald!

OSWALD. It's all decided. You must see that. It's useless to say anything. [REGINE *enters with an empty glass, which she keeps in her hand.*] Sit down, Regine.

[REGINE *looks inquiringly at* MRS. ALVING.]

MRS. ALVING. Sit down. [REGINE *sits down on a chair beside the dining-room door, still holding the empty glass in her hand.*] Oswald . . . what was that you were saying about the joy of life?

OSWALD. Yes, Mother, the joy of life. . . . You don't see much of that around this place. I never feel it here.

MRS. ALVING. Not even when you are with me?

OSWALD. Never when I'm at home. But you don't understand.

MRS. ALVING. Yes, I do . . . I'm beginning to understand . . . now.

OSWALD. That . . . and the joy of work, too. Well, they are the same thing, in fact. But people here don't know anything about that either.

MRS. ALVING. Perhaps you are right. Oswald, tell me more about this.

OSWALD. Well, all I mean is that people here are brought up to believe that work is a curse, and a sort of punishment for their sins; and that life is some kind of miserable affair, which the sooner we are done with the better for everybody.

MRS. ALVING. A vale of tears, I know. And we do our damnedest to make it that.

OSWALD. But people elsewhere simply won't have that. Nobody really believes in ideas of that sort any more. In other countries they think it's tremendous fun just to be alive at all. Mother, have you noticed how everything I've ever painted has turned on this joy of life? Always and without exception, this joy of life. Light and sunshine and a holiday spirit . . . and radiantly happy faces. That's why I'm frightened to stay at home with you.

MRS. ALVING. Frightened? What have you got to be frightened about, here with me?

OSWALD. I'm frightened that everything I care about would degenerate here into something ugly.

MRS. ALVING [*looks hard at him*]. You think *that* would happen?

OSWALD. I'm convinced it would. Live the same life here as abroad, yet it still wouldn't be the same life.

MRS. ALVING [*who has been listening intently, rises and says with big pensive eyes*]. Now I see the whole thing.

OSWALD. What do you see?

MRS. ALVING. Now I see for the first time. And now I can speak.

OSWALD [*rising*]. I don't understand you, Mother.

REGINE [*who has also risen*]. Perhaps I'd better go?

MRS. ALVING. No, stay here. Now I can speak. Now my boy must know everything. And then you can choose. Oswald! Regine!

OSWALD. Hush! The pastor. . . .

MANDERS [*enters by the hall door*]. There we are! We've had a most heart-warming time down there.

OSWALD. So have we.

MANDERS. Engstrand must be given help with his Seamen's Home. Regine must move in with him and lend a hand. . . .

REGINE. No, thank you, Pastor.

MANDERS [*only notices her now*]. What. . . ? Here, and with a glass in your hand!

REGINE [*quickly puts the glass down*]. Pardon!

OSWALD. Regine is leaving with me, Pastor.

MANDERS. Leaving with you!

OSWALD. Yes, as my wife . . . if she wants it that way.

MANDERS. But good heavens. . . !

REGINE. Don't blame me, Pastor.

OSWALD. Or else she stays here, if I stay.

REGINE [*involuntarily*]. Here!

MANDERS. I'm appalled at you, Mrs. Alving.

MRS. ALVING. Neither of these things will happen. Because now I can speak plainly.

MANDERS. But you mustn't. No, no, no!

MRS. ALVING. Oh yes I can, and I will. And nobody's ideals are going to suffer by it.

OSWALD. Mother, something's being kept from me! What is it?

REGINE [*listening*]. Mrs. Alving! Listen! They are shouting something out there.

[*She goes into the conservatory and looks out.*]

OSWALD [*over to the window, left*]. What's going on? Where's that glare coming from?

REGINE. The Orphanage is on fire!

MRS. ALVING [*towards the window*]. On fire!

MANDERS. On fire? Impossible. I've just been down there.

OSWALD. Where's my hat? Oh, never mind that . . . Father's Orphanage . . . !

[*He runs into the garden.*]

MRS. ALVING. My shawl, Regine! It's all in flames.

MANDERS. Dreadful! Mrs. Alving, *this* is a flaming judgement on this house of iniquity.

MRS. ALVING. Yes, of course. Come on, Regine.

[*She and* REGINE *hurry out through the hall.*]

MANDERS [*clasping his hands*]. And not insured!

[*He goes out the same way.*]

ACT THREE

The room as before. All the doors are standing open. The lamp is still burning on the table. It is dark outside, apart from a faint glow in the background, left.

MRS. ALVING, a large shawl over her head, is standing in the conservatory looking out. REGINE, also with a shawl round her, is standing a little behind her.

MRS. ALVING. Everything burnt. Burnt to the ground.

REGINE. The basement is still burning.

MRS. ALVING. Why doesn't Oswald come. There's nothing to save.

REGINE. Perhaps I should take him his hat down?

MRS. ALVING. Didn't he even have his hat?

REGINE [*pointing into the hall*]. No, it's hanging there.

MRS. ALVING. Leave it. He must be coming by now. I'll go and look myself.

[*She goes into the garden.*]

MANDERS [*enters from the hall*]. Isn't Mrs. Alving here?

REGINE. She's just gone into the garden.

MANDERS. This is the most terrible night I have ever known.

REGINE. Yes, it's a dreadful thing to happen, isn't it, Pastor?

MANDERS. Oh, don't talk about it! I hardly dare think about it even.

REGINE. But how can it have happened. . . ?

MANDERS. Don't ask me, Miss Engstrand! How should I know? You are not also wanting to. . . ? Isn't it enough that your father. . . ?

REGINE. What about him?

MANDERS. Oh, he's driving me to distraction.

ENGSTRAND [*enters from the hall*]. Pastor Manders. . . !

MANDERS [*turns round, startled*]. Are you after me in here, even?

ENGSTRAND. Yes, by God, I must. . . ! Oh, Lord! This is a terrible business, Pastor!

MANDERS [*walking up and down*]. I'm afraid it is!

REGINE. What is?

ENGSTRAND. Well, you see, it was that there service that did it. [*Aside.*] Now we've got him nicely, my girl. [*Aloud.*] And to think that I'm to blame for Pastor Manders being to blame for a thing like this!

MANDERS. But I assure you, Engstrand . . .

ENGSTRAND. But nobody else down there touched the candles apart from you, Pastor.

MANDERS [*halts*]. Yes, so you say. But I honestly can't remember ever having a candle in my hand.

ENGSTRAND. But I quite distinctly *saw* you take the candle and snuff it with your fingers and chuck the end away straight into some shavings.

MANDERS. You saw that?

ENGSTRAND. As plain as anything, I saw it.

MANDERS. I find that utterly incomprehensible. Besides, that is not a thing I'm in the habit of doing—snuffing candles out with my fingers.

ENGSTRAND. Yes, and horrible careless it looked too, I can tell you. But is it really all that serious, Pastor?

MANDERS [*walking restlessly up and down*]. Oh, don't ask me!

ENGSTRAND [*following him about*]. And you hadn't insured it either, eh, Pastor?

MANDERS [*still walking*]. No, no, no. I've told you.

ENGSTRAND. Not insured. And then to go straight away and set the whole place on fire! Lord, what rotten luck!

MANDERS [*mopping the sweat from his brow*]. You may very well say so, Engstrand.

ENGSTRAND. Fancy a thing like that happening to a charitable institution, something that was going to be such a boon to the whole district, as you might say. I don't suppose the papers are going to let *you* off very lightly, Pastor.

MANDERS. No, that's just what I'm thinking. That's just about the worst part of the whole affair. All these spiteful accusations and insinuations. . . ! Oh, it's terrible to think about!

MRS. ALVING [*coming from the garden*]. I can't get him to come away from the fire.

MANDERS. Ah, there you are, Mrs. Alving.

MRS. ALVING. Well, Pastor Manders, so you did get out of giving your speech.

MANDERS. Oh, I would have been only too glad. . . .

MRS. ALVING [*subdued*]. It's best things have turned out this way. That Orphanage wouldn't have done anybody any good.

MANDERS. Don't you think so?

MRS. ALVING. Do *you* think it would?

MANDERS. But it was a terrible calamity, all the same.

MRS. ALVING. Let's be businesslike about it, and not beat about the bush. . . . Are you waiting for Pastor Manders, Engstrand?

ENGSTRAND [*by the hall door*]. As a matter of fact I am.

MRS. ALVING. Have a seat, then, for the time being.

ENGSTRAND. Thanks, but I'd just as soon stand.

MRS. ALVING [*to* MANDERS]. You are leaving by the boat, presumably?

MANDERS. Yes. It leaves in an hour's time.

MRS. ALVING. Please take all the documents away with you again. I don't want to hear another word about this business. I've got other things to think about. . . .

MANDERS. Mrs. Alving. . . .

MRS. ALVING. Later on I'll send you authorization to clear things up as you think best.

MANDERS. I shall be only too delighted to see to that. The original terms of the bequest will have to be completely altered now, I'm afraid.

MRS. ALVING. Naturally.

MANDERS. Well, my idea at the moment is to arrange for the Solvik estate to be made over to the parish. The land cannot by any means be described as entirely valueless. It will always come in useful for something or other. And as for the interest on the capital in the bank, perhaps the best use I could put it to would be to support some scheme that might bring benefit to the town.

MRS. ALVING. Do just what you wish. It makes not the slightest difference to me.

ENGSTRAND. Don't forget my Seamen's Home, Pastor!

MANDERS. Ah, to be sure, there's something in what you say. Well, it must be given careful consideration.

ENGSTRAND. Oh, to hell with considering. . . . Oh Lord!

MANDERS [*with a sigh*]. And I'm afraid I don't know how much longer I'll have any say in these things. Or whether public opinion might not compel me to resign. It all depends on the result of the official inquiry into the cause of the fire.

MRS. ALVING. What's that you say?

MANDERS. And it's quite impossible to predict what those findings will be.

ENGSTRAND [*comes closer*]. Oh, no, it isn't. Because there's always Jacob Engstrand and me.

MANDERS. Yes, but . . . ?

ENGSTRAND [*in a low voice*]. And Jacob Engstrand isn't the sort to desert a worthy benefactor in his hour of need, as the saying goes.

MANDERS. Yes, but my dear fellow . . . how . . . ?

ENGSTRAND. Jacob Engstrand is a sort of guardian angel, like, as you might say, Pastor.

MANDERS. No, no. I honestly couldn't allow that.

ENGSTRAND. Oh, you just let things take their course. It's not the first time somebody I know has taken the blame for somebody else.

MANDERS. Jacob! [*Shakes him by the hand.*] Characters like you are rare. Well, you'll get support for your Seamen's Home, you can depend on it. [ENGSTRAND *tries to thank him, but cannot for emotion.* MANDERS *slings his satchel over his shoulder.*] Let's be off now. We'll travel together.

ENGSTRAND [*by the dining-room door, in a low voice to* REGINE]. Come on with me, lass! You could live like a queen!

REGINE [*tosses her head*]. *Merci!*

[*She goes out into the hall to fetch the pastor's things.*]

MANDERS. Goodbye, Mrs. Alving. And may I hope that very soon some sense of order and propriety will find its way into this house.

MRS. ALVING. Goodbye, Manders!

[*Seeing* OSWALD *enter from the garden, she goes straight towards the conservatory.*]

ENGSTRAND [*as he and* REGINE *help* MANDERS *on with his coat*]. Goodbye, my girl. And if you are ever in any difficulty, you know where to find Jacob Engstrand. [*In a low voice.*] Little Harbour Street, h'm...! [*To* MRS. ALVING *and* OSWALD.] And this place for seafaring men, it's going to be called the 'Captain Alving Home'. And if I can run it *my* way, I think I can promise it'll be a place worthy of the Captain's memory.

MANDERS [*in the doorway*]. H'm . . . h'm! Come along, my dear Engstrand. Goodbye, goodbye!

[*He and* ENGSTRAND *go out through the hall.*]

OSWALD [*goes over to the table*]. What place was that he was talking about?

MRS. ALVING. It's a sort of hostel he and Pastor Manders are thinking of starting.

OSWALD. It will burn down, just like all this.

MRS. ALVING. What gives you that idea?

OSWALD. Everything will burn. There'll be nothing left to remind people of Father. And here am I, burning down too.

[REGINE *looks at him, startled.*]

MRS. ALVING. Oswald! You shouldn't have stayed so long out there, my poor boy.

OSWALD [*sits at the table*]. I almost believe you are right.

MRS. ALVING. Let me dry your face, Oswald, you are all wet.

[*She dries his face with her handkerchief.*]

OSWALD [*not caring, looks fixedly ahead*]. Thank you, Mother.

MRS. ALVING. Aren't you tired, Oswald? Wouldn't you like a sleep, perhaps?

OSWALD [*fearfully*]. No, no . . . not sleep! I never sleep, I just pretend to. [*Dully.*] That will come soon enough.

MRS. ALVING [*looks anxiously at him*]. Yes, you really *are* ill, all the same, my darling boy.

REGINE [*tense*]. Mr. Alving ill?

OSWALD [*impatiently*]. And now shut all the doors! This deadly feeling of dread. . . .

MRS. ALVING. Shut them, Regine.

[REGINE *shuts the doors, and remains standing by the hall door.* MRS. ALVING *takes off her shawl, and* REGINE *does the same.* MRS. ALVING *draws a chair up near* OSWALD, *and sits down beside him.*]

MRS. ALVING. There now, I'm coming to sit beside you. . . .

OSWALD. Yes, do. And Regine must stay here too. Regine must always be near me. You'll give me a helping hand, Regine, won't you?

REGINE. I don't understand. . . .

MRS. ALVING. Helping hand?

OSWALD. Yes . . . when it's necessary.

MRS. ALVING. Oswald, haven't you got your mother to give you a helping hand?

OSWALD. You? [*Smiles.*] No, Mother, you'd never give me that sort of helping hand. [*Laughs dully.*] You! Ha! Ha! [*Looks earnestly at her.*] And yet who has a better right than you. [*Bursts out.*] Why can't you relax a bit with me, Regine? Why don't you call me Oswald?

REGINE [*softly*]. I don't think Mrs. Alving would like it.

MRS. ALVING. Very soon you can. Come over here and sit beside us. [REGINE *sits demurely and hesitantly on the other side of the table.*] And now, my darling, I am going to take a great burden off your poor, tormented mind . . .

OSWALD. You, Mother?

MRS. ALVING. . . . all the remorse and the self-reproach, as you called it, all those things that have been worrying you. . . .

OSWALD. You think you can?

MRS. ALVING. I can now, Oswald. Yes. You were talking earlier about the joy of living. And suddenly I seemed to see my whole life . . . everything in a new light.

OSWALD [*shakes his head*]. I don't understand a word of what you are saying.

MRS. ALVING. You should have seen your father when he was a young lieutenant. *He* had plenty of the joy of living, I can tell you!

OSWALD. Yes, I know.

MRS. ALVING. It cheered you up just to look at him. All that boundless energy and vitality he had!

OSWALD. Well. . . ?

MRS. ALVING. Well, there was this lively, happy boy—and at the time he *was* still like a boy—having to eat his heart out here in this little provincial town; pleasures of a kind it had to offer, but no real joy; no chance of any proper vocation, only an official position to fill; no sign of any kind of work he could throw himself into heart and soul—only business. He never had a single real friend capable of appreciating the joy of life and what it meant—nothing but a lot of lazy, drunken, hangers-on. . . .

OSWALD. Mother. . . !

MRS. ALVING. So then the inevitable happened.

OSWALD. What do you mean . . . the inevitable?

MRS. ALVING. You told me yourself this evening what would happen if you stayed at home.

OSWALD. Are you trying to say that Father. . . ?

MRS. ALVING. Your father could never find any outlet for this tremendous exuberance of his. And I didn't exactly bring very much gaiety into his home, either.

OSWALD. Didn't you?

MRS. ALVING. They'd taught me various things about duty and suchlike, and I'd simply gone on believing them. Everything seemed to come down to duty in the end—*my* duty and *his* duty and . . . I'm afraid I must have made the house unbearable for your poor father, Oswald.

OSWALD. Why did you never write to me about this?

MRS. ALVING. Until now I've never regarded it as anything I could bring myself to talk about to you—his son.

OSWALD. How did you regard it then?

MRS. ALVING [*slowly*]. I saw only one thing: that your father was a broken man before you were even born.

OSWALD [*in a smothered voice*]. Ah. . . !

[*He rises and goes across to the window.*]

MRS. ALVING. And day in and day out, one thought filled my mind: that in fact Regine belonged here in this house . . . just as much as my own son.

OSWALD [*turns quickly*]. Regine. . . !

REGINE [*jumps up startled, and says in a choking voice*]. Me. . . !

MRS. ALVING. Yes. Now you both know.

OSWALD. Regine!

REGINE [*to herself*]. So my mother was that sort.

MRS. ALVING. Your mother was in many ways a fine woman, Regine.

REGINE. Yes, but she was that sort, all the same. Well, sometimes I've thought as much, but. . . . Well, Mrs. Alving, please may I leave straight away?

MRS. ALVING. Do you really want to, Regine?

REGINE. Yes, I do that.

MRS. ALVING. You must please yourself, of course, but . . .

OSWALD [*walks over to* REGINE]. Leave now? But you belong here.

REGINE. *Merci*, Mr. Alving . . . well, now I suppose I can say Oswald. I must say *this* wasn't the way I'd imagined it happening.

MRS. ALVING. Regine, I haven't been altogether frank with you. . . .

REGINE. No, more's the pity! If I'd known Oswald had something wrong with him. . . . And anyway, now that there can never be anything serious between us. . . . No, you don't catch me staying out here in the country, working myself to death looking after invalids.

OSWALD. Not even somebody so close to you?

REGINE. Not likely. A poor girl's got to make the most of things while she's young. Or else you find yourself on the shelf before you know where you are. I've *also* got some of this joy of life as well, Mrs. Alving.

MRS. ALVING. Yes, I'm afraid so. But don't just throw yourself away, Regine.

REGINE. Oh, whatever will be, will be. If Oswald takes after his father, I probably take after my mother, I suppose. Mrs. Alving, may I ask if Pastor Manders knows all this about me?

MRS. ALVING. Pastor Manders knows everything.

REGINE [*busy putting on her shawl*]. Well, I'd better see what I can do about catching that boat, and getting away from here as quick as I can. The pastor's such a nice easy man to get on with. And it strikes me I've just as much right to a bit of that money as that rotten old carpenter.

MRS. ALVING. You're welcome to it, Regine.

REGINE [*looking fixedly at her*]. I think you might have brought me up like a gentleman's daughter, Mrs. Alving. It would have suited me a bit better than this. [*Tosses her head.*] Still, what the hell. . . ! What difference does it make! [*With a bitter glance at the unopened bottle.*] I'll be drinking champagne with the best yet, you see if I'm not.

MRS. ALVING. And if ever you need a home, Regine, come to me.

REGINE. No thank you, Mrs. Alving. Pastor Manders will look after me all right. And if the worst comes to the worst, I know a place I can make my home.

MRS. ALVING. Where is that?

REGINE. The Captain Alving Home.

MRS. ALVING. Regine . . . I can see it now . . . you are going to your ruin.

REGINE. Oh, get away! *Adieu!*

[*She nods and goes out through the hall.*]

OSWALD [*stands at the window looking out*]. Has she gone?

MRS. ALVING. Yes.

OSWALD [*mutters to himself*]. I think it's crazy, this.

MRS. ALVING [*goes and stands behind him and puts her hands on his shoulders*]. Oswald, my dear . . . has this been a big shock to you?

OSWALD [*turns his face towards her*]. All this about Father, you mean?

MRS. ALVING. Yes, your poor unhappy father. I'm so afraid it's been too much for you.

OSWALD. Whatever gives you that idea? Of course, it came as a great surprise; but fundamentally it doesn't make very much difference to me.

MRS. ALVING [*draws her hands back*]. Not much difference! That your father was so utterly unhappy!

OSWALD. Of course, I feel sorry for *him* just as I would for anybody else, but . . .

MRS. ALVING. Is that all! Your own father!

OSWALD [*impatiently*]. Oh, father . . . father! I never knew anything about my father. All I remember about him is that he once made me sick.

MRS. ALVING. What a terrible thought! Surely a child ought to love its father in spite of all?

OSWALD. What if a child has nothing to thank its father for? Never knew him? You don't really believe in this old superstition still, do you? And you so enlightened in other ways?

MRS. ALVING. You call that mere superstition. . . !

OSWALD. Yes, surely you realize that, Mother. It's simply one of those ideas that get around and . . .

MRS. ALVING [*shaken*]. Ghosts!

OSWALD [*walks across the room*]. Yes, call them ghosts if you like.

MRS. ALVING [*wildly*]. Oswald . . . then you don't love me either.

OSWALD. Well, at least I do know you. . . .

MRS. ALVING. Yes, you know me. But is that all!

OSWALD. And I also know how fond you are of me. And that's something I must be grateful to you for. And you can also be extremely useful to me, now I'm a sick man.

MRS. ALVING. Yes I can, can't I, Oswald! Oh, I could almost bless this illness that drove you home to me. I can see I haven't made you completely mine yet—I must still win you.

OSWALD [*impatiently*]. Yes, yes, yes, but these are just empty words. You must remember I'm a sick man, Mother. I can't be bothered very much with other people, I've got enough to think of with myself.

MRS. ALVING [*in a low voice*]. I shall be calm and patient.

OSWALD. And *cheerful*, Mother!

MRS. ALVING. Yes, my darling, you are right. [*She walks over to him.*] Now have I taken away all that remorse, those self-reproaches?

OSWALD. Yes, you have. But who now will take away the feeling of dread?

MRS. ALVING. Dread?

OSWALD [*walks across the room*]. Regine would have done it, just for the asking.

MRS. ALVING. I don't understand you. What's all this about dread . . . and about Regine?

OSWALD. Is it very late, Mother?

MRS. ALVING. It's early morning. [*She looks out from the conservatory.*] Dawn is already breaking over the mountains. And it's going to be fine, Oswald! In a little while you'll be able to see the sun.

OSWALD. I'm looking forward to that. Oh, there might be all sorts of things I could still take a delight in, and live for. . . .

MRS. ALVING. I should just think so!

OSWALD. Even if I can't work, I . . .

MRS. ALVING. Oh, but now you'll soon be able to work again, my darling. Now that you are rid of all those nagging and depressing thoughts that were worrying you.

OSWALD. Yes, you've made me stop imagining things now anyway, and that's a good thing. And if only I can get this last thing settled now. . . . [*Sits down on the sofa.*] Mother, we are going to have a talk . . .

MRS. ALVING. Yes, of course.

[*She pushes an armchair over to the sofa and sits close by him.*]

OSWALD. . . . and meanwhile the sun will be rising. And then you'll know. And then I'll no longer have this feeling of dread.

MRS. ALVING. What am I to know, did you say?

OSWALD [*without listening to her*]. Mother, earlier on this evening didn't you say there was nothing in the world you wouldn't do for me, if I asked you.

MRS. ALVING. Yes, that's what I said!

OSWALD. And you mean that, Mother?

MRS. ALVING. You can depend on me, my dear, darling boy. I have nothing to live for but you.

OSWALD. All right, then I'll tell you. . . . Mother, I know you are quite strong-minded. You must sit quite calmly when you hear what it is.

MRS. ALVING. What terrible thing is this. . . ?

OSWALD. You mustn't scream. Do you hear? Promise me? You'll sit and talk about it quite quietly? Promise me, Mother?

MRS. ALVING. Yes, yes, I promise. But tell me!

OSWALD. Well then, I must tell you that all this about being tired . . . about not being able to bear the thought of work . . . all this isn't the real illness. . . .

MRS. ALVING. What is the illness, then?

OSWALD. The disease I have inherited . . . [*He points to his forehead and adds softly.*] . . . has its seat here.

MRS. ALVING [*almost speechless*]. Oswald! No! no!

OSWALD. Don't scream. I couldn't bear it. Yes, Mother, it sits lurking in here. And it can break out any day, any time.

MRS. ALVING. Oh, how horrible. . . !

OSWALD. Keep calm. That's how things are with me. . . .

MRS. ALVING [*jumping up*]. It's not true, Oswald! It's impossible! It can't be!

OSWALD. I've already had one attack over there. It soon passed. But when they told me how I'd been, I suddenly felt so dreadfully, pitifully afraid. So I set off back home to you as quick as I could.

MRS. ALVING. So this is the feeling of dread. . . !

OSWALD. Yes, and it's so utterly revolting, don't you see. If only it had been some ordinary kind of fatal disease. . . . Because I'm not afraid to die, although I would like to live as long as I can.

MRS. ALVING. Of course, Oswald, you must!

OSWALD. But this is so horribly revolting. To be turned into a helpless child again. To have to be fed, to have to be. . . . Oh, it doesn't bear talking about!

MRS. ALVING. My child will have his mother to look after him.

OSWALD [*jumping up*]. No, never. That's exactly what I don't want. I can't bear the thought that I might lie like that for years . . . till I become old and grey. And in the meantime you might die and leave me. [*He sits in* MRS. ALVING's *chair*.] For the doctor said it wouldn't necessarily prove fatal immediately. He called it a kind of softening of the brain . . . or something like that. [*Smiles sadly*.] I think that expression sounds so nice. It always makes me think of cherry-red velvet curtains . . . something soft and delicate to the touch.

MRS. ALVING [*screams*]. Oswald!

OSWALD [*jumps up again and walks across the room*]. And now you have taken Regine away from me! If only I'd had her. She'd have given me this helping hand all right.

MRS. ALVING [*walks over to him*]. What do you mean by that, my darling. Is there anything in the world I wouldn't do for you?

OSWALD. When I came round again after that attack over there, the doctor said when it happened again—and it will happen again—there'd be no hope.

MRS. ALVING. How could he be so heartless. . . .

OSWALD. I demanded to know. I told him I had certain arrangements to make. . . . [*He smiles craftily*.] And so I had. [*He takes a little box out of his breast pocket*.] Mother, do you see this?

MRS. ALVING. What is it?

OSWALD. Morphine.

MRS. ALVING [*looks at him in terror*]. Oswald . . . my son!

OSWALD. I've got twelve tablets stored up. . . .

MRS. ALVING [*snatching at it*]. Give me that box, Oswald!

OSWALD. Not yet, Mother.

[*He puts the box back in his pocket*.]

MRS. ALVING. I can't bear this!

OSWALD. You must bear it. Now if I'd had Regine here, I'd have told her how things stood . . . and asked her for this last helping hand. She'd have helped me, I'm sure.

MRS. ALVING. Never!

OSWALD. If she saw me struck down by this ghastly thing, lying there helpless, like an imbecile child, beyond all hope of recovery. . . .

MRS. ALVING. Regine would never have done it, never!

OSWALD. Regine would have done it. Regine was so marvellously light-hearted. And she'd soon have got bored with looking after an invalid like me.

MRS. ALVING. Then thank God Regine isn't here!

OSWALD. Well then, now you'll have to give me this helping hand, Mother.

MRS. ALVING [*with a scream*]. Me!

OSWALD. There's nobody with a better right than you.

MRS. ALVING. Me! Your mother!

OSWALD. All the more reason.

MRS. ALVING. Me! Who gave you life!

OSWALD. I never asked you for life. And what sort of a life is this you've given me? I don't want it! Take it back!

MRS. ALVING. Help! Help!

[*She runs into the hall.*]

OSWALD. Don't leave me! Where are you going?

MRS. ALVING [*in the hall*]. To fetch the doctor, Oswald! Let me get out!

OSWALD [*also in the hall*]. You are not getting out. And nobody's getting in.

[*A key is turned.*]

MRS. ALVING [*comes in again*]. Oswald! Oswald! . . . my child!

OSWALD [*following her*]. If you love me, Mother . . . how can you let me suffer all this unspeakable terror!

MRS. ALVING [*after a moment's silence, says firmly*]. Here is my hand on it.

OSWALD. You will. . . ?

MRS. ALVING. If it becomes necessary. But it won't *be* necessary. No, no, it's quite impossible!

OSWALD. Well, let us hope so. And let's live together as long as we can. Thank you, Mother.

[*He sits in the armchair, which* MRS. ALVING *has moved over to the sofa. Day is dawning; the lamp is still burning on the table.*]

MRS. ALVING [*approaching him cautiously*]. Do you feel calmer now?

OSWALD. Yes.

MRS. ALVING [*bent over him*]. What terrible ideas they were to get into your head, Oswald. But all just imagination. All these upsets have been too much for you. But now you'll be able to have a good long rest. At home, with your mother beside you, my darling. Anything you want you shall have, just like when you were a little boy. There now. The attack's over. You see how quickly it went. Oh, I knew it would. . . . See what a lovely day we're going to have, Oswald? Brilliant sunshine. Now you'll be able to see the place properly.

[*She walks over to the table, and puts out the lamp. Sunrise. The glacier and the mountain peaks in the background gleam in the morning light.*]

OSWALD [*sits motionless in the armchair, with his back to the view; suddenly he says*]. Mother, give me the sun.

MRS. ALVING [*by the table, looks at him startled*]. What do you say?

OSWALD [*repeats dully and tonelessly*]. The sun. The sun.

MRS. ALVING [*across to him*]. Oswald, what's the matter with you? [OSWALD *seems to shrink in his chair, all his muscles go flaccid, his face is expressionless, and his eyes stare vacantly.* MRS. ALVING *quivers with terror.*] What is it? [*Screams.*] Oswald! What's the matter with you! [*Throws herself down on her knees beside him and shakes him.*] Oswald! Oswald! Look at me! Don't you know me?

OSWALD [*tonelessly as before*]. The sun. . . . The sun.

MRS. ALVING [*jumps up in anguish, tears at her hair with both hands, and shouts*]. I can't bear it! [*As though petrified, she whispers.*] I can't bear it! Never! [*Suddenly.*] Where's he put them? [*Hastily fumbling at his breast.*] Here! [*She shrinks back a step or two and screams.*] No, no, no! . . . Yes! . . . No, no!

[*She stands a few paces away from him, with her hands clutching her hair, staring at him in speechless horror.*]

OSWALD [*sits motionless as before, and says*]. The sun. . . . The sun.

HEDDA GABLER
[*Hedda Gabler*]

PLAY IN FOUR ACTS
(1890)

Translated by Jens Arup

CHARACTERS

JÖRGEN TESMAN, the holder of a University Fellowship in cultural history

MRS. HEDDA TESMAN, his wife

MISS JULIANE TESMAN, his aunt

MRS. ELVSTED

MR. BRACK, a judge

EJLERT LÖVBORG

BERTE, the Tesmans' maid

The action takes place in Tesman's villa on the west side of the town

ACT ONE

A spacious, handsome, and tastefully appointed reception room, decorated in dark colours. In the back wall there is a wide doorway with the hangings pulled back. This opening leads to a smaller room in the same style as the reception room. In the wall to the right of the outer room is a folding door leading to the hall. In the opposite wall, to the left, is a glass door, also with the curtains drawn aside. Through the windows we see part of a covered verandah outside, and trees in autumn colours. In the foreground stands an oval table, covered with a heavy cloth, and with chairs around it. Downstage by the right wall are a large, dark, porcelain stove, a high-backed armchair, an upholstered footrest, and two stools. Up in the right-hand corner, a corner sofa and a small round table. Downstage on the left, a little away from the wall, a sofa. Above the glass door, a piano. On either side of the doorway at the back is a what-not with objects in terra-cotta and majolica.—By the back wall of the inner room are a sofa, a table, and a couple of chairs. Over this sofa hangs the portrait of a handsome, elderly man in the uniform of a general. Over the table, a hanging lamp with a matt, milky-white glass shade.—All around the reception room there are numerous bunches of flowers arranged in vases and glasses. More lie on the tables. The floors of both rooms are covered with thick carpets.—Morning light. The sun is shining in at the glass door.

MISS JULIANE TESMAN, *with hat and parasol, comes in from the hall, followed by* BERTE, *who carries a bunch of flowers wrapped in paper.* MISS TESMAN *is a good-looking lady of benevolent aspect, some 65 years old, neatly but simply dressed in a grey costume.* BERTE *is a serving-maid getting on in years, with a plain and somewhat countrified exterior.*

MISS TESMAN [*stops just inside the room, listens and speaks softly*]. Well, I declare! I don't believe they are up yet!

BERTE [*similarly subdued*]. Why, that's what I said, Miss. So late the steamer was last night. And then afterwards! Gracious . . . all the things the young mistress wanted unpacked before she could get off to bed.

MISS TESMAN. Well, well . . . let them have a good rest and welcome. But we'll give them a breath of the fresh morning air when they do come down.

[*She crosses to the glass door and throws it wide open.*]

BERTE [*by the table, not knowing what to do with the flowers in her hand*]. I'm sure there isn't a decent place left for them. Maybe I'd better put them here, Miss.

[*She places the flowers on the front of the piano.*]

MISS TESMAN. And so now you've got yourself a new mistress, Berte my dear. The Lord knows, I found it more than hard to let you go.

BERTE [*close to tears*]. And what about me then, Miss? What am I to say! For so many years now I've been with you and Miss Rina.

MISS TESMAN. We must make the best of it, Berte. There's really no other way. Jörgen must have you in the house with him, you see. He simply must. You've always looked after him, ever since he was a little boy.

BERTE. Yes but, Miss, I get so worried about her, too, lying at home. The poor dear, she's quite helpless. And then with that new girl, now! She'll never learn to make things right for the poor lady, she won't.

MISS TESMAN. Oh, I'll soon get her into the way of it. And I'll see to most things myself, you may be sure. You needn't be so anxious for my poor sister's sake, my dear Berte.

BERTE. Yes, but then there's another thing too, Miss. I'm really so scared I'll never give satisfaction to the young mistress.

MISS TESMAN. Oh, Heavens . . . just to begin with of course there might be this and that. . . .

BERTE. Because she's ever so particular.

MISS TESMAN. Why, of course she is. General Gabler's daughter. The way she was used to having things in the General's time. Do you remember her riding along the road with her father? In that long black habit? And with a feather in her hat?

BERTE. I should think I would remember! . . . But I declare, I never once dreamed they'd make a match of it, her and Mr. Jörgen, not in those days I didn't.

MISS TESMAN. Nor I. . . . But now here's a point, Berte, while I remember it: you mustn't say mister about Jörgen from now on. He's a doctor.

BERTE. Yes, the lady did say about that too . . . last night . . . soon as they came in at the door. Is it really true then, Miss?

MISS TESMAN. Why certainly it's true. Just fancy, Berte . . . they made him a doctor abroad. Now, on the journey, you know. And I never knew the first thing about it . . . till he told me down there on the quay.

BERTE. Well, I should think he could get to be anything at all, he could. He's that clever. But I'd never have thought he'd have taken to doctoring people, too.

MISS TESMAN. Oh no, he's not that sort of doctor. . . . [*She nods significantly.*] And by the way, you'll probably have to call him something even finer pretty soon.

BERTE. Well I never! What sort of thing, Miss?

MISS TESMAN [*smiles*]. Hm . . . wouldn't you like to know! . . . [*Emotionally.*] Ah, dear God . . . if my sainted brother could look up from the grave and see what's become of his little boy! [*She looks around.*] But what's this, Berte . . . why on earth have you done that? Taken all the loose covers off?

BERTE. The lady told me to do it. She doesn't like loose covers on the chairs, she said.

MISS TESMAN. But will they be coming in here . . . I mean for every day?

BERTE. That's what it sounded like. The lady, that is. As for himself . . . the doctor . . . he didn't say anything.

[JÖRGEN TESMAN *enters from the right of the inner room, humming a tune and carrying an open, empty suitcase. He is a man of 33, of middle height and youthful appearance; slightly plump, his face round, open, and cheerful. Fair hair and beard. He wears glasses, and is dressed in comfortable, slightly slovenly, indoor clothes.*]

MISS TESMAN. Good morning, good morning, Jörgen!

TESMAN [*in the doorway*]. Aunt Julle! Dear Aunt Julle! [*Goes over and pumps her hand.*] Come all this way . . . so early in the morning! Eh?

MISS TESMAN. Well, of course I had to come and see how you've all settled in.

TESMAN. And you never even had a proper night's rest!

MISS TESMAN. Oh, that won't do me any harm.

TESMAN. Well, well, and you managed all right getting home from the quay, I hope? Eh?

MISS TESMAN. Oh yes, I did very well . . . thank Heavens. Mr. Brack was so very kind as to take me right to the door.

TESMAN. We were so dreadfully sorry we couldn't take you in the cab. But you could see for yourself. . . . Hedda had so many cases that had to come.

MISS TESMAN. Yes, she really did have a great many cases.

BERTE [*to* TESMAN]. Should I maybe go in and ask the mistress whether she wants me for anything?

TESMAN. No thank you, Berte . . . I don't think you'd better. If there is anything she'll ring, she said.

BERTE [*crossing to the right*]. All right, then.

TESMAN. Hey, wait a moment . . . take this along, will you.

BERTE [*taking the suitcase*]. I'll put it up in the loft.

[*She goes out at the hall door.*]

TESMAN. Just think, Auntie . . . the whole of that case was crammed full of nothing but notes. It's quite incredible, really, all the things I managed to dig up round about in those old archives. Fantastic old things that no one knew anything about. . . .

MISS TESMAN. Well to be sure, I don't expect you wasted your time on your honeymoon, did you, Jörgen?

TESMAN. I can assure you I didn't. But do take your hat off, Auntie. There now! Let me undo that ribbon. Eh?

MISS TESMAN [*as he does so*]. Oh, my dear . . . it's just as though you were home with us still.

TESMAN [*turning the hat around in his hand*]. My, my . . . that's a fine and fancy hat you've given yourself!

MISS TESMAN. I bought it because of Hedda.

TESMAN. Because of Hedda? Eh?

MISS TESMAN. Yes, so Hedda won't be ashamed of me, if we should happen to walk together in the street.

TESMAN [*patting her cheek*]. You always think of everything, don't you, Auntie Julle. [*He puts the hat on a chair by the table.*] And now . . . there we are . . . now we'll sit down on the sofa here. And we'll have a little chat until Hedda turns up.

[*They sit down. She puts her parasol in the corner by the sofa.*]

MISS TESMAN [*takes both his hands and looks at him*]. How wonderfully good it is to see you here again, as well as ever, and full of life, Jörgen! Ah . . . sainted Joachim's little boy!

TESMAN. For me too! To be with you again, Auntie Julle! You've always been both father and mother to me.

MISS TESMAN. Yes, I know you'll always have a soft spot in your heart for your old aunts.

TESMAN. But there's absolutely no improvement in Auntie Rina. Eh?

MISS TESMAN. Oh no, dear . . . we don't expect any, poor thing. She just lies there as she has done all these years. But God grant that I may keep her a little while yet! I don't know what I'd do without her, Jörgen. Especially now, you know, when I haven't got you to cope with any more.

TESMAN [*patting her back*]. There now, Auntie . . . !

MISS TESMAN [*suddenly switching to another tone*]. Well just think of it, so now you're a married man, Jörgen! . . . And to think that you'd be the one to walk off with Hedda Gabler! The lovely Hedda Gabler. Imagine it! So many admirers she always had around her!

TESMAN [*hums a bit and smirks*]. Yes, I dare say there are one or two of my good friends who wouldn't mind being in my shoes. Eh?

MISS TESMAN. And then that you were able to take such a honeymoon, too! Five months . . . almost six. . . .

TESMAN. Oh well . . . for me it was a sort of academic trip too, you know. I had to look through all those old records. And the books I had to plough through!

MISS TESMAN. Yes, I suppose you did. [*Lowers her voice confidentially.*] But tell me, now, Jörgen . . . isn't there anything . . . any other news you can tell me?

TESMAN. From the trip, you mean?

MISS TESMAN. Yes.

TESMAN. Well, I don't think there's much I didn't get into my letters. I was given a doctorate . . . but I told you about that last night.

MISS TESMAN. Oh, all those things, yes. But I mean to say . . . haven't you any . . . as it were . . . any prospects of . . .?

TESMAN. Prospects?

MISS TESMAN. Oh, good Heavens, Jörgen . . . after all I am your old aunt!

TESMAN. Why certainly I can talk of prospects.

MISS TESMAN. Oh!

TESMAN. I have the best prospect in the world of becoming professor, one of these days.

MISS TESMAN. Oh yes, professor. . . .

TESMAN. Or . . . I may as well say I'm certain to get it. But dear Auntie Julle . . . you know all this yourself!

MISS TESMAN [*suppressing a smile*]. Why, to be sure I do. You're quite right. [*Changing the subject.*] . . . But you were telling me about the journey. . . . It must have cost a pretty penny, Jörgen?

TESMAN. Oh well, the cost . . . that big fellowship helped quite a bit, you know.

MISS TESMAN. But I just can't imagine how you could make it do for both of you.

TESMAN. No, I suppose that would need a bit of imagination. Eh?

MISS TESMAN. And then when you're travelling with a lady. That makes everything so very much more expensive, I'm told.

TESMAN. Oh of course . . . it's bound to make a bit of difference. But Hedda had to have that trip, Aunt! She really had to. I couldn't do less.

MISS TESMAN. No, I suppose not. A honeymoon trip, that seems to be part of the trimmings, these days. . . . But tell me now . . . have you had a good look round the house?

TESMAN. Indeed I have. I've been up and about since dawn.

MISS TESMAN. Well, and how do you like it all?

TESMAN. Very much! Oh, very much indeed! There's just one thing, I don't quite know what we're going to do about those two empty rooms, you know, between the back room there and Hedda's bedroom.

MISS TESMAN [*with a smile*]. Ah, my dear Jörgen, you might find a use for them . . . when the time comes.

TESMAN. Why yes, Auntie Julle, you've got something there! As I gradually add to my collection of books, then. . . . Eh?

MISS TESMAN. Precisely, my dear boy. I was thinking of your books.

TESMAN. Most of all I'm pleased for Hedda, though. Before we got engaged she always said that old Lady Falk's villa was the only house she'd really like to live in.

MISS TESMAN. Yes, think of it . . . and then just after you'd gone away it came up for sale.

TESMAN. Yes, Aunt Julle, we really were lucky. Eh?

MISS TESMAN. But expensive, my dear Jörgen! It'll be a terrible expense for you . . . all this.

TESMAN [*looks at her rather crestfallen*]. Why yes, I suppose it will, Auntie?

MISS TESMAN. Oh my dear!

TESMAN. How much, do you think? Approximately? Eh?

MISS TESMAN. I simply can't tell you, before all the bills have come in.

TESMAN. Oh well, luckily Brack was able to get very favourable terms for me. He said as much when he wrote to Hedda.

MISS TESMAN. Yes, don't you worry about that, my boy. . . . Anyway, I've given security for the furniture and all the carpets.

TESMAN. Security? You have? But Auntie Julle . . . what sort of security could you offer?

MISS TESMAN. I made out a mortgage on the annuity.

TESMAN [*leaps up*]. What! On your . . . and Aunt Rina's annuity!

MISS TESMAN. Well, there didn't seem to be any other way of doing it, you know.

TESMAN [*places himself in front of her*]. But have you gone out of your mind, Auntie! That annuity . . . you and Aunt Rina, it's the only thing you've got to live on.

MISS TESMAN. There now . . . don't get so excited about it. It's just a formality, you know. Mr. Brack said so too, and he's a judge. He was the one who helped me to arrange the whole thing. Just a formality, he said.

TESMAN. Yes, that's all very well. But all the same . . .

MISS TESMAN. And now you're getting your own salary to draw on. And good gracious, if we did have to spend a little . . . ? A helping hand, just to begin with . . . ? Why, we'd be only too happy.

TESMAN. Oh, Auntie . . . you'll never stop sacrificing yourself for me!

MISS TESMAN [*rises and puts her hands on his shoulders*]. Isn't it the only joy I have in this world, to help you along your road, my darling boy? You, who have neither father nor mother to look to? And now we're very nearly there, my boy! There were some black days among the rest. But, thanks be to God, you've made good, Jörgen!

TESMAN. Yes, it's queer, really, the way it all turned out.

MISS TESMAN. Yes . . . and the people who stood in your way . . . and wanted to keep you back . . . you outran them all. They've fallen by the wayside, Jörgen! And your most dangerous adversary, he fell lower than any of them, he did. . . . And now he must lie on the bed he's made for himself . . . the poor depraved creature.

TESMAN. Have you heard anything of Ejlert? Since I went off, I mean.

MISS TESMAN. Only that he's supposed to have published a new book.

TESMAN. What's that! Ejlert Lövborg? Just recently, you mean? Eh?

MISS TESMAN. Yes, so they say. Do you think it's likely to amount to anything much? Now when your new book arrives . . . that'll be another matter, Jörgen! What's it going to be about?

TESMAN. It will be an account of the domestic crafts of mediaeval Brabant.

MISS TESMAN. Just think . . . and you can write about things like that!

TESMAN. Incidentally, it may be quite a while before I get it finished. There are all these extensive collections of material, you know, they all have to be sorted out first.

MISS TESMAN. Yes, collecting things and sorting them out . . . you've always been good at that. You're not Joachim's son for nothing!

TESMAN. I'm ever so keen to get going on it. Especially now, with my own comfortable and charming house to sit and work in.

MISS TESMAN. Ah, and most of all, now that you've won the wife of your heart, dear Jörgen.

TESMAN [embracing her]. Oh yes, Auntie Julle! Hedda . . . that's the most wonderful thing of all! [Looks towards the doorway.] But here she is, isn't she? Eh?

[HEDDA comes in from the left of the back room. She is a lady of 29. Her face and her figure are aristocratic and elegant in their proportions. Her complexion is of an even pallor. Her eyes are steel grey, and cold, clear, and dispassionate. Her hair is an attractive medium brown in colour, but not particularly ample. She is dressed in a tasteful, somewhat loose-fitting morning gown.]

MISS TESMAN [goes to meet her]. Good morning, dear Hedda! A very good morning to you!

HEDDA [offers her hand]. Good morning, dear Miss Tesman! Such an early visit. So very kind.

MISS TESMAN [*appearing somewhat put out*]. Well, and did the young mistress sleep well in her new home?

HEDDA. Thank you, I slept tolerably well.

TESMAN [*laughs*]. Tolerably! That's a good one, Hedda! You were sleeping like a log, you were, when I got up.

HEDDA. How fortunate. But then, Miss Tesman, one always has to get used to new things. Bit by bit. [*Looks towards the windows.*] Ugh . . . the maid's been and opened the verandah door. The place is flooded with sunlight.

MISS TESMAN [*moving towards the door*]. Well, let's shut it.

HEDDA. Oh no, don't do that! Dear Tesman, go and draw the curtains. That gives a softer light.

TESMAN [*at the door*]. So be it . . . so be it. . . . There you are, Hedda . . . now you've got both shade and fresh air.

HEDDA. Yes, we can do with a bit of fresh air. All these blessed flowers. . . . But dear Miss Tesman . . . won't you take a seat?

MISS TESMAN. No, thank you very much. Now I know everything's all right . . . thanks be to God! And I'd better be thinking of getting home again. To her, lying and waiting so patiently, poor dear.

TESMAN. You'll give her my love, won't you. And say I'll pop in to see her later in the day.

MISS TESMAN. Yes, yes, I'll tell her. Oh, here's another thing, Jörgen . . . [*She feels in her skirt pocket.*] I almost went and forgot it. I've got a little something for you.

TESMAN. What can it be, Aunt? Eh?

MISS TESMAN [*extracts a flat object wrapped in newspaper and hands it to him*]. There you are, my boy.

TESMAN [*opens it*]. Oh my goodness! . . . So you kept them for me, Auntie Julle! Hedda! Now isn't that nice of her, Hedda! Eh?

HEDDA [*by the right-hand whatnot*]. Of course, dear. What is it?

TESMAN. My old house shoes! My slippers, Hedda!

HEDDA. Ah yes. You mentioned them quite frequently on the trip, I remember.

TESMAN. Yes, I did miss them so. [*He goes to her.*] Here, just take a look at them, Hedda!

HEDDA [*crossing to the stove*]. Thank you, they wouldn't appeal to me.

TESMAN [*following her*]. Think of it . . . Aunt Rina lay there and embroidered them for me. Weak as she was. Oh, you can't imagine how many memories they have for me.

HEDDA [*by the table*]. But not for me, particularly.

MISS TESMAN. Why, Hedda's quite right about that, Jörgen.

TESMAN. Yes, but I do think, now that she's one of the family . . .

HEDDA [*interrupts*]. We'll never be able to manage with that maid, Tesman.

MISS TESMAN. Not manage with Berte?

TESMAN. My dear . . . why on earth should you say that? Eh?

HEDDA [*points*]. Look at that! She's left her old hat lying on the chair there.

TESMAN [*appalled, drops the slippers on the floor*]. But . . . but Hedda . . . !

HEDDA. Just think . . . somebody might come in and see it.

TESMAN. No but Hedda . . . that . . . that's Auntie Julle's hat!

HEDDA. Is it?

MISS TESMAN [*takes the hat*]. Yes indeed it's mine. And as it happens it isn't so very old either, my dear young lady.

HEDDA. I really didn't look at it so very closely, Miss Tesman.

MISS TESMAN [*ties on the hat*]. As a matter of fact I'm wearing it for the very first time. And that's God's truth.

TESMAN. And an awfully fine hat it is too. Really smart!

MISS TESMAN. Oh, that's as it may be, my dear Jörgen. [*Looks around.*] And my parasol . . . ? Here it is. [*She takes it.*] Because that happens to be mine too. [*Under her breath.*] Not Berte's.

TESMAN. A new hat and a new parasol! Think of that, Hedda!

HEDDA. Yes, really charming.

TESMAN. Yes, aren't they just? Eh? But Aunt, take a good look at Hedda before you go! Charming's the word for her, eh?

MISS TESMAN. Oh my dear, that's nothing new. Hedda's been lovely all her life.

[*She nods and starts across to the right.*]

TESMAN [*following her*]. Yes, but have you noticed how well and bonny she looks? I declare she's filled out beautifully on the trip.

HEDDA [*moves irritably*]. Oh, do you have to . . . !

MISS TESMAN [*has stopped and turned*]. Filled out?

TESMAN. Yes, Aunt Julle, you don't notice it so much when she's wearing that dress. But I . . . well, I have occasion to. . . .

HEDDA [*at the verandah door, impatiently*]. Oh, you don't have occasion for anything!

TESMAN. It must be the mountain air in the Tyrol. . . .

HEDDA [*curtly interrupting*]. I'm exactly the same as I was when we left.

TESMAN. Yes, that's what you say. But you aren't, you know. Can't you see it too, Auntie?

MISS TESMAN [*she has folded her hands and gazes at* HEDDA]. Lovely . . . lovely . . . lovely Hedda. [*She goes to* HEDDA, *takes her head and inclines it towards her with both hands, and kisses her hair.*] God bless you and keep you, Hedda Tesman. For Jörgen's sake.

HEDDA [*frees herself*]. Oh . . . ! Leave me be!

MISS TESMAN [*in quiet rapture*]. Every single day I'll come and visit you both.

TESMAN. Yes, Auntie, that'll be wonderful! Eh?

MISS TESMAN. Goodbye . . . goodbye!

[*She goes out at the hall door.* TESMAN *follows her out. The door stays half open, and we hear* TESMAN *repeating his message of love to Aunt Rina, and thanking again for the slippers.*

While this is going on HEDDA *walks about the room, raises her arms and clenches her fists as though in a frenzy. Then she draws the curtains back from the verandah door, stands there and looks out.*

After a while TESMAN *comes back and shuts the door behind him.*]

TESMAN [*picking up the slippers from the floor*]. What are you looking at, Hedda?

HEDDA [*calm and collected once more*]. I'm just looking at the leaves on the trees. They're so yellow. And so withered.

TESMAN [*rewraps the slippers and lays them on the table*]. Yes, well, it's September now, you know.

HEDDA [*ill at ease again*]. Why yes ... already it's ... it's September.

TESMAN. Don't you think Aunt Julle was odd, dear? Almost affected? What can have got into her, do you think? Eh?

HEDDA. Well, I hardly know her. Isn't she usually like that?

TESMAN. Why, no, not like she was just now.

HEDDA [*leaving the window*]. Do you think she was very put out about that hat business?

TESMAN. Oh, not so particularly. Perhaps a little just for a moment. ...

HEDDA. Well, what manner of behaviour is that, anyway, flinging her hat just anywhere in the drawing-room! It's not done.

TESMAN. Well, you may be quite sure that Aunt Julle won't do it again.

HEDDA. Oh, never mind. I'll propitiate her.

TESMAN. Oh my dear, sweet Hedda, if only you would!

HEDDA. When you go down there later you can invite her over for this evening.

TESMAN. Yes, certainly I will. And there's another thing, Hedda, that would make her so very happy.

HEDDA. Well?

TESMAN. Couldn't you bring yourself to give her a kiss when you meet? For my sake, Hedda? Eh?

HEDDA. Oh, don't ask me, Tesman, for God's sake. I've told you before, I just couldn't. I'll try to call her Aunt. And she'll have to be content with that.

TESMAN. Oh well . . . I just thought, now that you belong to the family, you . . .

HEDDA. Hm . . . I'm not at all sure . . .

[*She goes upstage towards the doorway.*]

TESMAN [*after a pause*]. Is there anything the matter with you, Hedda? Eh?

HEDDA. I was just looking at my old piano. It doesn't go with the rest of the things.

TESMAN. As soon as I get my first cheque, we'll see about getting it changed.

HEDDA. Oh no . . . not changed. I don't want to part with it. We'd better put it in the back room, there. And then we can get another one for this room. At a suitable moment, I mean.

TESMAN [*rather put out*]. Yes . . . I suppose that would be an alternative.

HEDDA [*takes the bunch of flowers from the piano*]. These flowers weren't here last night when we arrived.

TESMAN. Aunt Julle probably brought them.

HEDDA [*looks into the bouquet*]. A card. [*Takes it out and reads.*] 'Will come again later today.' Can you guess who it's from?

TESMAN. No. Who is it from? Eh?

HEDDA. It says 'Mrs. Carl Elvsted'.

TESMAN. Really! Mrs. Elvsted! Miss Rysing, as she used to be.

HEDDA. Exactly. That woman with the provoking hair that everyone made such a fuss of. An old flame of yours, too, I'm told.

TESMAN [*laughs*]. Oh, it didn't last long. And besides, that was before I met you, Hedda. But just think . . . that she should be back in town.

HEDDA. It's odd that she should come here. I hardly know her, apart from school.

TESMAN. No, and I haven't seen her for . . . oh good Lord, it must be years. I don't know how she can bear to be stuck right up there, so many miles away. Eh?

HEDDA [*thinks a moment, then suddenly speaks*]. I say, Tesman . . . wasn't it up there somewhere that he went . . . that . . . Ejlert Lövborg?

TESMAN. Yes, it must be just about there.

[BERTE *appears at the hall door.*]

BERTE. She's here again, ma'am, the lady who looked in with the flowers earlier on. [*She points.*] The ones you're holding, ma'am.

HEDDA. She is, is she. Well, be so good as to let her in.

[BERTE *opens the door to* MRS. ELVSTED *and goes out herself.*—MRS. ELVSTED *is a slight woman with soft, attractive features. Her eyes are light blue, large, round, and somewhat protruding, with a scared, questioning expression. Her hair is strikingly fair, almost whitish-yellow, and unusually rich and wavy. She is a couple of years younger than* HEDDA. *She wears a dark going-out dress, tastefully styled but not quite in the latest fashion.*]

HEDDA [*goes to meet her in a friendly manner*]. Good morning, my dear Mrs. Elvsted. How nice to see you once again.

MRS. ELVSTED [*nervous, trying to control herself*]. Yes, it's a long time now since we met.

TESMAN [*offering his hand*]. And since we met, too. Eh?

HEDDA. Thank you for your lovely flowers. . . .

MRS. ELVSTED. Oh, thank you. . . . I would have come here at once, yesterday afternoon. But then I heard you were abroad. . . .

TESMAN. You've just arrived in town? Eh?

MRS. ELVSTED. Yes. I got in about lunch time yesterday. Oh, I was quite in despair when I heard you were away.

HEDDA. In despair! But why?

TESMAN. But my dear Mrs. Rysing—Mrs. Elvsted I mean to say . . .

HEDDA. I hope there isn't anything wrong?

MRS. ELVSTED. Yes, there is. And I don't know another soul here, not anyone I could turn to, apart from you.

HEDDA [*puts the flowers on the table*]. Come . . . we'll sit down here on the sofa. . . .

MRS. ELVSTED. Oh, I can hardly keep still, let alone sit down!

HEDDA. Of course you can. Come along.

[*She persuades* MRS. ELVSTED *on to the sofa, and sits beside her.*]

TESMAN. Well? What is it then . . . ?

HEDDA. Is it something that's happened up at your place?

MRS. ELVSTED. Well . . . it both is and yet isn't. Oh, I do so hope you won't misunderstand me.

HEDDA. Well, in that case you'd better tell us all about it, from the beginning, Mrs. Elvsted.

TESMAN. After all, that's the reason why you came. Eh?

MRS. ELVSTED. Yes . . . yes of course it is. And so I'd better tell you . . . if you don't already know it . . . that Ejlert Lövborg is also in town.

HEDDA. Lövborg is . . . !

TESMAN. What, Ejlert Lövborg back again! Think of that, Hedda!

HEDDA. Yes, yes, I heard!

MRS. ELVSTED. He's been here now for about a week. Think of it . . . a whole week! In this dangerous place. Alone! And all the bad influences there are here.

HEDDA. But . . . excuse me, Mrs. Elvsted, but how can this possibly concern you?

MRS. ELVSTED [*gives her a scared look, then speaks quickly*]. He used to come and teach the children.

HEDDA. Your children?

MRS. ELVSTED. My husband's. I haven't got any.

HEDDA. Stepchildren, then.

MRS. ELVSTED. Yes.

TESMAN [*slightly incoherent*]. But was he sufficiently . . . I don't quite know how to put it . . . sort of . . . well, regular in his life and habits, so that he could be trusted with . . . ? Eh?

MRS. ELVSTED. For the last two years, there's been nothing that anyone could hold against him.

TESMAN. Hasn't there really? Think of that, Hedda!

HEDDA. Yes, I'm listening.

MRS. ELVSTED. Nothing at all, I assure you. Not in any way. But all the same. . . . Now that I know he's down here . . . in the big city. . . . And with so much money in his pocket. I'm so dreadfully worried about him.

TESMAN. Well, why didn't he stay where he was, then? With you and your husband? Eh?

MRS. ELVSTED. When the book came out, you see, he just couldn't contain himself any more, up there.

TESMAN. Why yes of course . . . Aunt Julle said he'd published a new book.

MRS. ELVSTED. Yes, a big new book, dealing with cultural development . . . sort of altogether. It's a fortnight ago, now. And then when it sold so many copies . . . and caused such an enormous stir . . .

TESMAN. Did it? Did it indeed? I suppose it was something he had tucked away from his good period, then.

MRS. ELVSTED. From before, you mean?

TESMAN. Yes.

MRS. ELVSTED. No, he wrote the whole thing while he was with us. Just now . . . during the last year.

TESMAN. Well, that really is good news, Hedda! Think of that!

MRS. ELVSTED. Oh yes, if only everything's all right!

HEDDA. Have you seen him here in town?

MRS. ELVSTED. No, not yet. It was so difficult, trying to discover his address. But this morning I got it at last.

HEDDA [*gives her a searching glance*]. You know, it seems a little odd that your husband . . . hm . . .

MRS. ELVSTED [*with a nervous start*]. That my husband? What?

HEDDA. That he should send you down to town on this errand. That he didn't come in himself to look after his friend.

MRS. ELVSTED. Oh no, no . . . my husband doesn't have the time. And then there was . . . some shopping I had to do.

HEDDA [*with a little smile*]. Oh, well, that's different, then.

MRS. ELVSTED [*gets up quickly, ill at ease*]. And now I beg of you, Mr. Tesman, please . . . receive Ejlert Lövborg well, if he comes here! And he's sure to. I know . . . you were such good friends before. And then you're both interested in the same subject. The same field of studies . . . so far as I understand it.

TESMAN. Well, it used to be before, anyway.

MRS. ELVSTED. Yes, and that's why I ask you so particularly, . . . please do . . . please would you keep an eye on him as well. You will, won't you Mr. Tesman . . . you promise you will.

TESMAN. Yes of course, I'll be only too happy, Mrs. Rysing . . .

HEDDA. Elvsted.

TESMAN. I'll certainly do absolutely everything I can for Ejlert. You may be sure of that.

MRS. ELVSTED. Oh, how very kind you are! [*She presses his hands.*] Thank you, Mr. Tesman, thank you! [*Alarmed.*] Yes, because my husband is so particularly fond of him!

HEDDA [*rising*]. You ought to write to him, Tesman. Perhaps he won't come on his own initiative.

TESMAN. Yes, wouldn't that be the best idea, Hedda? Eh?

HEDDA. And the sooner the better. You'd better do it now, at once.

MRS. ELVSTED [*beseechingly*]. Yes, if only you would!

TESMAN. I'll do it right away. Do you have his address, Mrs. . . . Mrs. Elvsted?

MRS. ELVSTED. Yes. [*She takes a piece of paper from her pocket and hands it to him.*] I wrote it there.

TESMAN. Good, good. I'll go in, then . . . [*He looks around*]. Oh yes, what happened to . . . ? Oh, there they are.

[*He picks up the packet with the slippers and is about to go.*]

HEDDA. Now be sure to write something really warm and friendly. A good long letter.

TESMAN. Yes, I'll do that.

MRS. ELVSTED. But for goodness' sake don't say that I asked you to invite him!

TESMAN. No, of course not . . . that goes without saying. Eh?

[*He goes out to the right through the back room.*]

HEDDA [*goes over to* MRS. ELVSTED, *smiles, and speaks in a low voice*]. There! Two birds with one stone.

MRS. ELVSTED. What do you mean by that?

HEDDA. Couldn't you see that I wanted him to leave us?

MRS. ELVSTED. Yes, to write the letter . . .

HEDDA. And so that I could speak to you alone.

MRS. ELVSTED [*flustered*]. What, about all this?

HEDDA. Exactly.

MRS. ELVSTED [*scared*]. But there isn't anything else, Mrs. Tesman! Really, nothing more to say!

HEDDA. Oh there is indeed. There's a great deal more. That's perfectly obvious. Come here . . . we'll sit down and have a nice talk about it.

[*She forces* MRS. ELVSTED *into the armchair by the stove, and sits down herself on one of the stools.*]

MRS. ELVSTED [*anxious, looking at her watch*]. But Mrs. Tesman, please . . . I should have left long ago.

HEDDA. Oh, you can't be in such an enormous hurry. . . . Well, then. Now you tell me a bit about your life at home.

MRS. ELVSTED. Oh, that's just the one thing I really didn't want to talk about.

HEDDA. But you can tell me, my dear . . . ? After all, we were at school together.

MRS. ELVSTED. Yes, but you were in the class above me. Oh, I was dreadfully frightened of you in those days!

HEDDA. Frightened? Of me?

MRS. ELVSTED. Oh, dreadfully frightened. When we met on the steps you always used to pull my hair.

HEDDA. No, did I really?

MRS. ELVSTED. Yes, and you once said you were going to burn it off.

HEDDA. Oh, that was just something I said, you know.

MRS. ELVSTED. Yes, but I was such a fool in those days. . . . And anyway, since then . . . we've grown such miles apart. We don't meet the same sort of people at all.

HEDDA. Well, we must try to bridge the gap again. We spoke freely to each other at school, at least, and we always called each other by our Christian names. . . .

MRS. ELVSTED. Oh, I'm sure you're wrong about that.

HEDDA. Oh no I'm not! I remember it perfectly. And so we'll be good friends again, like we were in the old days. [*She moves her chair closer.*] There! [*She kisses her cheek.*] From now on you're to call me Hedda.

MRS. ELVSTED [*presses and pats her hand*]. Oh, you're so kind and good to me! I'm just not used to such kind treatment.

HEDDA. There, now! And I'm going to call you my darling Thora.

MRS. ELVSTED. I'm called Thea.

HEDDA. Quite right. Of course. Thea, I meant. [*Looks at her sympathetically.*] And so you're not accustomed to kind treatment, my poor Thea? Not even in your own home?

MRS. ELVSTED. Oh, if only I had a home! But I haven't got one. Never had one.

HEDDA [*looks at her a little*]. I rather thought it must be something like that.

MRS. ELVSTED [*stares helplessly in front of her*]. Yes . . . yes . . . yes.

HEDDA. I don't quite remember how it was, now. But didn't you go up there in the first place as Mr. Elvsted's housekeeper?

MRS. ELVSTED. Oh, actually I was meant to be a governess. But his wife . . . in those days . . . she was an invalid . . . and usually stayed in bed. So I had to look after the house as well.

HEDDA. But then . . . after that . . . you became the mistress of the house.

MRS. ELVSTED [*heavily*]. Yes, I became his wife.

HEDDA. Let me see. . . . About how long ago would that be, now?

MRS. ELVSTED. That I got married?

HEDDA. Yes.

MRS. ELVSTED. That was five years ago.

HEDDA. That's right, five years it must be.

MRS. ELVSTED. Oh, those five years . . . ! Well, the last two or three at least. Oh, if only you knew, Mrs. Tesman . . .

HEDDA [*hits her lightly on the hand*]. Mrs. Tesman? Now that's naughty, Thea.

MRS. ELVSTED. Oh no, I'm sorry . . . Hedda. I'll try. But if only you could imagine what it was like. . . .

HEDDA [*casually*]. Ejlert Lövborg's been up there about three years, hasn't he?

MRS. ELVSTED [*looks at her uncertainly*]. Ejlert Lövborg? Yes . . . so he has.

HEDDA. Did you know him before that? From town?

MRS. ELVSTED. Hardly at all. Well, that is . . . I'd heard of him, of course.

HEDDA. But then up there . . . he used to come to your house quite often?

MRS. ELVSTED. Yes, he came over every day. He had to come and read with the children. Because in the long run I couldn't manage it all by myself.

HEDDA. No indeed, I can imagine. . . . And your husband . . . ? I suppose he travels quite a bit in his position?

MRS. ELVSTED. Well, of course . . . he's in charge of the whole administration of the district, so he has to keep an eye on things.

HEDDA [*leaning against the arm of the chair*]. Thea . . . poor, sweet Thea . . . now you must tell me all about it . . . as it really is.

MRS. ELVSTED. Well, what do you want to know?

HEDDA. Tell me, what's your husband really like, Thea? I mean, well . . . to be with? Does he treat you well?

MRS. ELVSTED [*evasively*]. He thinks he does everything for the best.

HEDDA. It just seems to me that he must be a little old for you. Over twenty years older, isn't he?

MRS. ELVSTED [*roused*]. Oh, that as well. Just everything about him! There's simply nothing . . . we just haven't a thought in common. We don't share a thing, he and I.

HEDDA. But isn't he fond of you all the same? In his own way?

MRS. ELVSTED. Oh, I don't know what he is. I think he just finds me useful. And then it doesn't cost much to keep me. I'm cheap.

HEDDA. That's foolish of you.

MRS. ELVSTED [*shakes her head*]. Can't be anything else. Not with him. I don't believe he thinks of anyone except himself. And then perhaps a bit the children.

HEDDA. And then he's fond of Ejlert Lövborg, Thea.

MRS. ELVSTED [*looks at her*]. Of Ejlert Lövborg! What gives you that idea?

HEDDA. But my dear . . . it seems to me that when he sends you all this way to town to look for him . . . [*Smiles almost imperceptibly.*] And besides, you told Tesman so yourself.

MRS. ELVSTED [*with a nervous laugh*]. Did I? Well, I suppose I did. [*A subdued outburst.*] No . . . I may as well make a clean breast of it at once! It's bound to come out anyway, in the end.

HEDDA. But Thea, my dear . . .?

MRS. ELVSTED. Brief and to the point, then! I never told my husband I was leaving.

HEDDA. What are you saying! Didn't he know you were leaving!

MRS. ELVSTED. Of course not. Anyway he wasn't at home. He'd gone on a tour of inspection. Oh, I just couldn't bear it any longer, Hedda! Not another minute! So terribly alone I'd have been, up there, from now on.

HEDDA. Well? And then?

MRS. ELVSTED. I just packed up a few of my belongings. The essentials. Without letting anyone see. And then I left.

HEDDA. Just like that?

MRS. ELVSTED. Yes. And took the train to town.

HEDDA. But my dear, sweet Thea . . . I don't know how you dared!

MRS. ELVSTED [*gets up from the chair and walks across the floor*]. Well what on earth else would you have me do?

HEDDA. But what do you think your husband will say when you go back?

MRS. ELVSTED. Back up there?

HEDDA. Yes, yes.

MRS. ELVSTED. I'll never go back up there.

HEDDA [*gets up, and goes closer to her*]. Then you've really . . . in all seriousness . . . run away from it all?

MRS. ELVSTED. Yes. I didn't think there was anything else I could do.

HEDDA. And then . . . that you left so openly.

MRS. ELVSTED. Oh, there's no hiding that sort of thing, anyway.

HEDDA. But what do you think people will say about you, Thea?

MRS. ELVSTED. Oh, they'll just have to say what they please. [*She sits depressed and exhausted on the sofa.*] I simply had to do what I did.

HEDDA [*after a short pause*]. And what's going to happen to you now? What are you going to do with yourself?

MRS. ELVSTED. I don't know yet. I just know that I must live here, where Ejlert Lövborg's living. . . . If I have to live at all.

HEDDA [*moves a chair across from the table, sits by her and strokes her hands*]. Tell me, Thea . . . how did it come about, this . . . this familiarity between you and Ejlert Lövborg?

MRS. ELVSTED. Oh, it just happened, bit by bit. I got a sort of control over him.

HEDDA. Really?

MRS. ELVSTED. He left off his old ways. Not because I asked him to. I never dared to do that. But he knew all right that I didn't like that sort of thing. And then he gave it up.

HEDDA [*concealing an involuntary sneer*]. And so you've reclaimed the prodigal . . . as they say . . . little Thea.

MRS. ELVSTED. Well, that's what he says, anyway. And he . . . for his part . . . he's made me into a sort of real person. Taught me to think . . . and to understand quite a lot of things.

HEDDA. Did he give you lessons too, then?

MRS. ELVSTED. No, not lessons, like that. But he talked to me. Talked of so fantastically many things. And then came that beautiful, happy time, when I shared his work! Was allowed to help him!

HEDDA. He let you help him?

MRS. ELVSTED. Yes! When he wrote anything, we always had to do it together.

HEDDA. Like two good companions, then.

MRS. ELVSTED [*animated*]. Companions! Yes, imagine, Hedda . . . that's what he used to say! . . . Oh, I ought to be so wonderfully happy. But I can't be, quite. For I can't be sure that it will really last.

HEDDA. Are you still so uncertain of him, then?

MRS. ELVSTED [*heavily*]. There's the shadow of a woman who stands between us.

HEDDA [*looks at her with keen interest*]. Who might that be?

MRS. ELVSTED. Don't know. Someone or other from . . . from his past. Someone he can't really forget.

HEDDA. What has he told you . . . about this?

MRS. ELVSTED. He's only ever once . . . sort of indirectly . . . touched on it.

HEDDA. Well! And what did he say?

MRS. ELVSTED. He said that when they parted, she threatened to shoot him with a pistol.

HEDDA [*cold and collected*]. Oh rubbish! People don't have such things here.

MRS. ELVSTED. No. And that's why I think it must be that red-haired singer, whom he once . . .

HEDDA. Yes, I suppose that's possible.

MRS. ELVSTED. Because I can remember someone telling me that she carried a loaded pistol.

HEDDA. Oh well . . . then it must be her, then.

MRS. ELVSTED [*wrings her hands*]. Yes but just think, Hedda . . . now I hear that that woman . . . she's in town again! Oh . . . I'm quite distracted. . . .

HEDDA [*glancing towards the back room*]. Sh! Here's Tesman coming. [*Gets up, and whispers.*] Thea . . . all this must be just between you and me.

MRS. ELVSTED [*jumping up*]. Oh yes . . . yes! For God's sake . . . !

[JÖRGEN TESMAN, *with a letter in his hand, comes from the right of the inner room.*]

TESMAN. There now . . . the epistle is signed and sealed.

HEDDA. That's splendid. But I think Mrs. Elvsted wants to go now. I won't be a moment. I'm just going as far as the garden gate.

TESMAN. Oh Hedda . . . do you think Berte could see to this?

HEDDA [*takes the letter*]. I'll tell her.

[BERTE *comes in from the hall.*]

BERTE. Mr. Brack is here and says please may he come in.

HEDDA. Yes, ask Mr. Brack to step inside. And then . . . I say, . . . then put this letter in the post box.

BERTE [*takes the letter*]. Yes, ma'am.

[*She opens the door for* MR. BRACK, *and goes out herself.* BRACK *is a gentleman of 45. Stocky, but well-built and elastic in his movements. His face roundish, with a good profile. Hair short, still almost black, and carefully dressed. Eyes lively and playful. Thick eyebrows, thick moustaches cut short at the ends. He is dressed in a stylish walking suit, perhaps a little too youthful in cut for a man of his age. He uses an eye-glass, which he now and again allows to fall.*]

BRACK [*bowing, his hat in his hand*]. Is it permissible to call so early in the day?

HEDDA. Of course it is.

TESMAN [*takes his hand*]. We're always glad to see you. [*He introduces.*] Mr. Brack . . . Miss Rysing. . . .

HEDDA. Oh . . . !

BRACK [*bows*]. Ah . . . delighted to make your acquaintance. . . .

HEDDA [*looks at him and laughs*]. How charming to view you by daylight, Mr. Brack!

BRACK. You find me . . . perhaps a little changed?

HEDDA. Yes, you look rather younger, I think.

BRACK. Accept my humble gratitude.

TESMAN. But what do you say to Hedda, then! Eh? Isn't she blossoming? She's positively . . .

HEDDA. Oh, pray leave me out of this. You'd do better to thank Mr. Brack for all the trouble he's taken . . .

BRACK. Oh, not at all . . . I do assure you it was a pleasure. . . .

HEDDA. Yes, you're a loyal soul. But my friend's standing here and dying to get away. Au revoir, Mr. Brack. I'll be back in a moment.

[*Mutual leave-taking.* MRS. ELVSTED *and* HEDDA *leave by the hall door.*]

BRACK. Well, now . . . and does everything come up to the lady's expectations?

TESMAN. Oh yes, and we can't thank you enough. That is . . . a little shifting back and forth may be necessary, I gather. And there are one or two things missing. We'll doubtless have to acquire a few trifles yet.

BRACK. Oh, will you? Really?

TESMAN. But we won't be putting you to any further trouble. Hedda said she'd take care of the necessary purchases herself. . . . But I say, shan't we sit down? Eh?

BRACK. Thank you, just for a moment. [*Sits by the table.*] There's a little matter I'd like to talk to you about, my dear Tesman.

TESMAN. Oh? Ah, I'm with you! [*He sits down.*] The entertainment has its serious side, no doubt. Eh?

BRACK. Oh, as yet there's no tearing hurry about the financial side. Though incidentally, I should be happier if we'd arranged things a little more modestly.

TESMAN. But that would have been quite out of the question! Think of Hedda, man! You, who know her so well. . . . I couldn't possibly have expected her to put up with a genteel suburb!

BRACK. Ah, no . . . there's the rub.

TESMAN. And then . . . fortunately . . . it can't be long before I get that appointment.

BRACK. Well, you know . . . these things have a habit of taking their time.

TESMAN. Perhaps you've heard some more about it? Eh?

BRACK. Nothing in any way definite, but . . . [*He breaks off.*] Oh, by the way, I do have one piece of news for you.

TESMAN. Oh?

BRACK. Your old friend Ejlert Lövborg is back in town.

TESMAN. I know that already.

BRACK. Oh? How did you come to know it?

TESMAN. She told us, the lady who just went out with Hedda.

BRACK. She did. What was her name again? I didn't quite catch . . .

TESMAN. Mrs. Elvsted.

BRACK. Aha . . . so that's who it was, then. Yes . . . I believe he stayed with them up there.

TESMAN. And just think . . . I was so delighted to hear that he's become quite a sober citizen again!

BRACK. Yes, that's what they say.

TESMAN. And he's supposed to have published a new book. Eh?

BRACK. Yes, by God he has!

TESMAN. And what's more, it's been very well received!

BRACK. It's been quite exceptionally well received.

TESMAN. Just think . . . isn't that wonderfully good news? That fellow, with all his extraordinary talents. . . . I was terribly convinced that he'd gone to the dogs for good.

BRACK. Yes, pretty nearly everyone thought the same.

TESMAN. But I just can't imagine what he's going to do with himself now! What on earth can he possibly find to live on? Eh?

[*During the last speech,* HEDDA *has come in from the hall.*]

HEDDA [*to* BRACK, *laughing a little scornfully*]. Tesman's for ever worrying about what people are going to find to live on.

TESMAN. Oh Heavens . . . we're sitting here talking about poor Ejlert Lövborg, my dear.

HEDDA [*looks at him quickly*]. Oh yes? [*Sits down in the armchair by the stove and asks indifferently.*] What's the matter with him?

TESMAN. Well . . . he must have spent all the money he inherited ages ago. And I don't suppose he can write a new book every year. Eh? Well, then . . . I really can't for the life of me see how he's going to exist at all.

BRACK. Perhaps I could tell you a little about that.

TESMAN. Oh?

BRACK. You must remember that he's got relations with quite a lot of influence.

TESMAN. Oh well, his relations . . . I'm afraid they've disowned him entirely.

BRACK. They used to regard him as the white hope of the family.

TESMAN. Yes, they used to, yes! But he's been and dished all that himself.

HEDDA. Who knows? [*She smiles faintly.*] Up at the Elvsteds' they've been busy reclaiming him. . . .

BRACK. And then there's this new book he's written. . . .

TESMAN. Oh well, I hope to goodness they will help him to get something. I've just written to him. Oh, Hedda, I asked him to come round this evening.

BRACK. But my dear Tesman, you're coming to my bachelor party this evening. You promised last night on the quay.

HEDDA. Had you forgotten, Tesman?

TESMAN. Yes, by all that's holy.

BRACK. In any case, I think you may rely on him to find an excuse.

TESMAN. Why should you think that? Eh?

BRACK [*a little hesitantly, rising and leaning his hands on the back of the chair*]. My dear Tesman. . . . And you too, madam. . . . I can no longer allow you to remain in ignorance of something that . . . that . . .

TESMAN. Something to do with Ejlert . . . ?

BRACK. Both him and yourself.

TESMAN. But come on then, Mr. Brack!

BRACK. You ought to prepare yourself for the discovery that your appointment may not come quite as soon as you hope and expect.

TESMAN [*jumps up in alarm*]. Has something happened to delay it? Eh?

BRACK. The appointment to the professorship might conceivably be contested by another candidate. . . .

TESMAN. Another candidate! Think of that, Hedda!

HEDDA [*leans further back in her chair*]. Ah, yes . . . yes!

TESMAN. But who on earth! Surely not . . . ?

BRACK. Quite correct. Ejlert Lövborg.

TESMAN [*clasps his hands together*]. No, no . . . this is quite unthinkable! Quite impossible! Eh?

BRACK. Hm . . . we may very well find it happening, all the same.

TESMAN. Oh but my dear sir . . . but that would be quite incredibly inconsiderate of him! [*He flings his arms about.*] Yes, because . . . just think . . . I'm a married man! We got married on our expectations, Hedda and I. Been and borrowed vast sums. We're in debt to Auntie Julle, too! Because, good God . . . the post was as good as promised to me. Eh?

BRACK. Come, come, come . . . you'll most probably get it, too. But only after a bit of competition.

HEDDA [*immobile in her chair*]. Just think, Tesman . . . it'll be quite a sporting event.

TESMAN. But my dearest Hedda, how can you take it all so calmly!

HEDDA [*as before*]. Oh, I don't at all. I await the result with breathless expectation.

BRACK. Well, anyway, Mrs. Tesman, it's as well that you should know how matters stand. I mean . . . before you embark on those little purchases you apparently threaten to make.

HEDDA. This can't change anything so far as that's concerned.

BRACK. No? Well, that's all right, then. I'll say goodbye! [*To* TESMAN.] When I take my constitutional this afternoon I'll step in and fetch you, shall I?

TESMAN. Oh yes, yes . . . I hardly know where I am.

HEDDA [*reclining, stretching out her hand*]. Goodbye, Mr. Brack! We look forward to your return.

BRACK. Many thanks. Goodbye, goodbye.

TESMAN [*escorting him to the door*]. Goodbye, my dear Mr. Brack! You really must excuse all this. . . .

[BRACK *goes out at the hall door.*]

TESMAN [*trails across the floor*]. Ah, Hedda . . . one should never go building castles in the air. Eh?

HEDDA [*looks at him and smiles*]. And do you?

TESMAN. Yes . . . it can't be denied . . . it was idiotically romantic to go and get married, and buy a house, just on expectations alone.

HEDDA. You may be right about that.

TESMAN. Well . . . at least we have got our lovely house, Hedda! Just think . . . the house we'd both set our hearts on. Our dream house, I might almost call it. Eh?

HEDDA [*rises slowly and tiredly*]. The agreement was that we were to live a social life. Entertain.

TESMAN. Yes, oh Heavens . . . I was so looking forward to it! Just think, to see you as the hostess . . . presiding over a select group of friends! Eh? . . . Well, well, well . . . for the time being we'll just have to be the two of us, Hedda. Just see Aunt Julle once in a while. . . . Oh, for you everything should have been so very . . . very different . . . !

HEDDA. And I suppose I won't get my footman just yet awhile.

TESMAN. Oh no . . . a manservant, you must see that that's quite out of the question.

HEDDA. And the saddle-horse I was to have had . . .

TESMAN [*appalled*]. The saddle-horse!

HEDDA. . . . I suppose I daren't even think of that, now.

TESMAN. No, God preserve us . . . that goes without saying!

HEDDA [*moving across*]. Oh, well . . . I've got one thing at least that I can pass the time with.

TESMAN [*ecstatic*]. Oh, thank the good Lord for that! And what might that be, Hedda? Eh?

HEDDA [*at the centre doorway, looking at him with concealed contempt*]. My pistols . . . Jörgen.

TESMAN [*alarmed*]. Pistols!

HEDDA [*with cold eyes*]. General Gabler's pistols.

[*She goes out to the left through the back room.*]

TESMAN [*runs to the doorway and shouts after her*]. No, for the love of God, my darling Hedda . . . don't touch those dangerous contraptions! For my sake, Hedda! Eh?

ACT TWO

The room at the Tesmans' as in the first Act, except that the piano has been removed and an elegant little writing-desk with a book-shelf put in its place. A small table has been placed by the sofa on the left. Most of the flowers have been removed. MRS. ELVSTED's *bunch of flowers stands on the large table in the foreground. . . . It is afternoon.*

HEDDA, *now dressed to receive visitors, is alone in the room. She is standing by the open glass door, loading a revolver-type pistol. Its companion lies in an open case on the writing-desk.*

HEDDA [*looks down into the garden and shouts*]. Hullo again, Mr. Brack!

BRACK [*down in the garden some distance away*]. Good afternoon to you, Mrs. Tesman!

HEDDA [*raises the pistol and takes aim*]. I'm going to shoot you, sir!

BRACK [*shouting down below*]. No-no-no! Don't stand there aiming right at me!

HEDDA. That's what comes of sneaking round the back!

[*She fires.*]

BRACK [*closer*]. Are you quite mad . . . !

HEDDA. Oh good Lord . . . did I hit you perhaps?

BRACK [*still outside*]. Stop fooling about, I tell you!

HEDDA. Come inside then, Mr. Brack.

[MR. BRACK, *already dressed for the evening's occasion, comes in through the glass door. He carries a light overcoat on his arm.*]

BRACK. What the devil . . . do you still play at that game? What are you shooting at?

HEDDA. Oh, I just stand here and shoot into the blue.

BRACK [*eases the pistol out of her hand*]. By your leave, my lady. [*Looks *at it.*] Ah yes . . . I seem to recognize this fellow. [*Looks around.*] Now then, where's the case? Ah, here. [*He replaces the pistol and shuts the case.*] And now we won't play with those toys any more today.

HEDDA. Well, what in God's name do you want me to do with myself?

BRACK. Haven't you had any visitors?

HEDDA [*shuts the verandah door*]. Not a soul. I suppose the crowd are all in the country still.

BRACK. And Tesman's not in either, perhaps?

HEDDA [*at the writing-desk, puts the pistol case in the drawer*]. No. As soon as he'd eaten he ran off to the aunts. He didn't expect you so soon.

BRACK. Hm . . . and I didn't think of that. Stupid of me.

HEDDA [*turns her head and looks at him*]. Why stupid?

BRACK. Because then I could have come out here . . . even a little earlier.

HEDDA [*crosses the floor*]. And then you'd have found no one at all. I've been in my room, changing after lunch.

BRACK. And isn't there the minutest chink in the door that would have permitted communication?

HEDDA. Why, you forgot to arrange one of those.

BRACK. That was also stupid of me.

HEDDA. Well, we'd better sit down here then. And wait. Because Tesman won't be home in a hurry.

BRACK. Well, well, good Heavens, I shall be patient.

[HEDDA *sits in the corner of the sofa.* BRACK *lays his coat over the nearest chair and seats himself, but keeps his hat in his hand. A short pause. They look at one another.*]

HEDDA. Well?

BRACK [*in the same tone*]. Well?

HEDDA. I asked first.

BRACK [*leans forward slightly*]. Well, my lady, what do you say to a comfortable little gossip.

HEDDA [*leans further back in the sofa*]. Doesn't it seem to you that it's an eternity since we talked together? Oh . . . I don't count those few words last night and this morning.

BRACK. But . . . between ourselves? Just the two of us, you mean?

HEDDA. Well, yes. More or less.

BRACK. I've gone around here day after day longing for you to come back again.

HEDDA. And for the matter of that, I've been longing for the same thing.

BRACK. You have? Really, my lady? And I was convinced you were having a wonderful time on the trip!

HEDDA. Oh, magnificent!

BRACK. But Tesman was always saying so in his letters.

HEDDA. Yes, he was! He's absolutely in his element if he's given leave to grub around in libraries. And sit copying out ancient parchments . . . or whatever they are.

BRACK [*a little maliciously*]. After all, that is his particular *raison d'être*. Part of it, anyway.

HEDDA. Yes, that's it. So it was all very fine for him. . . . But for me! Oh no, my dear Brack . . . for me it was horribly tedious!

BRACK [*sympathizing*]. Was it really as bad as all that?

HEDDA. Oh yes, use your imagination . . . ! For six months on end, never meeting anyone who knew anybody in our circle. Who could talk about our own affairs.

BRACK. Well, no . . . I'd have felt the want of that myself.

HEDDA. And then the most unbearable thing of all . . .

BRACK. Well?

HEDDA. . . . everlastingly having to be together with . . . with the self-same person. . . .

BRACK [*nods assentingly*]. Day in and day out . . . yes. Think of it . . . at all possible times of the . . .

HEDDA. I said everlastingly.

BRACK. So be it. But I should have thought that in the case of our estimable Tesman, it would have been possible to . . .

HEDDA. Tesman is . . . an academic, my dear sir.

BRACK. Undeniably.

HEDDA. And academics aren't a bit amusing as travelling-companions. Not in the long run, anyway.

BRACK. Not even . . . the academic with whom one happens to be . . . in love?

HEDDA. Ugh . . . don't use that glutinous word!

BRACK [*pulled up*]. What's this, my lady!

HEDDA [*half laughingly, half bitterly*]. Well, you ought to have a try at it! Hearing about the history of civilization day in and day out. . . .

BRACK. Everlastingly.

HEDDA. Yes-yes-yes! and then this stuff about mediaeval domestic crafts . . . ! That's the most sickening of the lot!

BRACK [*looks at her inquiringly*]. But, tell me . . . how am I then to account for the fact that . . . ? Hm. . . .

HEDDA. That Jörgen Tesman and I made a match of it, you mean?

BRACK. Well, let's put it that way.

HEDDA. Oh, Heavens, does it seem to you so strange, then?

BRACK. Both yes and no . . . my lady.

HEDDA. I'd really danced myself tired, my dear sir. I had had my day . . . [*She gives a little shudder.*] Oh, no . . . I'm not going to say that. Nor think it, either.

BRACK. With respect, madam, you've no reason to.

HEDDA. Oh . . . reason. . . . [*She sums him up with her look.*] And Jörgen Tesman . . . you must allow that he's a most worthy person in every way.

BRACK. Oh, solid worth. Heaven preserve us.

HEDDA. And I can't see that there's anything specifically ridiculous about him. . . . Or what do you say?

BRACK. Ridiculous? No-o . . . I wouldn't say that exactly. . . .

HEDDA. Well. But then he's a most diligent research worker, at any rate! . . . And after all, he might get somewhere with it in time, in spite of everything.

BRACK [*looks at her a little uncertainly*]. But I thought you believed, like everybody else, that he'd make a really outstanding man.

HEDDA [*with a tired expression*]. Yes, so I did. . . . And then when he came along and was so pathetically eager to be allowed to support me. . . . I don't really see why I shouldn't let him?

BRACK. Well of course, if you put it like that. . . .

HEDDA. It was more than any of my other gallant friends were prepared to do, dear Mr. Brack.

BRACK [*laughs*]. Ah, I regret I can't answer for all the others. But as for myself, as you know I've always observed a . . . a certain respect for the bonds of holy matrimony. In a general sort of way, my lady.

HEDDA [*banteringly*]. Well no, I never really had any very high hopes of you.

BRACK. I demand no more than a nice intimate circle of acquaintances, where I can rally round with advice and assistance, and where I'm allowed to come and go as . . . as a trusted friend. . . .

HEDDA. Of the master of the house, you mean?

BRACK [*inclines his head*]. Candidly . . . of the lady, for choice. But naturally of the man as well. D'you know . . . this sort of . . . let me put it, this sort of triangular relationship . . . it's really highly convenient for all concerned.

HEDDA. Yes, I'd have been glad of a third on the trip, often enough. Ugh . . . sitting there, just two people alone in the compartment . . . !

BRACK. Fortunately, the nuptial journey is at an end. . . .

HEDDA [*shakes her head*]. The journey'll be a long one . . . a long one yet. I've just come to a stopping-place on the line.

BRACK. Well, then you jump out. And move around a little, my lady.

HEDDA. I'll never jump out.

BRACK. Are you quite sure?

HEDDA. Yes. Because there's always someone there who'll . . .

BRACK [*laughing*]. . . . who'll look at your legs, you mean?

HEDDA. Exactly.

BRACK. Oh well, good Lord. . . .

HEDDA [*with a gesture of dismissal*]. Don't like it. . . . Then I'd sooner stay where I am . . . in the compartment. Two people alone together.

BRACK. Well then, if somebody else climbs into the compartment.

HEDDA. Ah yes . . . that's quite another thing!

BRACK. A trusted and sympathetic friend . . .

HEDDA. . . . who can converse on all manner of lively topics . . .

BRACK. . . . and who's not in the least academic!

HEDDA [*with an audible sigh*]. Yes, that really is a relief.

BRACK [*hears the front door opening and listens*]. The triangle is completed.

HEDDA [*half aloud*]. And the train drives on.

[JÖRGEN TESMAN, *in a grey walking suit and with a soft hat, comes in from the hall. He has quite a number of unbound books under his arm and in his pockets.*]

TESMAN [*goes up to the table by the corner sofa*]. Poof . . . hot work dragging all these around. [*He puts down the books.*] To put it elegantly, I'm sweating, Hedda. Why, what's this . . . you're here already, Mr. Brack? Eh? Berte didn't tell me anything about that.

BRACK [*gets up*]. I came up through the garden.

HEDDA. What are those books you've got there?

TESMAN [*turns a few pages*]. Oh, new academic publications that I simply had to have.

HEDDA. Academic publications?

BRACK. Aha, they're academic publications, Mrs. Tesman.

[BRACK *and* HEDDA *exchange a knowing smile.*]

HEDDA. Do you need still more academic publications?

TESMAN. Oh yes, my dear Hedda . . . can't get too many of those. One must keep up with everything that's written.

HEDDA. Yes, I suppose one must.

TESMAN [*searching among the books*]. And look here . . . here we are, I've got hold of Ejlert Lövborg's new book, too. [*He holds it out.*] Perhaps you'd like to have a look at it, Hedda? Eh?

HEDDA. No thank you. Or . . . yes, perhaps I will, later on.

TESMAN. I glanced at a few pages on my way up.

BRACK. Well, and what did you think of it, then? . . . From the academic point of view?

TESMAN. I think it's remarkable how soberly he's argued it. He never used to write like this before. [*Gathers up the books.*] But now I'm going to go in with all this. It'll be a joy to cut the pages . . . ! And then I'll have to get into some other clothes. [*To* BRACK.] I take it we don't have to leave straight away, do we? Eh?

BRACK. No indeed . . . there's no hurry for a long while yet.

TESMAN. Ah well, I'll take my time then. [*Goes with the books, but stops in the doorway and turns.*] Oh, while I think of it, Hedda . . . Aunt Julle won't be able to come this evening.

HEDDA. Won't she? Is it because of that affair with the hat, perhaps?

TESMAN. Oh, good gracious! How can you think that of Auntie Julle? Just think . . . ! But the thing is Aunt Rina's so very ill, you see.

HEDDA. She always is.

TESMAN. Yes, but today she was quite exceptionally bad, poor thing.

HEDDA. Well, then it's only reasonable that the other one should stay with her. I'll have to make the best of it.

TESMAN. And you can't imagine, Hedda, how overjoyed Aunt Julle was in spite of everything . . . because you looked so well from the trip!

HEDDA [*half under her breath, getting up*]. Oh, these everlasting aunts!

TESMAN. Eh?

HEDDA [*crossing to the glass door*]. Nothing.

TESMAN. Oh, all right then.

[*He goes out through the back room to the right.*]

BRACK. What was that about a hat?

HEDDA. Oh, it was to do with Miss Tesman this morning. She'd put her hat down there on the chair. [*Looks at him and smiles.*] And I pretended I thought it was the maid's.

BRACK [*shakes his head*]. But my dearest lady, how could you do such a thing! To that harmless old soul!

HEDDA [*nervously, walking across*]. Oh, you know how it is . . . these things just suddenly come over me. And then I can't resist them. [*Flings herself down in the armchair by the stove.*] Oh, I don't know myself how to explain it.

BRACK [*behind the armchair*]. You're not really happy . . . that's probably what it is.

HEDDA [*looking straight ahead*]. And I don't really know why I should be . . . happy. Or perhaps you might be able to tell me?

BRACK. Yes . . . among other things, because you've got just the home you wanted.

HEDDA [*looks up at him and laughs*]. Do you also believe that fairy story?

BRACK. Why, isn't there anything in it?

HEDDA. Oh yes . . . there's something in it.

BRACK. Well?

HEDDA. There's this much in it, that I used Tesman as an escort to take me home from evening parties last summer. . . .

BRACK. Ah, regrettably . . . I had to go quite a different way.

HEDDA. True enough, you were going a rather different way, last summer.

BRACK [*laughs*]. Touché, my lady! Well . . . but you and Tesman, then . . . ?

HEDDA. Yes, well then we came past this house one evening. And Tesman, poor fellow, was floundering and dithering. Because he couldn't think of anything to talk about. So I felt sorry for the poor erudite man. . . .

BRACK [*smiles sceptically*]. Did you? Hm. . . .

HEDDA. Yes, by your leave sir, I did. And then . . . to help him along a bit . . . I happened to say, just on the impulse, that I'd like to live here in this villa.

BRACK. No more than that?

HEDDA. Not that particular evening.

BRACK. But afterwards, then?

HEDDA. Ah yes. My impulsiveness had its consequences, my dear Mr. Brack.

BRACK. Unfortunately . . . impulsiveness does that only too frequently, my lady.

HEDDA. Thank you! But in this ardour for Lady Falk's villa Jörgen Tesman and I met in mutual understanding, you see! It brought on engagement and marriage and honeymoon and the whole lot. Ah well, Mr. Brack . . . as one makes one's bed one must lie on it . . . I almost said.

BRACK. But this is delicious! And perhaps you didn't really care about the place at all?

HEDDA. No, God knows I did not.

BRACK. Well, but now, then? Now that we've arranged everything a bit comfortably for you!

HEDDA. Ugh . . . I think it smells of lavender and pot-pourri in all the rooms. . . . But perhaps Auntie Julle brought that smell in with her.

BRACK [*laughs*]. No, I think it's more probably a relic of the late lamented Lady Falk.

HEDDA. Yes, it has a sort of odour of death. Like a bouquet the day after a ball. [*Clasps her hands at the back of her neck, leans back in the chair and looks at him.*] Ah, dear Mr. Brack . . . you just can't imagine how excruciatingly bored I'll be, out here.

BRACK. Don't you think that for you too, my lady, life might have something or other up its sleeve?

HEDDA. Anything . . . in any way inviting?

BRACK. Well of course that would be best.

HEDDA. Lord knows what sort of thing that would be. I often wonder whether . . . [*She breaks off.*] But that wouldn't be any good either.

BRACK. Who knows? Let me hear about it.

HEDDA. Whether I could get Tesman to go in for politics, I mean.

BRACK [*laughs*]. Tesman! Oh now seriously . . . anything like politics, he wouldn't be any . . . manner of use at that.

HEDDA. No, I don't suppose he would. . . . But don't you think I might get him to do it, all the same?

BRACK. Well . . . what possible satisfaction could that give you? When he's no good? Why should you want him to?

HEDDA. Because I'm bored, d'you hear! [*After a pause.*] So you think it would be quite out of the question for Tesman to end up as Prime Minister?

BRACK. Hm . . . you know, my lady . . . to do that he'd have to be quite a rich man, for a start.

HEDDA [*rises impatiently*]. Yes, there we have it! It's these paltry circumstances I've landed up in . . . ! [*She moves across.*] That's what makes life so pitiful! So positively ludicrous! . . . Because that's what it is.

BRACK. I think it's something else that's the trouble.

HEDDA. What, then?

BRACK. You've never had to go through any really stirring experience.

HEDDA. Anything serious, you mean?

BRACK. Yes, I suppose one could put it that way too. But now . . . it might come.

HEDDA [*tosses her head*]. Oh, you're thinking of all the commotion about this wretched professorship! But that'll be Tesman's own affair. I'm not going to give it a thought.

BRACK. No–no, well we won't talk about that. But then when you're faced with ... what I may ... perhaps a little pompously ... refer to as a sacred and ... and exacting responsibility? [*Smiles.*] A new responsibility, my little lady.

HEDDA [*angry*]. Be quiet! You'll never see anything of the sort!

BRACK [*carefully*]. We'll talk about it in a year's time ... at the very latest.

HEDDA [*shortly*]. I've no aptitude for any such thing, Mr. Brack. No responsibilities for me, thank you!

BRACK. Why shouldn't you, like most other women, have a natural aptitude for a vocation that ... ?

HEDDA [*at the glass door*]. Oh, be quiet, I say! ... I've often thought there's only one thing in the world I'm any good at.

BRACK [*moves closer*]. And what might that be, may I venture to ask?

HEDDA [*standing and looking out*]. Boring myself to death. So now you know. [*Turns, looks towards the inner room, and laughs.*] Ah yes, right enough! Here comes the professor.

BRACK [*cautioning her in a low voice*]. Now, now, now, my lady!

[JÖRGEN TESMAN, *dressed for the party, holding his gloves and his hat, comes in from the right of the back room.*]

TESMAN. Hedda ... did Ejlert Lövborg send to say he wasn't coming? Eh?

HEDDA. No.

TESMAN. Well then, you'll see, he'll be here in a moment.

BRACK. Do you really think he'll come?

TESMAN. Yes, I'm almost sure of it. Because I don't think you can have been right about what you said this morning.

BRACK. Oh?

TESMAN. Well at any rate Auntie Julle said she couldn't see how he could possibly think of putting himself up against me, as things are. Think of that!

BRACK. Well, then everything's perfectly all right.

TESMAN [*puts his hat, with the gloves inside, on a chair to the right*]. Yes, but you won't mind if we give him as long as possible.

BRACK. Oh, we've got any amount of time. Nobody'll be coming to my place until seven or half past.

TESMAN. Well, we can keep Hedda company until then. And see what happens. Eh?

HEDDA [*carrying* BRACK's *overcoat and hat over to the corner sofa*]. And if the worst comes to the worst Mr. Lövborg can always stay here with me.

BRACK [*wants to carry his things himself*]. Allow me, Mrs. Tesman! . . . What do you mean by the worst?

HEDDA. If he won't go with you and Tesman.

TESMAN [*looks at her uncertainly*]. But, dearest Hedda . . . do you think it would be quite the thing for him to stay with you? Eh? Remember Aunt Julle can't come.

HEDDA. No, but Mrs. Elvsted's coming. And we'll all three have a nice cup of tea together.

TESMAN. Oh well, then, that's quite all right!

BRACK [*smiles*]. And perhaps that arrangement would be the most wholesome thing for him.

HEDDA. How so?

BRACK. Oh, come, Mrs. Tesman, you've twitted me often enough about my little bachelor parties. Only to be recommended, wasn't it, to men of the most steadfast principles?

HEDDA. But surely Mr. Lövborg is steadfast enough now. A prodigal reformed. . . .

[BERTE *appears at the hall door.*]

BERTE. Ma'am, there's a gentleman who wants to come in. . . .

HEDDA. Let him come.

TESMAN [*quietly*]. I'm sure it's him! Think of it!

[EJLERT LÖVBORG *comes in from the hall. He is slim and lean; the same age as* TESMAN, *but looks older and a little haggard. Hair and beard dark brown, face longish and pale, patches of colour on either cheekbone. He is dressed in an elegant, black, and quite new suit. Dark gloves and a top hat in his hands. He remains standing close to the door and bows hurriedly. He seems a little embarrassed.*]

TESMAN [*goes to him and pumps his hand*]. My dear Ejlert . . . so we meet again in spite of everything!

EJLERT LÖVBORG [*speaks in a low voice*]. Thanks for the letter, Tesman. [*Approaches* HEDDA.] May I take your hand as well, Mrs. Tesman?

HEDDA [*taking the hand he offers*]. So pleased you came, Mr. Lövborg. [*With a gesture.*] I wonder if you two gentlemen . . . ?

LÖVBORG [*with a slight inclination*]. Mr. Brack, I believe.

BRACK [*following suit*]. How do you do. Some years ago now. . . .

TESMAN [*to* LÖVBORG, *his hands on* LÖVBORG'*s shoulders*]. And now you must behave just as if you were at home, Ejlert! Isn't that right, Hedda? . . . And I hear you're going to settle here in town again? Eh?

LÖVBORG. That is so.

TESMAN. Well, and why not indeed? Hey listen . . . I've got hold of your new book. But I just haven't had a moment to read it yet.

LÖVBORG. You might as well save yourself the bother.

TESMAN. Why do you say that?

LÖVBORG. Because there's nothing much to it.

TESMAN. Oh but . . . what a thing for you to say!

BRACK. But it's been enormously praised, they tell me.

LÖVBORG. That was just what I wanted. So I wrote a book that nobody could disagree with.

BRACK. Very sensible.

TESMAN. Yes but, my dear Ejlert . . . !

LÖVBORG. Because I'm trying now to build up a position for myself. Starting over again.

TESMAN [*a bit embarrassed*]. Why yes, I suppose you are? Eh?

LÖVBORG [*smiles, puts down his hat and pulls a packet wrapped in paper from his coat pocket*]. But when this one comes out . . . Jörgen Tesman . . . then you're to read it. Because this is the real thing. I put some of myself into this one.

TESMAN. Really? And what's that about?

LÖVBORG. It's the continuation.

TESMAN. The continuation? Of what?

LÖVBORG. Of the book.

TESMAN. The new one?

LÖVBORG. Of course.

TESMAN. Yes but, my dear Ejlert . . . it carries on right to the present day!

LÖVBORG. That is so. And this one deals with the future.

TESMAN. With the future! But ye gods, we don't know anything about that!

LÖVBORG. No. But there are one or two things to be said about it, all the same. [*Opens the packet.*] Here, look at this. . . .

TESMAN. But that isn't your writing.

LÖVBORG. I dictated it. [*Turns the leaves.*] It's in two sections. The first is about the social forces involved, and this other bit . . . [*He ruffles the pages further on.*] . . . that's about the future course of civilization.

TESMAN. Amazing! It just wouldn't enter my head to write about anything like that.

HEDDA [*at the glass door, drumming her fingers on the pane*]. Hm. . . . No-no.

LÖVBORG [*wraps up the papers again, and puts the packet on the table*]. I brought it along so that I could read you a bit this evening.

TESMAN. Well yes, that was frightfully decent of you, old man. But this evening . . . ? [*Looks at* BRACK.] I don't really know if we can manage it. . . .

LÖVBORG. Well, some other time then. There's no hurry.

BRACK. I ought to tell you, Mr. Lövborg . . . there's going to be a little entertainment at my place this evening. More or less in honour of Tesman, you understand. . . .

LÖVBORG [*looks for his hat*]. Ah . . . in that case I won't . . .

BRACK. No, just a moment. Wouldn't you do me the very great honour of joining us?

LÖVBORG [*shortly and firmly*]. No, I'm afraid I can't. Thank you very much indeed.

BRACK. Oh, come along! Do be persuaded. We'll be quite a small and select gathering. And I guarantee that it'll be 'lively', as my la— . . . as Mrs. Tesman expresses it.

LÖVBORG. I don't doubt it. But all the same . . .

BRACK. Then you could bring along your manuscript and read to Tesman over at my place. There are plenty of rooms.

TESMAN. Yes, just think, Ejlert . . . what about that! Eh?

HEDDA [*intervenes*]. But my dear, when Mr. Lövborg doesn't want to! I'm sure that Mr. Lövborg would far sooner stay where he is and take a bit of supper with me.

LÖVBORG [*looks at her*]. With you, Mrs. Tesman?

HEDDA. And then with Mrs. Elvsted.

LÖVBORG. Oh. . . . [*Casually.*] I met her for a moment this afternoon.

HEDDA. Did you? Well, she's coming out here. And so you'll almost have to stay, Mr. Lövborg. Because otherwise there'll be no one to see her home.

LÖVBORG. That's true. Well, thank you very much, Mrs. Tesman . . . I'll stay here then.

HEDDA. Then I'll just have a word with the maid. . . .

[*She goes to the hall door and rings.* BERTE *comes in.* HEDDA *speaks to her quietly and points towards the inner room.* BERTE *nods and goes out again.*]

TESMAN [*while this is going on, to* LÖVBORG]. Tell me, Ejlert . . . is it this new subject . . . this business about the future . . . that you'll be lecturing about?

LÖVBORG. Yes.

TESMAN. Because I heard at the bookseller's that you're giving a series of lectures here this autumn.

LÖVBORG. I am. You mustn't hold it against me, Tesman.

TESMAN. No, no, of course I wouldn't dream of it. But . . . ?

LÖVBORG. I can see that for you this must be rather an embarrassment.

TESMAN [*dejected*]. Oh well, I can't possibly expect you to . . .

LÖVBORG. But I shall wait till you've received your appointment.

TESMAN. You'll wait till . . . ! Yes but . . . yes but . . . aren't you going to compete for it? Eh?

LÖVBORG. No. I only intend to outshine you. In reputation.

TESMAN. But, good Heavens . . . so Auntie Julle was right after all! There . . . I said she would be! Hedda! Just think, Hedda . . . Ejlert Lövborg isn't going to stand in our way at all!

HEDDA [*shortly*]. Our way? Leave me out of it.

[*She goes upstage towards the back room, where* BERTE *is placing a tray with decanters and glasses on the table.* HEDDA *nods her approval and comes forward again.* BERTE *goes out.*]

TESMAN [*while this is going on*]. Well, Mr. Brack, what about that! . . . What do you say? Eh?

BRACK. Well, I say that honour and reputation . . . hm . . . these things certainly have their appeal. . . .

TESMAN. Yes of course they do. But all the same . . .

HEDDA [*looks at* TESMAN *with a cold smile*]. You stand there looking as if you'd been struck by lightning.

BRACK. And it was quite a thunderstorm that passed over us, Mrs. Tesman.

HEDDA [*points to the back room*]. Now, would all you gentlemen like to go inside and take a glass of cold punch?

BRACK [*looks at his watch*]. By way of an hors d'œuvre? That wouldn't be a bad idea.

TESMAN. Excellent, Hedda! Just what we need! I really feel in the mood for something now.

HEDDA. You'll have some too, Mr. Lövborg.

LÖVBORG [*dismissing the subject*]. No thank you. Not for me.

BRACK. But good Lord . . . there's nothing lethal about cold punch, let me tell you.

LÖVBORG. Not perhaps for everyone.

HEDDA. Well then, I'll entertain Mr. Lövborg in the meanwhile.

TESMAN. All right, dear Hedda, you do that.

[TESMAN *and* BRACK *go into the inner room, sit down, drink punch, smoke cigarettes, and carry on an animated conversation during the following scene.* EJLERT LÖVBORG *remains standing by the stove.* HEDDA *goes to the desk.*]

HEDDA [*in a slightly loud voice*]. And now if you like I'll show you some photographs. We took an excursion through the Tyrol . . . Tesman and I . . . on our way home.

[*She produces an album, and, laying it on the small table, sits down at the upper end of the sofa.* EJLERT LÖVBORG *comes closer, stops, and looks at her. Then he takes a chair and sits on her left, with his back to the inner room.*]

HEDDA [*opens the album*]. Do you see this range of mountains, Mr. Lövborg? That is the Ortler Group. Tesman wrote it underneath the picture. There you are: The Ortler Group at Meran.

LÖVBORG [*who has not once taken his eyes off her, says softly and slowly*]. Hedda . . . Gabler!

HEDDA [*with a quick sidelong glance at him*]. Now! Sh!

LÖVBORG [*softly repeats*]. Hedda Gabler!

HEDDA [*looks in the album*]. That was once my name. When . . . when we two used to know each other.

LÖVBORG. And from now on . . . and for the rest of my life . . . I must stop saying Hedda Gabler.

HEDDA [*still turning the pages*]. Yes, you must. And I think you'd better start practising at once. The sooner the better, I should say.

LÖVBORG [*with bitterness in his voice*]. Hedda Gabler married. And married to . . . Jörgen Tesman!

HEDDA. Yes . . . that's the way of it.

LÖVBORG. Oh Hedda . . . darling Hedda, how could you throw yourself away like that?

HEDDA [*with a sharp look*]. Now. None of that!

LÖVBORG. None of what?

[TESMAN *comes in and goes towards the sofa.*]

HEDDA [*hears him coming and says indifferently*]. And this, Mr. Lövborg, was taken in the Ampezzo Valley. Just look at those rock formations. [*Looks amiably up at* TESMAN.] What were those peculiar mountains called, dear?

TESMAN. Let me look. Ah, those are the Dolomites.

HEDDA. That's right! . . . those are the Dolomites, Mr. Lövborg.

TESMAN. Oh, Hedda . . . I just wanted to ask if you wouldn't like a little punch in here all the same? For yourself at least. Eh?

HEDDA. Yes, thank you very much. And maybe a few cakes.

TESMAN. No cigarettes?

HEDDA. No.

TESMAN. Very good.

[*He goes into the back room and away to the right.* BRACK *sits within, occasionally keeping an eye on* HEDDA *and* LÖVBORG.]

LÖVBORG [*quietly, as before*]. Answer me then, dearest Hedda, how could you go and do such a thing?

HEDDA [*apparently immersed in the album*]. If you continue to address me like that I shan't speak to you at all.

LÖVBORG. Even when we're alone, won't you let me?

HEDDA. I can't dictate your thoughts, Mr. Lövborg. But you will speak to me with respect.

LÖVBORG. Ah, I see. Because of your love . . . for Jörgen Tesman.

HEDDA [*glances sideways at him and smiles*]. Love? That's good!

LÖVBORG. Not love, then!

HEDDA. But no kind of unfaithfulness! I'll have none of that.

LÖVBORG. Hedda . . . answer one single question. . . .

HEDDA. Sh!

[TESMAN, *with a tray, comes in from the back room.*]

TESMAN. Here we are! This is what you've been waiting for!

[*He puts the tray on the table.*]

HEDDA. Why don't you leave that to the maid?

TESMAN [*fills the glasses*]. Because I think it's such fun to wait on you, Hedda.

HEDDA. But now you've filled them both. And Mr. Lövborg doesn't want . . .

TESMAN. No, but Mrs. Elvsted must be here soon.

HEDDA. Oh yes, that's true . . . Mrs. Elvsted. . . .

TESMAN. Had you forgotten her? Eh?

HEDDA. We're so taken up with this. [*Shows him a picture.*] Do you remember that little village?

TESMAN. Ah, that's the one below the Brenner Pass! That was where we stayed the night . . .

HEDDA. . . . and met all those lively summer visitors.

TESMAN. Yes, that's the place. Just think . . . if only you could have been with us, Ejlert! Well then!

[*He goes in again and sits down by* BRACK.]

LÖVBORG. Answer me just this one question, Hedda . . .

HEDDA. Well?

LÖVBORG. Was there no love in your relationship to me either? Not a trace . . . not a suspicion of love in that either?

HEDDA. Can there have been, I wonder? My memory is that we were two good companions. Really sincere friends. [*Smiles.*] You were especially candid.

LÖVBORG. You were the one who wanted it like that.

HEDDA. When I think back to that time, wasn't there something beautiful, something attractive . . . something courageous too, it seems to me . . . about this . . . this secret intimacy, this companionship that no one even dreamed of.

LÖVBORG. There was, Hedda, wasn't there! . . . When I came up to your father's in the afternoons. . . . And the General used to sit by the window, reading the papers . . . his back towards us . . .

HEDDA. And we sat in the corner sofa . . .

LÖVBORG. Always with the same magazine in front of us . . .

HEDDA. Yes . . . for want of an album.

LÖVBORG. Yes, Hedda . . . and then when I used to confess to you . . . ! Told you things about myself that none of the others knew at that time. Sat there and admitted that I'd been out on the razzle for whole days and nights. For days on end. Oh, Hedda . . . what power was it in you that forced me to reveal all those things?

HEDDA. Do you think it was a power in me?

LÖVBORG. Well, how else can I explain it? And all those . . . those roundabout questions you used to put to me . . .

HEDDA. And which you were so quick to understand. . . .

LÖVBORG. That you could sit and ask like that! Quite confidently!

HEDDA. Roundabout questions, if you please.

LÖVBORG. Yes, but confidently all the same. Cross-examine me about . . . about all those things!

HEDDA. And that you could answer, Mr. Lövborg.

LÖVBORG. Yes, that's just what I find so incredible . . . now afterwards. But tell me then, Hedda . . . wasn't it love at the back of it all? Wasn't it on your part a desire to absolve me . . . when I came to you and confessed? Wasn't that a part of it?

HEDDA. No, not exactly.

LÖVBORG. Why did you do it, then?

HEDDA. Do you find it so hard to understand that a young girl . . . when it can happen like that . . . in secret . . .

LÖVBORG. Well?

HEDDA. That she should want to find out about a world that . . .

LÖVBORG. That . . . ?

HEDDA. . . . that she isn't supposed to know anything about?

LÖVBORG. So that was it!

HEDDA. That as well . . . I rather think it was that as well.

LÖVBORG. Our common lust for life. But then why couldn't that at least have gone on?

HEDDA. That was your own fault.

LÖVBORG. It was you who broke it off.

HEDDA. Yes, because there was an imminent danger that the game would become a reality. Shame on you, Ejlert Lövborg, how could you offer such violence to . . . to your confidential companion!

LÖVBORG [*presses his fists together*]. Oh, why didn't you play it out! Why didn't you shoot me down, as you threatened!

HEDDA. I'm too much afraid of a scandal.

LÖVBORG. Yes, Hedda, at bottom you're a coward.

HEDDA. An awful coward. [*In a different tone.*] Which was lucky for you. And now you've consoled yourself so beautifully up at the Elvsteds'.

LÖVBORG. I know what Thea's told you.

HEDDA. And perhaps you told her something about us?

LÖVBORG. Not a word. She's too stupid to understand anything like that.

HEDDA. Stupid?

LÖVBORG. She's stupid about things like that.

HEDDA. And I'm a coward. [*Leans a little closer to him, and without meeting his eyes says softly.*] But now I'm going to confess something to you.

LÖVBORG [*in suspense*]. What?

HEDDA. That I didn't dare to shoot you . . .

LÖVBORG. Yes!

HEDDA. . . . that wasn't my worst cowardice . . . that evening. . . .

LÖVBORG [*looks at her for a moment, takes her meaning, and whispers passionately*]. Oh Hedda! Hedda Gabler! Now I think I see what it was that lay behind our companionship! You and I . . . ! So it was your lust for life . . .

HEDDA [*quietly, with a sharp glance at him*]. Have a care! Don't assume any such thing!

[*It has started to get dark. The hall door is opened by* BERTE.]

HEDDA [*claps the album shut and cries out with a smile*]. At last! Thea, my dear . . . come in then!

[MRS. ELVSTED *comes in from the hall. She is dressed for a social occasion. The door shuts behind her.*]

HEDDA [*on the sofa, stretching out her arms towards* MRS. ELVSTED]. Dearest Thea . . . you can't imagine how I've been longing for you to come!

[MRS. ELVSTED, *in passing, exchanges a greeting with the gentlemen in the inner room; then crosses to the table and gives* HEDDA *her hand.* EJLERT LÖVBORG *has stood up. He and* MRS. ELVSTED *exchange a nod of greeting without speaking.*]

MRS. ELVSTED. Shouldn't I go in and have a word with your husband?

HEDDA. Oh, don't worry. Let them stay where they are. They'll be gone soon.

MRS. ELVSTED. Are they going?

HEDDA. Yes, they're going out on the spree.

MRS. ELVSTED [*quickly, to* LÖVBORG]. But not you?

LÖVBORG. No.

HEDDA. Mr. Lövborg . . . he'll stay here with us.

MRS. ELVSTED [*takes a chair and makes to sit down beside* LÖVBORG]. Oh, it's good to be here!

HEDDA. No you don't, Thea my pet! Not there! You come over here like a good girl. I want to be in the middle.

MRS. ELVSTED. All right, just as you please.

[*She goes round the table and sits on the sofa on* HEDDA'*s right.* LÖVBORG *resumes his chair.*]

LÖVBORG [*after a little pause, to* HEDDA]. Isn't she lovely to sit and look at?

HEDDA [*passes a hand lightly over* MRS. ELVSTED'*s hair*]. Just to look at?

LÖVBORG. Yes. Because we two . . . she and I . . . we're really good companions. We trust each other completely. And so we can sit and talk together in full confidence.

HEDDA. Nothing roundabout, Mr. Lövborg?

LÖVBORG. Oh, well . . .

MRS. ELVSTED [*quietly, clinging to* HEDDA]. Oh, how happy I am, Hedda! Because, do you know what he also says . . . he says I've inspired him, too.

HEDDA [*looking at her with a smile*]. Does he really say that, Thea?

LÖVBORG. And then she has the courage to act, Mrs. Tesman!

MRS. ELVSTED. Oh Heavens . . . me, courage!

LÖVBORG. Infinite courage . . . for her companion.

HEDDA. Oh courage . . . oh yes! If only one had that.

LÖVBORG. What, then, do you mean?

HEDDA. Then life might be liveable, in spite of everything. [*Switches to another tone.*] But now, Thea my dear . . . now you must let me give you a glass of cold punch.

MRS. ELVSTED. No thank you . . . I never drink anything like that.

HEDDA. Well, then you must, Mr. Lövborg.

LÖVBORG. Thank you, not for me either.

MRS. ELVSTED. No, he doesn't either!

HEDDA [*looks at him steadily*]. But when I want you to?

LÖVBORG. Makes no difference.

HEDDA [*laughs*]. And so I've got no power over you at all? Is that it?

LÖVBORG. Not where that's concerned.

HEDDA. But quite seriously, I do think you should have some all the same. For your own sake.

MRS. ELVSTED. Oh, but Hedda . . . !

LÖVBORG. How do you mean?

HEDDA. Or rather, because of other people.

LÖVBORG. Oh?

HEDDA. Otherwise people might so easily get the idea that you're not . . . not really confident, really sure of yourself.

MRS. ELVSTED [*quietly*]. Oh, no Hedda, no . . . !

LÖVBORG. People can think whatever they like . . . for the time being.

MRS. ELVSTED [*happy*]. Yes, that's right!

HEDDA. It was so obvious with Mr. Brack just now.

LÖVBORG. What do you mean?

HEDDA. He smiled so contemptuously when you didn't dare to join them in there at the table.

LÖVBORG. Didn't I dare! I quite naturally preferred to stay here and talk to you.

MRS. ELVSTED. Of course he did, Hedda!

HEDDA. Well, Mr. Brack wasn't to know that. And I also saw the way he smiled and glanced at Tesman when you didn't dare to go along to this wretched little party, either.

LÖVBORG. Dare! Do you say I didn't dare!

HEDDA. I don't. But that's the way Mr. Brack understood it.

LÖVBORG. Let him.

HEDDA. So you're not going?

LÖVBORG. I'll stay with you and Thea.

MRS. ELVSTED. Yes, Hedda . . . of course he's going to stay!

HEDDA [*nods and smiles approvingly at* LÖVBORG]. Firm as a rock, then. A man who is steadfast in his principles. Well, that's how a man should be! [*Turns to* MRS. ELVSTED *and pats her.*] There, wasn't that what I said this morning when you came in here in such a state of desperation. . . .

LÖVBORG [*pulled up*]. Desperation?

MRS. ELVSTED [*in a panic*]. Hedda . . . oh but Hedda . . . !

HEDDA. Just look at him! There isn't the slightest need for you to go about in mortal terror . . . [*She breaks off.*] There! Now we can all be lively!

LÖVBORG [*shocked*]. But . . . what is all this, Mrs. Tesman?

MRS. ELVSTED. Oh God, oh God, Hedda! What are you saying? What are you trying to do?

HEDDA. Hush, now! That odious Mr. Brack has got his eye on you.

LÖVBORG. So you were in mortal terror. On my account.

MRS. ELVSTED [*quietly wailing*]. Oh, Hedda . . . now you've really made me unhappy!

LÖVBORG [*looks at her steadily for a moment. His face is tense*]. So that was my companion's confident belief in me.

MRS. ELVSTED [*piteously*]. Oh, my dear, you must let me explain . . . !

LÖVBORG [*takes one of the full punch glasses, raises it, and says quietly, in a hoarse voice*]. Your health, Thea!

[*He empties the glass, puts it down, and picks up the other.*]

MRS. ELVSTED [*quietly*]. Oh Hedda, Hedda . . . how could you have wanted this to happen?

HEDDA. I wanted it? Don't be absurd!

LÖVBORG. And yours too, Mrs. Tesman! Thanks for the truth. Here's to it!

[*He drinks and makes to refill the glass.*]

HEDDA [*putting her hand on his arm*]. Now, now . . . no more for the moment. Remember you're going to a party.

MRS. ELVSTED. No, no, no!

HEDDA. Quiet! They're sitting there looking at you.

LÖVBORG [*puts down the glass*]. Thea . . . be honest with me. . . .

MRS. ELVSTED. Yes!

LÖVBORG. Did your husband know you were coming down to look for me?

MRS. ELVSTED [*wrings her hands*]. Oh Hedda . . . did you hear what he asked me?

LÖVBORG. Did you arrange it between you that you should come to town to keep an eye on me? Or maybe it was the old man himself who suggested it? Aha, now I've got it . . . he wanted me back in the office again! Or was he short of a fourth at cards?

MRS. ELVSTED [*quietly, painfully*]. Oh Lövborg, Lövborg . . . !

LÖVBORG [*grabs a glass and starts to fill it*]. And here's one to old Elvsted, too!

HEDDA [*firmly*]. No more now. Remember you're going out to read to Tesman.

LÖVBORG [*quietly, putting down the glass*]. I'm sorry, Thea. I've made a fool of myself. Taking it like that, I mean. Don't be angry with me, my dear . . . dear companion. I'll show you . . . both you and the others . . . that however worthless I may have been in the past, I . . . I've found my feet again! With your help, Thea.

MRS. ELVSTED [*ecstatically happy again*]. Oh, thank God . . . !

[*In the meanwhile* BRACK *has been looking at his watch. He and* TESMAN *get up and come into the drawing-room.*]

BRACK [*taking his hat and coat*]. Well, Mrs. Tesman, our time is up.

HEDDA. I suppose it is.

LÖVBORG [*getting up*]. Mine too, Mr. Brack.

MRS. ELVSTED [*quietly and imploringly*]. Oh Lövborg . . . don't do it!

HEDDA [*pinches her arm*]. They can hear you!

MRS. ELVSTED [*crying out faintly*]. Ow!

LÖVBORG [*to* BRACK]. You were so kind as to invite me.

BRACK. Oh, so you've changed your mind?

LÖVBORG. Yes, if I may.

BRACK. A very great pleasure. . . .

LÖVBORG [*pockets his manuscript and addresses* TESMAN]. Because there are one or two things I'd like to show you before I hand it in.

TESMAN. Just think . . . that'll be wonderful! . . . But I say, Hedda, how will you get Mrs. Elvsted home then? Eh?

HEDDA. Oh, we'll manage somehow.

LÖVBORG [*looking at the ladies*]. Mrs. Elvsted? Why, naturally I'll come back and fetch her. [*Goes closer.*] Somewhere about ten o'clock, Mrs. Tesman. Will that suit you?

HEDDA. Yes, that'll be splendid.

TESMAN. Oh well, then everything's in order. But you mustn't expect me so early, Hedda.

HEDDA. Oh that's all right. Just you stay as long as . . . ever you like.

MRS. ELVSTED [*with suppressed anxiety*]. Mr. Lövborg . . . I'll stay here then, till you come.

LÖVBORG [*his hat in his hand*]. Why of course.

BRACK. And now, gentlemen, let the revels commence! I trust it will be lively, as a certain lovely lady has it.

HEDDA. Ah, if only that lovely lady could come along as an invisible onlooker . . . !

BRACK. Why invisible?

HEDDA. So as to hear a little of your liveliness . . . unexpurgated, Mr. Brack.

BRACK [*laughs*]. Ah, now that's something I wouldn't recommend to the lovely lady!

TESMAN [*also laughing*]. That's a good one, Hedda! Think of that!

BRACK. Well, goodbye, goodbye, ladies!

LÖVBORG [*bowing in departure*]. About ten, then.

[BRACK, LÖVBORG, *and* TESMAN *go out at the hall door. Simultaneously* BERTE *comes in from the back room with a lighted lamp, which she places on the large table, and goes out the way she came.*]

MRS. ELVSTED [*has got up, and wanders uneasily about the room*]. Hedda . . . Hedda . . . how is all this going to end!

HEDDA. Ten o'clock . . . and back he'll come. I can just see him. With vine leaves in his hair. Flushed and confident. . . .

MRS. ELVSTED. Yes, oh I do so hope it's like that.

HEDDA. And then, my dear . . . then he'll be master of himself again. He'll be a free man for the rest of his life.

MRS. ELVSTED. Oh yes, oh God . . . if only he would come back, just as you see him.

HEDDA. He'll come . . . just exactly like that! [*She gets up and goes closer to her.*] You may doubt him as much as you please. I believe in him. And then we'll be able to see . . .

MRS. ELVSTED. You've got some reason for all this, Hedda!

HEDDA. Yes, I have. For once in my life I want to feel that I control a human destiny.

MRS. ELVSTED. But surely you do already?

HEDDA. I don't, and I never have done.

MRS. ELVSTED. But what about your husband?

HEDDA. Yes, that would really be something, wouldn't it. Oh, if only you knew how destitute I am. And you're allowed to be so rich! [*She passionately grips* MRS. ELVSTED *in her arms.*] I think I'll burn your hair off after all.

MRS. ELVSTED. Let me go! Let me go! I'm frightened of you, Hedda!

BERTE [*in the doorway*]. Everything's ready, ma'am, in the dining-room.

HEDDA. Good. We're coming.

MRS. ELVSTED. No, no, no! I'd sooner go home alone! Now, at once!

HEDDA. Nonsense! First you're going to have some tea, you little goose. And then . . . at ten o'clock . . . then Ejlert Lövborg will come . . . with vine leaves in his hair.

[*She pulls* MRS. ELVSTED *towards the doorway almost by main force.*]

ACT THREE

*The room at the Tesmans'. The curtains are drawn across the
centre doorway, and also at the glass door. The lamp, with a shade,
and half turned down, is alight on the table. The door of the stove
stands open; the fire within has almost burnt itself out.*

    MRS. ELVSTED, *wrapped in a large shawl and with her feet on a
footstool, is reclining in the armchair close to the stove.* HEDDA,
still fully dressed, is lying asleep on the sofa with a rug over her.

MRS. ELVSTED [*after a pause, starts up in the chair and listens anxiously.
Then she sinks back wearily and wails quietly*]. Still not back! Oh
God . . . oh God . . . still not back!

    [BERTE *comes tiptoeing carefully in at the hall door. She carries a letter
in her hand.*]

MRS. ELVSTED [*turns and whispers urgently*]. Well . . . has anybody come?

BERTE [*quietly*]. Yes, a young woman just came with this letter.

MRS. ELVSTED [*quickly, stretching out her hand*]. A letter! Give it to me!

BERTE. No, ma'am, it's for Dr. Tesman.

MRS. ELVSTED. Oh. . . .

BERTE. It was Miss Tesman's maid who brought it. I'll put it on the
table here.

MRS. ELVSTED. Yes, do that.

BERTE [*puts down the letter*]. Perhaps I'd best put out the lamp. It's
smoking a bit.

MRS. ELVSTED. Yes, put it out. It'll soon be light now.

BERTE [*dousing the lamp*]. It's broad daylight.

MRS. ELVSTED. Yes, daylight! And still not back . . . !

BERTE. Oh, bless you, ma'am . . . I knew this would happen.

MRS. ELVSTED. You knew it?

BERTE. Yes, when I saw that a certain person was back in town. . . . And then when he went off with them. We know what to expect of that gentleman.

MRS. ELVSTED. Not so loud. You'll wake Mrs. Tesman.

BERTE [*looks at the sofa and sighs*]. Oh the poor dear . . . let her have her sleep. . . . Shan't I put a bit more on the fire?

MRS. ELVSTED. Thank you, not on my account.

BERTE. All right, then.

[*She goes out quietly at the hall door.*]

HEDDA [*is woken by the closing of the door and looks up*]. What's that . . . !

MRS. ELVSTED. It was just the maid. . . .

HEDDA [*looks around*]. Here . . . ! Oh yes, I remember . . . [*Sits up on the sofa, stretches and rubs her eyes.*] What's the time, Thea?

MRS. ELVSTED [*looks at her watch*]. It's gone seven.

HEDDA. When did Tesman come in?

MRS. ELVSTED. He isn't back yet.

HEDDA. Not back yet?

MRS. ELVSTED [*getting up*]. No one came at all.

HEDDA. And we sat there watching and waiting till four in the morning. . . .

MRS. ELVSTED [*wringing her hands*]. Oh, and how I did wait for him!

HEDDA [*yawns, and speaks with her hand over her mouth*]. Ah well . . . we could have saved ourselves the trouble.

MRS. ELVSTED. Did you sleep at all?

HEDDA. Oh yes . . . I think I slept quite well. Didn't you?

MRS. ELVSTED. Not a wink. I just couldn't, Hedda! It was quite impossible.

HEDDA [*gets up and goes towards her*]. Now, now, now! There's nothing to worry about. It's quite obvious what's happened.

MRS. ELVSTED. Well, what has happened, then? Just tell me that!

HEDDA. Well, naturally, they must have carried on till all hours at Mr. Brack's . . .

MRS. ELVSTED. Yes, Oh God . . . I suppose they did. But all the same . . .

HEDDA. And then of course Tesman didn't want to come home and make a din and ring the bell in the middle of the night. [*Laughs.*] Perhaps he didn't want to show himself either . . . right on top of a night like that.

MRS. ELVSTED. But for goodness' sake . . . where else could he have gone?

HEDDA. He obviously went along up to the aunts to sleep it off there. They still have his old room.

MRS. ELVSTED. No, there at least he can't be. Because just now a letter came for him from Miss Tesman. It's lying there.

HEDDA. Oh? [*Looks at the writing on the envelope.*] Yes, it's from Auntie Julle all right, in her own fair hand. Well, he must have stopped over at Mr. Brack's, then. And Ejlert Lövborg, he's sitting there reading aloud . . . with vine leaves in his hair.

MRS. ELVSTED. Oh, Hedda, you're just saying all this, you don't really believe it yourself.

HEDDA. You really are a little ninny, Thea.

MRS. ELVSTED. Yes, I suppose I am, really.

HEDDA. And you look tired to death.

MRS. ELVSTED. Yes, I am tired to death.

HEDDA. And so you're to do as I tell you. You're to go into my room and lie down on the bed for a little while.

MRS. ELVSTED. Oh no, no . . . anyway I wouldn't sleep.

HEDDA. Of course you would.

MRS. ELVSTED. Yes, but your husband must be back soon. And then I must hear at once . . .

HEDDA. I'll let you know when he comes.

MRS. ELVSTED. Do you promise me, Hedda?

HEDDA. Yes, yes, that's all right. Just you go in and sleep till then.

MRS. ELVSTED. Thank you. Well, I'll try, then.

[*She goes out through the inner room.*]

[HEDDA *goes over to the glass door and draws the curtains aside. Full daylight streams into the room. She then takes a small looking-glass from the desk, inspects herself and arranges her hair. Then she crosses to the hall door and presses the bell.*]

[*After a short while* BERTE *comes to the door.*]

BERTE. Did you ring, ma'am?

HEDDA. Yes, be so good as to put some more on the stove. I'm cold.

BERTE. Gracious . . . straight away, ma'am . . . I'll have it hot in a moment.

[*She rakes the embers together and puts in a piece of wood.*]

BERTE [*stops and listens*]. That was the front door, ma'am.

HEDDA. Then go and attend to it. I'll look after the fire myself.

BERTE. It'll soon burn up.

[*She goes out at the hall door.*]

[HEDDA *kneels on the footstool and puts more wood into the stove.*]

[*After a little while* JÖRGEN TESMAN *comes in from the hall. He looks tired and rather serious. Creeps on tiptoe towards the doorway, and is about to slip in through the curtains.*]

HEDDA [*at the stove, without looking up*]. Good morning.

TESMAN [*turning*]. Hedda! [*Comes closer.*] But what on earth . . . are you up already! Eh?

HEDDA. Yes, I was up very early this morning.

TESMAN. And I was so sure you'd be sound asleep still! Think of that, Hedda!

HEDDA. Don't talk so loudly. Mrs. Elvsted is lying down in my room.

TESMAN. Did Mrs. Elvsted stay the night!

HEDDA. Well, nobody came to fetch her.

TESMAN. No, I suppose not.

HEDDA [*shuts the stove door and gets up*]. Well, and did you have a good time at Mr. Brack's?

TESMAN. Were you worried about me? Eh?

HEDDA. Good gracious no . . . I wouldn't dream of it. But I asked if you'd had a good time.

TESMAN. Yes, I suppose. For once in a way. . . . But most to begin with, I thought. Then Ejlert read to me. We got there an hour too soon . . . think of that! And Brack had to arrange things. But then Ejlert read to me.

HEDDA [*sits to the right of the table*]. Well? Tell me about it. . . .

TESMAN [*sits on a stool by the stove*]. Oh Hedda, you've no idea, it's going to be ever so good! One of the most remarkable books ever written, I'd almost say. Think of that!

HEDDA. Yes, yes, I don't care so much about that . . .

TESMAN. There's something I'm bound to confess, Hedda. When he'd finished reading . . . something ugly came over me.

HEDDA. Something ugly?

TESMAN. I sat and envied Ejlert that he'd been able to write such a thing. Think of that, Hedda!

HEDDA. Yes, yes, I'm thinking.

TESMAN. And then to know that . . . with all his talents . . . unfortunately he's quite beyond hope of reform, all the same.

HEDDA. I suppose you mean he's got more courage than the rest?

TESMAN. No, good Lord . . . he just can't keep himself under control at all, you know.

HEDDA. Well, and what happened then . . . in the end?

TESMAN. Yes, well, I'd almost have described it as an orgy, Hedda.

HEDDA. Did he have vine leaves in his hair?

TESMAN. Vine leaves? No, I didn't see anything like that. But he made a long and incoherent speech about the woman who had inspired him in his work. Yes, that's how he expressed it.

HEDDA. Did he say who that was?

TESMAN. No, he didn't. But I can only imagine that it must have been Mrs. Elvsted. You mark my words!

HEDDA. Well . . . and where did you part company with him?

TESMAN. On the way back to town. We broke up . . . the last of us . . . all together. And Brack came along too to get some fresh air. And then, you see, we agreed that we'd better see Ejlert home. Well, you know, he had quite a few drinks inside him!

HEDDA. I suppose he had.

TESMAN. But now comes the most remarkable thing, Hedda! Or the saddest, I suppose I should say. Oh . . . I'm almost ashamed . . . on Ejlert's behalf . . . to tell you about it. . . .

HEDDA. Well, then . . . ?

TESMAN. Yes, well as we were going along, you see, I happened to fall back a bit behind the others. Just for a minute or two . . . think of it!

HEDDA. Yes, yes, good Lord, but . . . ?

TESMAN. And then as I was hurrying along to catch up . . . well, do you know what I found in the gutter? Eh?

HEDDA. How on earth should I know?

TESMAN. Don't tell anyone, will you, Hedda. Do you hear? Promise me that, for Ejlert's sake! [*He pulls a packet wrapped in paper out of his coat pocket.*] Just think . . . I found this.

HEDDA. Isn't that the packet he had with him here yesterday?

TESMAN. That's it, it's his precious, irreplaceable manuscript! And he's just gone along and dropped it . . . without noticing. Just think of it, Hedda! It's quite pathetic. . . .

HEDDA. But why didn't you give the packet back to him at once?

TESMAN. No, I didn't dare to do that . . . when he was in that condition. . .

HEDDA. Didn't you tell any of the others that you'd found it either?

TESMAN. Oh no, no. You must see I couldn't have done that, for Ejlert's sake.

HEDDA. So nobody knows at all that you've got Ejlert Lövborg's papers?

TESMAN. No. And no one must get to know it.

HEDDA. What did you talk to him about, afterwards?

TESMAN. I didn't get to talk to him at all. Because as we got into the town we quite lost him . . . him and two or three others. Think of that!

HEDDA. Oh? I suppose they saw him home, then.

TESMAN. Yes, so it seemed. And Brack went off, too.

HEDDA. And what did you get up to then . . . afterwards?

TESMAN. Oh, I went with some of the others, and one of the fellows took us up to his place and gave us morning coffee. Or night coffee, I suppose I should say. Eh? But now as soon as I've rested a bit . . . and when poor old Ejlert has had a chance to sleep it off . . . I must go in and give him this.

HEDDA [*stretches out her hand for the packet*]. No . . . don't give it back! Not straight away, I mean. Let me read it first.

TESMAN. No, my dear, sweet Hedda, I swear I just daren't do that.

HEDDA. You daren't?

TESMAN. No . . . because you can just imagine, he'll be quite desperate when he wakes up and finds he's lost his manuscript. Because this is the only copy he's got, you know! He told me so himself.

HEDDA [*looks at him keenly*]. But can't a thing like that be rewritten? Over again, I mean?

TESMAN. No, I don't think that would do at all. Because the inspiration . . . you see . . .

HEDDA. Yes, yes . . . that's it, I suppose . . . [*Casually.*] Oh, by the way . . . there's a letter for you.

TESMAN. A letter? Just think . . . !

HEDDA [*passes it to him*]. It came early this morning.

TESMAN. From Auntie Julle! What can it be? [*He puts the manuscript down on the other stool, opens the letter, glances through it, and jumps up.*] Oh, Hedda . . . she writes that poor Auntie Rina is at the point of death!

HEDDA. Well, it was to be expected.

TESMAN. And if I want to see her again, I must hurry. I'll rush over at once.

HEDDA [*suppressing a smile*]. You'll rush, will you?

TESMAN. Oh Hedda, my dearest . . . if only I could persuade you to come too! Just think!

HEDDA [*gets up and answers tiredly but firmly*]. No, no, don't ask me. I don't want to look at sickness and death. I must be free of everything that's ugly.

TESMAN. Oh well, for God's sake then . . . ! [*Rushes about.*] My hat . . . ! My coat . . . ? Oh, in the hall. . . . Oh, I do so hope I'm not going to be too late, Hedda? Eh?

HEDDA. You'd better rush, then. . . .

[BERTE *appears at the hall door.*]

BERTE. Mr. Brack is outside and asks if he can come in.

TESMAN. Now! No, I can't possibly see him now.

HEDDA. But I can. [*To* BERTE.] Ask Mr. Brack to come inside.

[BERTE *goes.*]

HEDDA [*quickly, whispering*]. The papers, Tesman!

[*She whips the packet off the stool.*]

TESMAN. Yes, give them to me!

HEDDA. No, no, I'll look after them till you come back.

[*She goes to the desk and puts the packet in the bookshelf.* TESMAN *stands there in a flap, unable to get his gloves on.*]

[MR. BRACK *comes in from the hall.*]

HEDDA [*nods to him*]. Well, you are an early bird.

BRACK. Yes, am I not? [*To* TESMAN.] Are you going out again?

TESMAN. Yes, I have to go to the aunts. Just think . . . the one who's ill, she's dying, poor thing.

BRACK. Good Lord, is she really? But then you musn't stand here talking to me. At such a serious moment. . . .

TESMAN. Yes, I really must rush. . . . Goodbye! Goodbye!

[*He hurries out at the hall door.*]

HEDDA [*comes closer*]. It seems it was decidedly lively at your place last night, Mr. Brack.

BRACK. I haven't even had time to change my clothes, my lady.

HEDDA. You haven't either?

BRACK. As you see. But what has Tesman told you of the events of the night?

HEDDA. Oh, nothing much. That he went somewhere and drank coffee.

BRACK. Yes, I know about that coffee party. Ejlert Lövborg wasn't there though, I believe?

HEDDA. No, they'd seen him home first.

BRACK. Tesman too?

HEDDA. No, but a few of the others, he said.

BRACK [*smiles*]. Jörgen Tesman really is a credulous soul, my lady.

HEDDA. Yes, God knows he is. But is there something behind all this?

BRACK. Yes, you might say there is.

HEDDA. Well! Let's sit down, dear Mr. Brack. Then you'll tell it better.

[*She sits to the left of the table.* BRACK *sits down at the table close to her.*]

HEDDA. Well, then?

BRACK. There were particular reasons why I wanted to keep track of my guests . . . or rather, of certain of my guests last night.

HEDDA. And perhaps Ejlert Lövborg was among them?

BRACK. I have to confess . . . he was.

HEDDA. Now you really begin to intrigue me. . . .

BRACK. Do you know where he and a few of the others spent what was left of the night, my lady?

HEDDA. Tell me . . . if it bears telling.

BRACK. Oh yes, it may be told. Well, they adorned a particularly animated soirée.

HEDDA. One of the lively kind?

BRACK. One of the very liveliest.

HEDDA. A bit more about this, Mr. Brack . . .

BRACK. Lövborg had also been invited earlier. I happened to know about it. But at that time he declined the invitation. Because now he's put on a new man, as you know.

HEDDA. Up at the Elvsteds', yes. But he went all the same?

BRACK. Well you see, my lady . . . most unfortunately the inspiration took him up at my place last night. . . .

HEDDA. Yes, the spirit did move him, so I'm told.

BRACK. Moved him somewhat vehemently. And, well . . . then he had second thoughts about it, I assume. Because we men, you know, we're not always so firm in our principles as we ought to be.

HEDDA. Oh, I don't doubt that you provide an exception, Mr. Brack. But Lövborg . . . ?

BRACK. Well, to cut a long story short . . . he finally adjourned to Mademoiselle Diana's salon.

HEDDA. Mademoiselle Diana's?

BRACK. Mademoiselle Diana was giving the aforesaid soirée. For a select circle of friends and admirers.

HEDDA. Is that a red-haired woman?

BRACK. Most decidedly.

HEDDA. A sort of a . . . singer?

BRACK. Oh yes . . . among other things. And moreover a mighty huntress . . . of men . . . my lady. You must have heard of her. Ejlert Lövborg was one of her most ardent champions . . . in the days of his glory.

HEDDA. And how did it all end, then?

BRACK. Not altogether amicably, it appears. Mademoiselle Diana, I understand, passed from the tenderest possible welcome to actual violence.

HEDDA. Against Lövborg?

BRACK. Yes. He maintained that she, or one of the members of her entourage, had robbed him. He said that he'd lost a pocket-book. And other things as well. In short, he appears to have kicked up the devil of a row.

HEDDA. And what happened then?

BRACK. What happened then was a general mêlée, involving both ladies and gentlemen. Fortunately the police arrived at last.

HEDDA. The police came, too?

BRACK. Yes. But I fear this will have been a costly interlude for that imbecile Lövborg.

HEDDA. Oh!

BRACK. Apparently he put up a spirited resistance. Struck an officer of the law over the head, and tore his tunic. So he had to go along to the police station too.

HEDDA. How do you know all this?

BRACK. The police told me themselves.

HEDDA [*looking away*]. So that was how it was. He didn't have vine leaves in his hair.

BRACK. Vine leaves, my lady?

HEDDA [*in a different voice*]. But tell me now, Mr. Brack . . . why should you show such an elaborate interest in Ejlert Lövborg?

BRACK. In the first place, I can't be altogether indifferent if it comes out, when the case is heard, that he came straight from my place.

HEDDA. There'll be a court case, then?

BRACK. Naturally. But it isn't really that so much. No, the fact is I felt it my duty, as a friend of the house, to give you and your husband a full account of his nocturnal escapades.

HEDDA. And why should you feel that, Mr. Brack?

BRACK. Well, I have a pretty shrewd suspicion that he intends to use you as a sort of screen.

HEDDA. Why, what gives you that idea?

BRACK. Oh good Heavens . . . we're not blind, my lady. Use your eyes! This Mrs. Elvsted person, she won't be leaving town in such a hurry.

HEDDA. Well, and if there is anything between those two, I suppose there are plenty of other places where they can meet.

BRACK. No private household. From now on every decent home will be closed to Ejlert Lövborg once again.

HEDDA. And mine ought to be too, you mean?

BRACK. Yes. I must admit I'd find it extremely awkward if this fellow were to become a constant visitor here. If this superfluous and . . . and unsuitable individual were to insinuate himself into . . .

HEDDA. Into the triangle?

BRACK. Just so. For me it would be like becoming homeless.

HEDDA [*looks at him with a smile*]. So . . . you want to be the only cock in the yard, is that it?

BRACK [*nods slowly and lowers his voice*]. Yes, that's what I want. And I'll fight for that end . . . with every means at my disposal.

HEDDA [*her smile fading*]. You're quite a formidable person . . . when it comes to the point.

BRACK. You think so?

HEDDA. Yes, I'm beginning to think so, now. And I'm content . . . so long as you don't have any sort of hold over me.

BRACK [*laughs equivocally*]. Ah yes, my lady . . . you may be right about that. Who knows, in such a case I might be capable of . . . one thing and another.

HEDDA. Really, Mr. Brack! You sound almost as though you mean to threaten me.

BRACK [*rising*]. Oh, far from it! This triangle . . . well, you know, it's best when it's fortified and defended by mutual consent.

HEDDA. I agree with you.

BRACK. Well, now I've said what I wanted to say. And I'd better see about getting back home. Goodbye, my lady!

[*He moves towards the glass door.*]

HEDDA [*getting up*]. Are you going through the garden?

BRACK. Yes, it's a bit nearer for me.

HEDDA. Yes, and then it's round the back way.

BRACK. Very true. I've no objection to going round the back way. At times it can be quite stimulating.

HEDDA. When there's target practice going on, you mean?

BRACK [*at the door, laughing*]. Oh, nobody shoots their tame farmyard cocks!

HEDDA [*also laughing*]. Ah no, when they've only got one of them. . . .

[*Laughing, they nod their farewells. He leaves. She shuts the door behind him.*]

[HEDDA *stands for a moment with a serious expression, looking out. Then she crosses to the centre doorway and looks in through the curtains. Then moves to the desk, takes* LÖVBORG's *packet out of the bookcase, and is about to look at the papers.* BERTE's *voice, raised in altercation, is heard from the hall.* HEDDA *turns and listens. Then she quickly locks the manuscript away in a drawer and puts the key on the writing-pad.*]

[EJLERT LÖVBORG, *wearing his overcoat and holding his hat, flings open the hall door. He looks somewhat confused and excited.*]

LÖVBORG [*turned towards the hall*]. And I tell you that I must go in! And that's that!

[*He shuts the door, turns, and sees* HEDDA. *He controls himself at once, and bows.*]

HEDDA [*at the desk*]. Well, Mr. Lövborg, you're a little late in calling for Thea.

LÖVBORG. Or a little early in calling on you. I apologize.

HEDDA. How do you know she's still here?

LÖVBORG. They told me at her lodgings that she'd been out all night.

HEDDA [*crosses to the table*]. Did you notice anything in particular when they told you that?

LÖVBORG [*looks at her questioningly*]. Notice anything?

HEDDA. I mean, did they seem to be drawing any inferences at all?

LÖVBORG [*suddenly understands*]. Oh yes, of course, you're right! I'm dragging her down with me! But as it happens I didn't notice anything. . . . I suppose Tesman isn't up yet?

HEDDA. No . . . I don't think . . .

LÖVBORG. When did he come in?

HEDDA. Very late.

LÖVBORG. Did he tell you anything?

HEDDA. Yes, he said it was a very gay party at Mr. Brack's.

LÖVBORG. Nothing else?

HEDDA. No, I don't think so. But I was frightfully sleepy. . . .

[MRS. ELVSTED *comes in through the curtains at the back.*]

MRS. ELVSTED [*comes towards him*]. Oh, Lövborg! At last . . . !

LÖVBORG. Yes, at last. And too late.

MRS. ELVSTED [*looks at him anxiously*]. What's too late?

LÖVBORG. Everything's too late now. I'm finished.

MRS. ELVSTED. Oh, no, no . . . don't say that!

LÖVBORG. You'll say the same yourself when you hear. . . .

MRS. ELVSTED. I don't want to hear anything!

HEDDA. Perhaps you'd prefer to speak to her alone? Because if so I'll go.

LÖVBORG. No, stay . . . I beg you to stay.

MRS. ELVSTED. But I don't want to hear about it, I tell you!

LÖVBORG. I'm not going to talk about what happened last night.

MRS. ELVSTED. What is it then . . . ?

LÖVBORG. It's just this, that it's all over between us now.

MRS. ELVSTED. All over!

HEDDA [*involuntarily*]. I knew it!

LÖVBORG. Because I have no use for you any more, Thea.

MRS. ELVSTED. And you can stand there and say that! No use for me any more! Can't I help you now as I did before? Aren't we going to go on working together?

LÖVBORG. I don't intend to do any more work.

MRS. ELVSTED [*yielding to despair*]. What am I to do with my life, then?

LÖVBORG. You must try to live your life as though you had never known me.

MRS. ELVSTED. Oh, but I can't!

LÖVBORG. See if you can, Thea. You must go back home. . . .

MRS. ELVSTED [*in rebellion*]. That I'll never do! Wherever you are, that's where I want to be! I won't be packed off like this! I want to be right here! To be together with you when the book comes out.

HEDDA [*half aloud, tensely*]. Ah yes . . . the book!

LÖVBORG [*looks at her*]. My book and Thea's. Because that's what it is.

MRS. ELVSTED. Yes, that's what I feel that it is. And therefore I have a right to be together with you when it comes! I want to see you praised and honoured again. And the joy . . . I want to share the joy of it with you.

LÖVBORG. Thea . . . our book will never be published.

HEDDA. Ah!

MRS. ELVSTED. Not published!

LÖVBORG. It's impossible now.

MRS. ELVSTED [*in dreadful foreboding*]. Lövborg . . . what have you done to the manuscript!

HEDDA [*looks at him in suspense*]. Yes, the manuscript . . . ?

MRS. ELVSTED. Where is it!

LÖVBORG. Oh Thea. . . . Don't ask me to tell you that.

MRS. ELVSTED. Yes, yes, I want to know. I've got the right to know. At once.

LÖVBORG. The manuscript. . . . Well, then . . . I've torn the manuscript into a thousand pieces.

MRS. ELVSTED [*shrieks*]. Oh no, no . . . !

HEDDA [*involuntarily*]. But that's not . . . !

LÖVBORG [*looks at her*]. Not true, you think?

HEDDA [*collects herself*]. Oh well . . . of course. If you say so yourself. But it sounded so fantastic. . . .

LÖVBORG. True all the same.

MRS. ELVSTED [*wrings her hands*]. Oh God . . . oh God, Hedda . . . torn his own work to pieces!

LÖVBORG. I've torn my own life to pieces. So I might as well tear up my life's work as well.

MRS. ELVSTED. And you did that last night!

LÖVBORG. Yes, I tell you. Into a thousand pieces. And scattered them out in the fjord. A long way out. At least the water's clean and salt out there. They'll drift with the current and the wind. And after a while they'll sink. Deeper and deeper. Like I will, Thea.

MRS. ELVSTED. I want you to know, Lövborg, what you've done to the book. . . . For the rest of my life it'll be for me as though you'd killed a little child.

LÖVBORG. You're right. It was like killing a child.

MRS. ELVSTED. But how could you then . . . ! The child was mine, it was also mine.

HEDDA [*almost inaudibly*]. The child . . .

MRS. ELVSTED [*sighs deeply*]. So there's an end of it. Well, I'm leaving now, Hedda.

HEDDA. But you're not going back . . .?

MRS. ELVSTED. Oh, I don't know myself what I'll do. There's nothing but darkness ahead of me.

[*She goes out at the hall door.*]

HEDDA [*stands for a while and waits*]. So you're not going to take her home, Mr. Lövborg?

LÖVBORG. I? Through the streets? And let everybody see her walking with me?

HEDDA. Well, I don't know what else happened last night. But was it so utterly irrevocable?

LÖVBORG. It won't stop at last night. I know that well enough. But then there's another thing, I just can't be bothered with that kind of a life either. Not now again. She's broken my courage, and my defiance.

HEDDA [*looking straight ahead*]. So that silly little fool has had her fingers in a man's destiny. [*Looks at him.*] But how could you treat her so callously, all the same?

LÖVBORG. Oh, don't say I was callous!

HEDDA. To destroy everything that's filled her mind and her heart for all this long time! Don't you call that callous?

LÖVBORG. I can tell you the truth, Hedda.

HEDDA. The truth?

LÖVBORG. Promise me first . . . give me your word that Thea will never know what I'm going to tell you now.

HEDDA. I give you my word.

LÖVBORG. Well. Then I'll tell you that what I was saying just now wasn't the truth.

HEDDA. About the manuscript?

LÖVBORG. Yes. I didn't tear it up. And I didn't throw it in the fjord, either.

HEDDA. No. . . . But . . . where is it then?

LÖVBORG. I've destroyed it all the same. Destroyed it utterly, Hedda!

HEDDA. I don't understand this.

LÖVBORG. Thea said that for her it was as though I had killed a child.

HEDDA. Yes . . . so she did.

LÖVBORG. But to kill his child . . . that's not the worst thing a father can do.

HEDDA. Not the worst?

LÖVBORG. No. I wanted to spare Thea the worst.

HEDDA. And what is this worst thing, then?

LÖVBORG. Look, Hedda, suppose a man . . . in the early hours of the morning . . . came home to his child's mother after a wild and senseless debauch and said: now listen . . . I've been here and I've been there. To all sorts of places. And I had our child along with me. All over the place. And I've lost him. Just like that. Christ alone knows where he's got to, or who's got hold of him.

HEDDA. Oh but . . . when all's said and done . . . this was only a book. . . .

LÖVBORG. Thea's soul was in that book.

HEDDA. Yes, I can understand that.

LÖVBORG. And so you must understand also that Thea and I . . . that there isn't any future for us any more.

HEDDA. And what are you going to do, then?

LÖVBORG. Nothing. Just put an end to it all. The sooner the better.

HEDDA [*takes a step towards him*]. Ejlert Lövborg . . . listen to me. . . . Couldn't you let it happen . . . beautifully?

LÖVBORG. Beautifully? [*Smiles.*] Crowned with vine leaves, as you used to imagine?

HEDDA. Oh no. I don't believe in those vine leaves any more. But beautifully all the same! Just for this once! . . . Goodbye. You must go now. And never come here again.

LÖVBORG. Goodbye, Mrs. Tesman. And remember me to your husband.

[*He is about to leave.*]

HEDDA. No, wait! I want to give you something to remember me by.

[*She goes to the desk and opens the drawer, and takes out the pistol case. Then she comes back to* LÖVBORG *with one of the pistols.*]

LÖVBORG [*looks at her*]. That! Is that what you want me to have?

HEDDA [*nods slowly*]. Do you recognize it? It was aimed at you, once.

LÖVBORG. You should have used it then.

HEDDA. Well . . . ! You use it now.

LÖVBORG [*sticking the pistol in his breast pocket*]. Thank you.

HEDDA. And beautifully, Ejlert Lövborg. Promise me that!

LÖVBORG. Goodbye, Hedda Gabler.

[*He goes out at the hall door.*]

[HEDDA *listens at the door for a moment. Then she goes to the desk and takes out the packet with the manuscript, peeps inside the wrappers for a moment, takes some of the leaves half way out and looks at them. Then she takes it all over to the armchair by the stove and sits down. After a while she opens the stove door, and unwraps the packet.*]

HEDDA [*throws one of the folded sheets into the fire and whispers to herself*]. Now I'm burning your child, Thea! With your curly hair! [*Throws a few more sheets into the stove.*] Your child and Ejlert Lövborg's. [*Throws in the rest.*] I'm burning . . . burning your child.

ACT FOUR

The same room at the Tesmans'. It is evening. The outer room is in darkness. The lamp over the table in the inner room is alight. The curtains at the glass door are drawn.

HEDDA, dressed in black, is walking aimlessly about the darkened room. Then she goes into the inner room and is lost to view to the left of the doorway. A few chords from the piano are heard. Then she emerges again and goes back into the reception room.

BERTE comes in from the right of the inner room, carrying a lighted lamp, which she places on the table by the corner sofa in the reception room. Her eyes show signs of weeping, and she has black bands in her cap. Goes out quietly and carefully to the right. HEDDA crosses to the glass door, draws the curtains aside a little, and looks out into the darkness.

After a little while MISS TESMAN comes in from the hall, dressed in mourning and wearing a hat and veil. HEDDA goes to meet her and gives her her hand.

MISS TESMAN. Yes, Hedda, I come dressed in the colour of mourning. For now my poor sister has passed away at last.

HEDDA. I am already aware of it, as you see. Tesman sent me a note.

MISS TESMAN. Yes, he promised he would. But I felt all the same that here to Hedda . . . in this house of life . . . I must bring the tidings of death myself.

HEDDA. That was extremely kind of you.

MISS TESMAN. Oh, but Rina shouldn't have been taken just now. This is no time for mourning, not in Hedda's house.

HEDDA [*avoiding the subject*]. She died quite peacefully, Miss Tesman?

MISS TESMAN. Oh, she passed over so quietly . . . and so gently. And it was such a blessed joy to her that she could see Jörgen once again. And could say goodbye to him properly. He isn't home yet?

HEDDA. No. He wrote that I wasn't to expect him straight away. But do sit down.

MISS TESMAN. No, thank you, my dear . . . dear Hedda. I should have liked to. But I have so little time. Now I have to attend to her and prepare her as well as I may. She shall go to her grave looking her best.

HEDDA. Is there nothing I can do?

MISS TESMAN. Oh, you mustn't think of it! No, that's not fit work for Hedda Tesman's hands. Nor a fit subject for her thoughts, either. Not at this time.

HEDDA. Oh thoughts . . . they can't be curbed so easily. . . .

MISS TESMAN [*continuing*]. Ah yes, dear God, that's how it goes. We'll be sewing linen for poor Rina; and soon there'll be sewing to be done here too, I fancy. But that'll be of a different kind . . . thanks be to God.

[JÖRGEN TESMAN *comes in at the hall door.*]

HEDDA. Well, so you're here at last.

TESMAN. You here, Auntie Julle? With Hedda? Think of that!

MISS TESMAN. I was just going away again, my dear boy. Well, and did you manage to see to it all?

TESMAN. Oh, I'm awfully afraid I'll have forgotten the half of it. I'll have to dash over and see you again tomorrow. I'm all at sixes and sevens today. I just can't think straight.

MISS TESMAN. But Jörgen, my own boy, you mustn't take it like that.

TESMAN. I mustn't? Well, how else, then?

MISS TESMAN. You must be glad, even in your grief. Glad of what has come to pass. As I am.

TESMAN. Oh yes, yes. You're thinking of Auntie Rina.

HEDDA. It will be a little lonely for you now, Miss Tesman.

MISS TESMAN. Why yes, just to begin with. But not for so very long, I sincerely hope. Poor Rina's little room won't be left empty, you may be sure of that!

TESMAN. Oh? Who are you thinking of putting in there, then? Eh?

MISS TESMAN. Oh, there's always some poor invalid or other who needs a bit of care and attention, unfortunately.

HEDDA. Would you really take on another burden of that kind?

MISS TESMAN. Burden! Oh, God forgive you, child . . . this hasn't been a burden to me.

HEDDA. But in the case of a total stranger . . .

MISS TESMAN. Oh, you soon get friendly with people when they're sick. And besides, I also do need to have someone to live for. Ah well, God is good . . . and I fancy there'll soon be a few things for an old aunt to do here in this house, too.

HEDDA. Oh, don't think about us.

TESMAN. Yes, just think how fine it would be if we all three. . . . Yes . . . if only . . .

HEDDA. If only . . . ?

TESMAN [*ill at ease*]. Oh, never mind. It'll all turn out all right, I expect. Let's hope so. Eh?

MISS TESMAN. Well, well. I expect you young people have lots of things you want to talk about. [*Smiles.*] And perhaps Hedda has something to tell you, too, Jörgen. Goodbye, my dears! I must get back home to Rina. [*She turns at the door.*] Yes, dear God, how strange to think! Now Rina's both here with me, and also with sainted Joachim.

TESMAN. Yes, just think of that, Auntie Julle! Eh?

[MISS TESMAN *goes out at the hall door.*]

HEDDA [*coldly appraising* TESMAN]. I almost think you're more upset about this death than she is.

TESMAN. Oh, it's not just Aunt Rina. I'm so frightfully worried about Ejlert.

HEDDA [*quickly*]. Have you heard anything about him?

TESMAN. I was going to run over to see him this afternoon, to tell him that the manuscript's in good hands.

HEDDA. Well? Didn't you catch him?

TESMAN. No. He wasn't at home. But afterwards I met Mrs. Elvsted, and she said he'd been here early this morning.

HEDDA. Yes, just after you left.

TESMAN. And that he said that he'd torn up the manuscript. Eh?

HEDDA. Yes, that's what he said.

TESMAN. But, good Heavens above, the man must have been raving! And then you didn't dare to let him have it back, I suppose, Hedda?

HEDDA. No, he didn't get it.

TESMAN. But you did tell him we'd got it?

HEDDA. No. [*Quickly.*] Did you tell Mrs. Elvsted?

TESMAN. No. I didn't like to. But you ought to have said it to him. Just think, he might go and do something desperate! Give me the manuscript, Hedda! I'll rush over with it at once. Where have you got it?

HEDDA [*cold and immobile, supporting herself on the armchair*]. I haven't got it any more.

TESMAN. You haven't got it! But for God's sake . . . what do you mean?

HEDDA. I've burnt it up . . . all of it.

TESMAN [*jumps up in alarm*]. Burnt . . . you've burnt it! Burnt Ejlert Lövborg's manuscript!

HEDDA. Don't shout like that. The maid might hear you.

TESMAN. Burnt! But good God! . . . No, no, no . . . this is quite impossible!

HEDDA. Well, it's true, for all that.

TESMAN. Yes, but . . . do you know what it is that you've done, Hedda? It's a felony . . . it's misappropriation of lost property! Think of that! Yes, you just go and ask Mr. Brack, he'll tell you.

HEDDA. I think you'd be well advised not to talk about it . . . either to Mr. Brack or anyone else.

TESMAN. But how could you go and do anything so utterly fantastic!

How on earth did you come to do such a thing? What got into you? Answer me, Hedda! Eh?

HEDDA [*suppressing an almost imperceptible smile*]. I did it for your sake, Jörgen.

TESMAN. For my sake!

HEDDA. When you came home this morning and told me how he'd read to you . . .

TESMAN. Yes, yes, what about it?

HEDDA. You admitted that you envied him for it.

TESMAN. Oh Heavens above, I didn't mean it so literally.

HEDDA. All the same. I couldn't bear the thought that someone else should put you in the shade.

TESMAN [*exclaiming, torn between doubt and happiness*]. Hedda . . . oh gracious . . . is this really true! . . . Yes, but . . . yes, but . . . I never knew you loved me like that, Hedda, not in that way. Think of that!

HEDDA. Well, then I suppose I'd better tell you that . . . that just at this time . . . [*Breaks off passionately.*] Oh no, no . . . you can go and ask your Auntie Julle. She'll tell you all about it.

TESMAN. Oh, I almost think I know what it is, Hedda! [*Claps his hands together.*] Oh good Heavens . . . is it really possible! Eh!

HEDDA. Don't shout like that. The maid can hear you.

TESMAN [*laughing in the excess of his joy*]. The maid! Oh, Hedda, you really are priceless! The maid . . . why that's Berte! I'll go out and tell Berte myself!

HEDDA [*clenches her hands as though in desperation*]. Oh, it'll kill me . . . it'll kill me, all this!

TESMAN. All what, Hedda? Eh?

HEDDA [*coldly, in control again*]. All this . . . this farce . . . Jörgen.

TESMAN. Farce? But it's just that I'm so happy. But, perhaps. . . . Well, perhaps I'd better not tell Berte, then.

HEDDA. Oh yes . . . why not do the thing properly.

TESMAN. No, no, not just yet. But at least I'll have to tell Aunt Julle. And that you've started to call me Jörgen, too! Think of it. Oh, Auntie Julle really will be pleased!

HEDDA. When she hears that I've burnt Ejlert Lövborg's papers . . . for your sake?

TESMAN. Oh, good Lord yes . . . the papers! No, of course, nobody must get to know about that. But your burning zeal on my behalf, Hedda . . . Auntie Julle really must hear about that! I say though, I wonder, is that sort of thing usual with young wives, d'you think? Eh?

HEDDA. I think it would be a good idea if you asked Auntie Julle about that, too.

TESMAN. Yes, yes, I'll do that some time. [*Looks uneasy and thoughtful again.*] No, but this business with the manuscript! Good Lord, it's . . . it's quite awful, really, to think of poor Ejlert.

[MRS. ELVSTED, *dressed as for her first visit, with hat and coat, comes in at the hall door.*]

MRS. ELVSTED [*greets them hurriedly and speaks in agitation*]. Oh my dear Hedda, do excuse me for coming back again.

HEDDA. What's happened to you, Thea?

TESMAN. Is it something to do with Ejlert Lövborg again? Eh?

MRS. ELVSTED. Oh yes . . . I'm so dreadfully afraid that he may have met with an accident.

HEDDA [*grips* MRS. ELVSTED'S *arm*]. Oh . . . do you think so!

TESMAN. Oh, but good Heavens . . . why should you think that, Mrs. Elvsted?

MRS. ELVSTED. Oh, yes, I heard them talking about him at the lodging house . . . just as I came in. There are the most incredible rumours about him going around today.

TESMAN. Yes, just think, I heard something too! And yet I can testify that he went straight off home to bed. Think of that!

HEDDA. Well . . . what were they saying then, at the boarding house?

MRS. ELVSTED. Oh, I didn't really discover anything at all. Either because they didn't really know the particulars or else. . . . They all stopped talking when they saw me. And I didn't dare to ask.

TESMAN [*anxiously pacing around*]. We can only hope . . . we can only hope you were mistaken, Mrs. Elvsted!

MRS. ELVSTED. No, no I'm sure it was him they were talking about. And then I heard one of them say something that sounded like hospital or . . .

TESMAN. Hospital!

HEDDA. Oh no . . . that can't be possible!

MRS. ELVSTED. Oh, I was so horribly frightened for him. And then I went up to his lodgings and asked after him there.

HEDDA. You could bring yourself to do that, Thea!

MRS. ELVSTED. Well, and what else was I to do? Because it seemed to me I just couldn't go on, not knowing.

TESMAN. But I suppose you didn't find him there, either? Eh?

MRS. ELVSTED. No. And the people knew nothing whatever about him. He hadn't been home since yesterday afternoon, they said.

TESMAN. Yesterday! Fancy their saying that!

MRS. ELVSTED. Oh God, I'm so sure that something must have happened to him!

TESMAN. I say, Hedda . . . what if I go into town, and make a few inquiries round about . . . ?

HEDDA. No, no . . . you'd better not get mixed up in this.

[MR. BRACK, *carrying his hat in his hand, comes in at the hall door, which* BERTE *opens and closes again behind him. He looks serious and bows without speaking.*]

TESMAN. Oh, Mr. Brack, you're here are you? Eh?

BRACK. Yes, I had to come up and see you again this evening.

TESMAN. I can see that you've heard from Aunt Julle.

BRACK. Yes, I also received her message.

TESMAN. Isn't it terribly sad? Eh?

BRACK. Oh, my dear Tesman, that's as you choose to take it.

TESMAN [*looks at him uneasily*]. Is there something else, perhaps?

BRACK. Yes, there is.

HEDDA [*in suspense*]. Bad news, Mr. Brack?

BRACK. Also as you choose to take it, Mrs. Tesman.

MRS. ELVSTED [*in a spontaneous outburst*]. Oh, it's to do with Ejlert Lövborg!

BRACK [*looks at her*]. Why should you think that, madam? Perhaps you know something already . . . ?

MRS. ELVSTED [*confused*]. No, no, I know absolutely nothing; but . . .

TESMAN. Well, good gracious man, let's have it then!

BRACK [*shrugs his shoulders*]. Well then . . . I regret to say . . . Ejlert Lövborg has been taken to the hospital. He is not expected to live.

MRS. ELVSTED [*crying out*]. Oh my God, my God . . . !

TESMAN. To the hospital! And not expected . . . !

HEDDA [*involuntarily*]. So soon . . . !

MRS. ELVSTED [*wailing*]. And we . . . we weren't even reconciled when we parted, Hedda!

HEDDA [*whispers*]. Now Thea . . . Thea!

MRS. ELVSTED [*taking no notice of her*]. I must go to him! I must see him alive!

BRACK. It's no use, madam. No one is allowed to see him.

MRS. ELVSTED. Oh, but at least tell me what's happened to him! What's the matter with him?

TESMAN. Surely he can't have . . . himself . . . ! Eh?

HEDDA. Yes, I'm certain he did.

MRS. ELVSTED. Oh Hedda . . . how can you . . . !

BRACK [*who is watching her all the time*]. Regrettably your guess is correct, Mrs. Tesman.

MRS. ELVSTED. Oh, but how dreadful!

TESMAN. Did it himself! Think of that!

HEDDA. Shot himself!

BRACK. Correctly guessed again, Mrs. Tesman.

MRS. ELVSTED [*trying to pull herself together*]. When did this happen, Mr. Brack?

BRACK. This afternoon. Between three and four.

TESMAN. Yes, but, good Lord . . . where did he do it, then? Eh?

BRACK [*a little uncertainly*]. Where? Well, I . . . suppose it was at his lodgings.

MRS. ELVSTED. No, that can't be right. I was there myself at about half past six.

BRACK. Well, somewhere else then. I don't exactly know about that. I just know that he was found. . . . He had shot himself . . . in the breast.

MRS. ELVSTED. Oh, but how dreadful! That he should end like that!

HEDDA [*to* BRACK]. He was shot in the breast?

BRACK. Yes . . . as I said.

HEDDA. Not in the temple?

BRACK. In the breast, Mrs. Tesman.

HEDDA. Well . . . the breast is good, too.

BRACK. I beg your pardon, Mrs. Tesman?

HEDDA [*evasively*]. Oh no . . . nothing.

TESMAN. And the wound may be fatal, you say? Eh?

BRACK. The wound will undoubtedly be fatal. Most probably it's all over already.

MRS. ELVSTED. Yes, yes, I feel that it is! It's all over! All over! Oh, Hedda . . . !

TESMAN. Yes but tell me then . . . how did you come to hear of all this?

BRACK [*briefly*]. Through the police, a . . . man there I had to see.

HEDDA [*triumphantly*]. At last . . . a really courageous act!

TESMAN [*alarmed*]. But good Lord . . . what are you saying, Hedda?

HEDDA. I say that there is beauty in this deed.

BRACK. Hm, Mrs. Tesman . . .

TESMAN. Beauty! Think of that!

MRS. ELVSTED. Oh, Hedda, how can you call a thing like that beautiful?

HEDDA. Ejlert Lövborg has settled accounts with himself. He had the courage to do . . . what had to be done.

MRS. ELVSTED. Oh no, it couldn't possibly have been like that! He must have done what he did in a fit of madness.

TESMAN. In desperation, it must have been!

HEDDA. It wasn't like that. I am quite certain of it.

MRS. ELVSTED. Yes, it was! A fit of madness! Like when he tore our book to pieces!

BRACK [*pulled up*]. The book? The manuscript, you mean? Did he tear it to pieces?

MRS. ELVSTED. Yes, he did that last night.

TESMAN [*whispering softly*]. Oh Hedda, we'll never get clear of this.

BRACK. Hm, how very extraordinary.

TESMAN [*drifting about the stage*]. Think of it! That Ejlert should end his life like that! And not even to leave behind him the work that would have made his name immortal. . . .

MRS. ELVSTED. Oh, if only it could be put together again!

TESMAN. Yes, if only it could! I'd give anything on earth . . .

MRS. ELVSTED. Perhaps it can, Mr. Tesman.

TESMAN. What do you mean?

MRS. ELVSTED [*searching in her skirt pocket*]. Look here. I kept the notes, all the notes he used when he dictated.

HEDDA [*a step closer*]. Ah . . . !

TESMAN. You kept them, Mrs. Elvsted! Eh?

MRS. ELVSTED. Yes, they're all here. I took them with me when I left. And they've just stayed in my pocket. . . .

TESMAN. Oh, let me see them!

MRS. ELVSTED [*gives him a handful of small papers*]. But they're in such a muddle. All just anyhow.

TESMAN. Just think, if we could manage it all the same! Perhaps if we two were to have a go at it between us . . .

MRS. ELVSTED. Oh, yes, let's try at least . . .

TESMAN. It must be done! It shall be done! I'll devote my life to this work!

HEDDA. You, Jörgen? Your life?

TESMAN. Yes, or at any rate the time I have at my disposal. My own material will just have to wait. Hedda . . . you understand me? Eh? I owe this to Ejlert's memory.

HEDDA. Perhaps you do.

TESMAN. And now, my dear Mrs. Elvsted, we must pull ourselves together. God knows, there's no point in crying over spilt milk. Eh? We must try to contemplate the matter calmly. . . .

MRS. ELVSTED. Yes, Mr. Tesman, I'll do my best.

TESMAN. Well, come along then. We must look at these jottings at once. Now, where shall we sit? Here? No, there, in the back room. You'll excuse us, Mr. Brack! You come along with me, Mrs. Elvsted.

MRS. ELVSTED. Oh God . . . if only it could be done!

[TESMAN *and* MRS. ELVSTED *go into the inner room. She removes her hat and coat. They both sit at the table under the hanging lamp, and immerse themselves in an eager examination of the papers.* HEDDA *goes across to the stove and sits in the armchair. After a while* MR. BRACK *joins her.*]

HEDDA [*softly*]. Ah, Mr. Brack . . . what a sense of release it gives, this affair of Ejlert Lövborg.

BRACK. Release, my lady? Well, of course, for him it's a release. . . .

HEDDA. I mean, for me. It's a liberation to know that an act of spontaneous courage is yet possible in this world. An act that has something of unconditional beauty.

BRACK [*smiles*]. Hm . . . my very dear lady . . .

HEDDA. Oh, I know what you're going to say. Because you're something of an academic too, in your own line, like . . . well!

BRACK [*looks at her steadily*]. Ejlert Lövborg was more to you perhaps than you are willing to admit, even to yourself. Or am I mistaken?

HEDDA. I don't answer that kind of question. I just know that Ejlert Lövborg had the courage to live his life in his own fashion. And then now . . . this! This beautiful act. That he had the courage to take his leave of life . . . so early.

BRACK. It pains me, my lady . . . but I am compelled to disabuse you of a beautiful illusion.

HEDDA. Illusion?

BRACK. Which you would in any case have been deprived of fairly soon.

HEDDA. And what might that be?

BRACK. He didn't shoot himself . . . intentionally.

HEDDA. Not intentionally!

BRACK. No. This business with Ejlert Lövborg didn't happen quite as I described it.

HEDDA [*in suspense*]. Did you keep something back? What is it?

BRACK. For the sake of that poor Mrs. Elvsted I made use of a few circumlocutions.

HEDDA. What, then?

BRACK. In the first place, he is already dead.

HEDDA. At the hospital?

BRACK. Yes. Without recovering consciousness.

HEDDA. And what else?

BRACK. That the affair did not take place at his lodgings.

HEDDA. Well, that doesn't really make any difference.

BRACK. Does it not? Because as it happens . . . Ejlert Lövborg was found shot in . . . in Mademoiselle Diana's boudoir.

HEDDA [*is about to jump up, but sinks back again*]. No, that's impossible, Mr. Brack! He can't have gone there again today!

BRACK. He went there this afternoon. He wanted to recover something that he said they'd taken. He was talking wildly about a child that had been lost. . . .

HEDDA. Oh . . . so that was why . . .

BRACK. I imagined that he might have been referring to his manuscript. But that he apparently destroyed himself. So it must have been his pocket-book, then.

HEDDA. I suppose so. . . . And so . . . he was found there.

BRACK. Yes, there. With a discharged pistol in his breast pocket. The bullet had wounded him fatally.

HEDDA. In the breast.

BRACK. No . . . he was shot in the abdomen.

HEDDA [*looks up with an expression of revulsion*]. That as well! Oh. . . . Everything I touch seems destined to turn into something mean and farcical.

BRACK. There is a further detail, my lady. Another circumstance that might be classified as somewhat distasteful.

HEDDA. And what's that?

BRACK. The pistol that was found on his body . . .

HEDDA [*holding her breath*]. Well! What about it!

BRACK. It must have been stolen.

HEDDA [*jumps up*]. Stolen! No! That isn't true!

BRACK. There is no possible alternative. He must have stolen it. . . . Sh!

[TESMAN *and* MRS. ELVSTED *have got up from the table in the inner room and come out to the reception room.*]

TESMAN [*with papers in both hands*]. Oh, Hedda . . . it's almost impossible for me to see in there under the lamp. Think of that!

HEDDA. Yes, I'm thinking.

TESMAN. Do you think we might be allowed to sit at your desk for a bit? Eh?

HEDDA. Yes, of course you can. [*Quickly.*] No, wait a moment! Let me clear away some of these things first.

TESMAN. Oh, don't worry about that, Hedda. There's plenty of room.

HEDDA. No, no, let me take all these away. I'll put them on the piano. There you are!

[*She has pulled an object, covered with sheets of music, out of the bookcase; she adds a few more sheets and carries the whole pile off to the left of the inner room.* TESMAN *puts the papers on the desk, and brings over the lamp from the corner table. He and* MRS. ELVSTED *sit down and proceed with their work.* HEDDA *returns.*]

HEDDA [*behind* MRS. ELVSTED's *chair, lightly caressing her hair*]. Well, Thea, my sweet . . . and how is the Ejlert Lövborg memorial getting on?

MRS. ELVSTED [*looks up at her, discouraged*]. Oh goodness . . . it's going to be dreadfully difficult to sort it out.

TESMAN. It must be possible. It simply has to be. And this . . . putting other people's papers in order . . . that's just the sort of thing I'm good at.

[HEDDA *goes across to the stove and sits on one of the stools.* BRACK *stands over her, leaning against the armchair.*]

HEDDA [*whispers*]. What were you saying about the pistol?

BRACK [*quietly*]. That it must have been stolen.

HEDDA. And why must it have been?

BRACK. Because any other explanation ought to be impossible, my lady.

HEDDA. Indeed.

BRACK [*looks at her*]. Ejlert Lövborg was evidently here this morning. Isn't that so?

HEDDA. Yes.

BRACK. Were you alone with him?

HEDDA. Yes, for a while.

BRACK. And did you not leave the room while he was here?

HEDDA. No.

BRACK. Think carefully. Were you not out of the room even for a moment?

HEDDA. Yes, perhaps just for a moment . . . out in the hall.

BRACK. And where was the case with your pistols during this time?

HEDDA. It was locked in . . .

BRACK. Well, my lady?

HEDDA. The case was standing over there on the writing table.

BRACK. Have you looked at it since then to see whether both pistols are still in place?

HEDDA. No.

BRACK. You don't need to look. I saw the pistol that was found on Lövborg. And I recognized it immediately, from yesterday. And from before that, too.

HEDDA. Have you got the pistol?

BRACK. No, it is in the hands of the police.

HEDDA. And what will the police do with it?

BRACK. Try to discover who owns it.

HEDDA. And do you think they will be successful?

BRACK [*bends over her and whispers*]. No, Hedda Gabler . . . not if I hold my tongue.

HEDDA [*looks at him apprehensively*]. And if you don't . . . what then?

BRACK [*shrugs his shoulders*]. There is always the possibility that the pistol was stolen.

HEDDA [*with determination*]. I'd sooner die!

BRACK [*smiles*]. People say such things. But they don't do them.

HEDDA [*without answering*]. And so . . . as the pistol was not stolen. And when the owner is discovered. What happens then?

BRACK. There will be an unpleasant scandal . . . Hedda.

HEDDA. A scandal!

BRACK. Yes, a scandal . . . the one thing you are afraid of. You will of course be required to go into the witness box. Both you and Mademoïselle Diana. She will have to explain how the event took place. Whether the wound was inflicted accidentally or deliberately. Was he about to pull the pistol out of his pocket in order to threaten her? And did it then go off? Or did she seize the pistol out of his hand, shoot him down, and then stick the weapon back in his pocket? I wouldn't put it past her. She's a spirited wench, is this Mademoiselle Diana.

HEDDA. But all this revolting business has nothing to do with me.

BRACK. No. But you will be obliged to tell the court why you gave Ejlert Lövborg the pistol. And what inference will be drawn from the fact that you did give it to him?

HEDDA [*lowers her head*]. That's true. I didn't think of that.

BRACK. Well, fortunately there is nothing to fear so long as I keep silence.

HEDDA [*looks up at him*]. And so I am in your power, Mr. Brack. From now on I am at your mercy.

BRACK [*whispers more softly*]. Dearest Hedda . . . believe me . . . I shall not abuse the position.

HEDDA. In your power, all the same. Subject to your will and your demands. No longer free! [*She gets up violently.*] No! That's a thought that I'll never endure! Never.

BRACK [*looks at her half tauntingly*]. One generally acquiesces in what is inevitable.

HEDDA [*returns the look*]. Perhaps you're right.

[*She crosses to the writing desk.*]

HEDDA [*suppresses an involuntary smile, and imitates* TESMAN'*s intonation*]. Well? Is it going to work out, Jörgen? Eh?

TESMAN. Heaven knows, my love. At any rate it's going to take us months.

HEDDA [*as before*]. Well, think of that! [*She passes her fingers lightly through* MRS. ELVSTED'*s hair*.] Isn't this strange for you, Thea? Now you're sitting here together with Tesman . . . as you used to sit with Ejlert Lövborg.

MRS. ELVSTED. Oh yes, oh God . . . if only I could inspire your husband in the same way.

HEDDA. Oh, I expect it will come . . . in time.

TESMAN. Yes, d'you know what, Hedda . . . it really does seem to me that I'm beginning to feel something of the sort. But you go and sit down again, now, with Mr. Brack.

HEDDA. And is there nothing I can do to help you two?

TESMAN. No, nothing at all. [*Turns his head.*] We'll just have to rely on you, dear Mr. Brack, to keep Hedda company!

BRACK [*with a look to* HEDDA]. It will be a pleasure indeed.

HEDDA. Thank you. But tonight I'm tired. I'm going to go in and lie down a bit on the sofa.

TESMAN. Yes, you do that my dear. Eh?

[HEDDA *goes into the inner room and pulls the curtains together behind her. A short pause. Suddenly she is heard to play a wild dance tune on the piano.*]

MRS. ELVSTED [*starts up from her chair*]. Oh . . . what's that!

TESMAN [*runs to the doorway*]. But Hedda, my dear . . . don't play dance music, not tonight! Do think of Aunt Rina! And of Ejlert, too!

HEDDA [*puts her head out between the curtains*]. And of Auntie Julle. And of all the rest of them. . . . I shall be silent in future.

[*She draws the curtains together again.*]

TESMAN [*at the desk*]. I don't think it's good for her to see us at this melancholy task. I'll tell you what, Mrs. Elvsted . . . you'll have to move in to Aunt Julle's. Then I'll come up in the evenings. And then we can sit and work there. Eh?

MRS. ELVSTED. Yes, perhaps that would be the best. . . .

HEDDA [*from the inner room*]. I can hear what you're saying, Tesman. And how am I supposed to survive the evenings out here?

TESMAN [*leafing through the papers*]. Oh, I expect Mr. Brack will be kind enough to look in now and again.

BRACK [*in the armchair, shouts cheerfully*]. I'll gladly come every single evening, Mrs. Tesman! Don't you worry, we'll have a fine time out here together!

HEDDA [*clearly and distinctly*]. Yes, you're looking forward to that, aren't you, Mr. Brack? Yourself as the only cock in the yard. . . .

[*A shot is heard within.* TESMAN, MRS. ELVSTED, *and* BRACK *all start to their feet.*]

TESMAN. Oh, now she's playing about with those pistols again.

[*He pulls the curtains aside and runs in.* MRS. ELVSTED *follows.* HEDDA *lies stretched out dead on the sofa. Confusion and shouting.* BERTE, *in alarm, comes in from the right.*]

TESMAN [*yelling at* BRACK]. Shot herself! Shot herself in the temple! Think of that!

BRACK [*half prostrate in the armchair*]. But, good God Almighty . . . people don't do such things!

THE MASTER BUILDER

[Bygmester Solness]

PLAY IN THREE ACTS
(1892)

Translated by James McFarlane

CHARACTERS

HALVARD SOLNESS, master builder

MRS. ALINE SOLNESS, his wife

DR. HERDAL, the family doctor

KNUT BROVIK, sometime architect, now working for Solness

RAGNAR BROVIK, his son, a draughtsman

KAJA FOSLI, his niece, a book-keeper

HILDE WANGEL

Other women

People in the street

The action takes place in Solness's house

ACT ONE

A plainly furnished office in SOLNESS's *house. In the left wall, double doors lead out to the hall. On the right is the door to the inner rooms of the house. In the back wall, an open door to the drawing office. Downstage, left, a desk with books, papers, and writing materials. Upstage from the door, a stove. In the corner, right, a sofa with a table and a couple of chairs. On the table, a water carafe and glasses. Downstage, right, a smaller table with a rocking-chair and an armchair. Shaded lamps are burning on the table in the office, on the table in the corner, and on the desk.*

Within the drawing office sit KNUT BROVIK *and his son* RAGNAR, *busy with plans and calculations.* KAJA FOSLI *is standing at the desk in the office, writing in the ledger.* KNUT BROVIK *is a thin old man, with white hair and beard. He is dressed in a rather threadbare but well preserved black coat. He wears spectacles and a white cravat which has gone rather yellow.* RAGNAR BROVIK *is in his thirties, well dressed, fair-haired, with a slight stoop.* KAJA FOSLI *is a slightly-built girl in her early twenties, neatly dressed but rather delicate looking. She is wearing a green eye-shade. All three work for a while in silence.*

KNUT BROVIK [*suddenly gets up from the drawing table as though in distress and comes forward into the doorway, breathing heavily and with difficulty*]. Oh, I can't stand this much longer!

KAJA [*goes across to him*]. You must be feeling pretty bad tonight, are you, Uncle?

BROVIK. Oh, I think it gets worse every day.

RAGNAR [*has risen and comes over*]. You'd better go home, Father. Try and get some sleep. . . .

BROVIK [*impatiently*]. Go to bed, you mean? Do you want me to suffocate?

KAJA. Well, take a little walk, then.

RAGNAR. Yes, do that. I'll come with you.

BROVIK [*vehemently*]. I'm not leaving before he gets back. Tonight there's going to be some plain speaking with . . . [*With suppressed bitterness.*] . . . with him . . . with the boss.

KAJA [*fearfully*]. Oh no, Uncle! . . . Please let that wait!

RAGNAR. Yes, better wait, Father!

BROVIK [*struggling for breath*]. Ah . . . ah . . . ! I doubt if I've got much time for waiting.

KAJA [*listening*]. Sh! I can hear him coming up the steps.

[*All three go back to their work again. Short silence.* HALVARD SOLNESS, *master builder, enters by the hall door. He is a man of mature years, strong and vigorous, with close-cut curly hair, dark moustache, and dark bushy eyebrows. He wears a grey-green jacket, buttoned-up, with a high collar and broad revers. On his head he has a soft grey felt hat, and he has a couple of folders under his arm.*]

SOLNESS [*by the door, points towards the drawing office and asks in a whisper*]. Have they gone?

KAJA [*in a low voice, shaking her head*]. No.

[*She takes off her eye-shade.* SOLNESS *walks across the room, throws his hat on a chair, lays the folders on the table by the sofa, and comes over towards the desk again.* KAJA *continues to write but seems nervous and uneasy.*]

SOLNESS [*aloud*]. What's that you are entering up, Miss Fosli?

KAJA [*starts*]. Oh, it's just something that . . .

SOLNESS. Let me see. [*He bends over her, pretending to look at the ledger, and whispers.*] Kaja?

KAJA [*in a low voice, still writing*]. Yes?

SOLNESS. Why do you always take that eye-shade off when I come in?

KAJA [*as before*]. Because I look so awful with it on.

SOLNESS [*with a smile*]. And that's something you don't want, eh, Kaja?

KAJA [*half glancing up at him*]. Not for anything in the world. Not in *your* eyes.

SOLNESS [*gently stroking her hair*]. Poor, poor little Kaja. . . .

KAJA [*moving her head away*]. Sh! . . . They can hear you!

[SOLNESS *strolls across the room to the right, turns and stops by the door into the drawing office.*]

SOLNESS. Has anybody been here asking for me?

RAGNAR [*gets up*]. Yes, the young couple who want that villa built out at Løvstrand.

SOLNESS [*growling*]. Oh, them? Well, *they'll* have to wait. I haven't got the plans straight in my mind yet.

RAGNAR [*comes closer, rather hesitantly*]. They were rather anxious to have the drawings soon.

SOLNESS [*as before*]. Oh Lord, yes! That's what they always want!

BROVIK [*looks up*]. Because they're just dying to move into a place of their own, they said.

SOLNESS. Yes, yes! We know *that*. They're prepared to make do with anything. Find themselves . . . somewhere to live. Any kind of place to move into, that's all. But not a *home*. No thank you! If that's how it is, let them go to somebody else. Tell them *that* the next time they come.

BROVIK [*pushes his spectacles up on to his forehead and looks at him aghast*]. To somebody else? Would you turn down a commission like that?

SOLNESS [*impatiently*]. Yes, damn it, yes! If that's the way it is. . . . Rather that than go and build any old thing. [*Bursts out.*] Anyway, I don't know anything about these people!

BROVIK. They're substantial enough. Ragnar knows them. He's a friend of the family. Thoroughly substantial people.

SOLNESS. Oh, substantial . . . substantial! That isn't what I mean at all. Good Lord . . . don't *you* understand me now, either? [*Angrily.*] I don't want anything to do with these strangers. They can go to somebody else—anybody they like—I don't care.

BROVIK [*gets up*]. Do you seriously mean that?

SOLNESS [*sulkily*]. Yes, I do . . . For once.

[*He walks across the room.* BROVIK *exchanges a glance with* RAGNAR *who makes a warning gesture, and then comes forward into the other room.*]

BROVIK. I'd like a few words with you, if I may?

SOLNESS. Certainly.

BROVIK [*to* KAJA]. Go along in there for a moment, Kaja.

KAJA [*uneasily*]. But, Uncle . . .

BROVIK. Do as I say, child. And shut the door after you.

[KAJA *goes reluctantly into the drawing office, glancing anxiously and imploringly at* SOLNESS, *and shuts the door.*]

BROVIK [*lowers his voice*]. I don't want these poor children to know how bad I am.

SOLNESS. Yes, you are not looking too well these days.

BROVIK. I won't last much longer. I get weaker and weaker every day.

SOLNESS. Sit down a moment.

BROVIK. Thank you, may I?

SOLNESS [*moves the armchair a little for him*]. Here you are. Well?

BROVIK [*after sitting down with difficulty*]. Well, it's this question of Ragnar. This is what's worrying me most. What's to become of him?

SOLNESS. Your son will of course remain with me—as long as he wants to, that is.

BROVIK. But that's just the point. He doesn't want to. He doesn't feel he can any longer.

SOLNESS. Well, he's making pretty good money, I'd have thought. But if he feels he wants more, I wouldn't say 'no' to . . .

BROVIK. No, no! It's not that at all! [*Impatiently.*] It's about time he had the chance of doing some independent work.

SOLNESS [*without looking at him*]. Do you think Ragnar has the ability necessary for that?

BROVIK. That's what's so terrible. The fact is I've begun to have doubts about the boy. Because you've never once said a single encouraging word about him. All the same, I can't help feeling there *is* something there. He *must* have some ability.

SOLNESS. But he hasn't really learnt anything . . . thoroughly, I mean. Except how to draw.

BROVIK [*looks at him with suppressed hatred and says hoarsely*]. You hadn't learnt much about the business either, when you were working for me. But that didn't stop you from launching out. [*Breathing with difficulty.*] Or from getting on. You went and left me standing . . . and a lot of other people as well.

SOLNESS. Well, things just ran my way.

BROVIK. You're right. Everything ran your way. So surely you haven't the heart to let me die . . . without seeing something of what Ragnar can do. And I also very much want to see them married . . . before I go.

SOLNESS [*sharply*]. Does *she* want that?

BROVIK. Not Kaja so much. But Ragnar talks about it every day. [*Pleads.*] You must . . . you *must* let him try doing something on his own! I *must* see something the boy has done himself! Do you hear?

SOLNESS [*irritably*]. But, damn it, commissions like that don't just grow on trees!

BROVIK. He could have a very nice commission right now. Quite a big job.

SOLNESS [*startled and uneasy*]. Could he?

BROVIK. If you would give your approval.

SOLNESS. What sort of a job is it?

BROVIK [*a little hesitantly*]. He could get the job building that villa at Løvstrand.

SOLNESS. *That*! But I'm going to build that myself!

BROVIK. But *you're* not particularly interested in it.

SOLNESS [*flares up*]. Not interested! Who says I'm not?

BROVIK. You said so yourself, just now.

SOLNESS. Oh, you shouldn't pay any attention to what I . . . *say*. Could Ragnar get the job of building that villa?

BROVIK. Yes. He knows the family, you see. And then—just for the fun of it more or less—he's drawn up plans and estimates and such like. . . .

SOLNESS. And these plans, are they pleased with them? The people who are going to live there?

BROVIK. Yes. As long as you're ready to look them over and approve them. . . .

SOLNESS. And then they would get Ragnar to build their home for them?

BROVIK. They liked his ideas very much indeed. They felt they were getting something quite new, they said.

SOLNESS. Aha! *New*! Not the sort of old-fashioned rubbish *I* generally build!

BROVIK. They thought it was somehow different.

SOLNESS [*with suppressed bitterness*]. So it was Ragnar they came to see —while I was out!

BROVIK. They came to talk to you. To ask if you might be willing to withdraw. . . .

SOLNESS [*flaring up*]. Withdraw! Me!

BROVIK. As long as you felt that Ragnar's drawings . . .

SOLNESS. I!—Withdraw in favour of your son!

BROVIK. Withdraw from the agreement, they meant.

SOLNESS. It comes to the same thing! [*Laughs bitterly.*] So that's it! Halvard Solness—he's to start backing down now, eh? Making way for younger men. Much younger men, maybe? Just get out of the way! Out of the way!

BROVIK. Good Heavens, surely there's room here for more than just one. . . ?

SOLNESS. Oh, there isn't all that much room to spare round here. Well, that's as may be. But I'm never going to back down! I'll never give way to anybody! Never of my own free will. Never in this world will I do *that*!

BROVIK [*rises with difficulty*]. Have I to die like this? An unhappy man, without any proof that I was right to have faith and confidence in Ragnar? Without ever seeing a single example of his work? Must I do this?

SOLNESS [*half turns to one side and mutters*]. H'm! Stop asking me these things now.

BROVIK. I won't! Answer me! Must I die so miserably?

SOLNESS [*seems to battle with himself, then says in a low but firm voice*]. You must die as best you can.

BROVIK. So be it.

[*He walks across the room.*]

SOLNESS [*follows him, half in desperation*]. Don't you understand? There's nothing else *I* can do! I am what I am! And I can't change myself!

BROVIK. No, no! I suppose you can't. [*He sways and stops beside the sofa table.*] Could I have a glass of water?

SOLNESS. Of course. [*Pours a glass and hands it to him.*]

BROVIK. Thanks.

[*He drinks and puts the glass down.* SOLNESS *walks across to the door into the drawing office and opens it.*]

SOLNESS. Ragnar! You'd better come and take your father home.

[RAGNAR *gets up quickly. He and* KAJA *come into the office.*]

RAGNAR. What is it, Father?

BROVIK. Take my arm. Now let's go.

RAGNAR. All right. Get your things, Kaja.

SOLNESS. Miss Fosli is to stay behind. Just for a moment. There's a letter I want written.

BROVIK [*looks at* SOLNESS]. Good night. Sleep well—if you can.

SOLNESS. Good night.

> [BROVIK *and* RAGNAR *go out by the door into the hall.* KAJA *walks over to the desk.* SOLNESS *stands with bowed head by the armchair, right.*]

KAJA [*uncertainly*]. Is it some letter . . . ?

SOLNESS [*shortly*]. No, of course it isn't. [*Looks sternly at her.*] Kaja!

KAJA [*frightened, in a low voice*]. Yes?

SOLNESS [*points with a commanding finger at the floor*]. Come over here! At once!

KAJA [*hesitating*]. Yes.

SOLNESS [*as before*]. Closer!

KAJA [*obeying*]. What do you want me for?

SOLNESS [*looks at her for a moment*]. Is it you I'm to thank for all this?

KAJA. No, no! You mustn't think that!

SOLNESS. So now you want to go and get married.

KAJA [*in a low voice*]. Ragnar and I have been engaged four or five years now, and . . .

SOLNESS. And now you think it's time you did something about it. Isn't that so?

KAJA. Ragnar and Uncle say I must. So I suppose I'll have to.

SOLNESS [*more gently*]. And you're also really quite fond of Ragnar, aren't you, Kaja?

KAJA. I was very fond of Ragnar once. . . . Before I came here to work for you.

SOLNESS. But not any longer? Not at all?

KAJA [*passionately clasps her hands and holds them out to him*]. Oh, you know very well there's only one person I care about now! There's nobody else in the whole wide world! I'll never care for anybody else!

SOLNESS. That's what you say. Yet you are going to leave me. Leave me sitting here, alone with everything.

KAJA. But couldn't I stay on here with you, even if Ragnar . . . ?

SOLNESS [*with a deprecating gesture*]. No, no, that certainly can't be done. If Ragnar goes off and starts up on his own account, he'll be needing you himself.

KAJA [*wringing her hands*]. Oh, I don't see how I *can* be separated from you. It seems so utterly impossible!

SOLNESS. Then see if you can't get Ragnar to drop these stupid ideas. Go and marry him as much as you like . . . [*Changes his tune.*] Well, what I mean is—get him to stay on in this good job he's got with me. Because then I'll be able to keep you too, Kaja my dear.

KAJA. Oh yes, how lovely it would be if things worked out like that!

SOLNESS [*takes her head in his hands and whispers*]. You see, I can't do without you. I must have you here near me every single day.

KAJA [*in rapture*]. Oh God! Oh God!

SOLNESS [*kisses her hair*]. Kaja! Kaja!

KAJA [*sinks at his feet*]. Oh, how good you are to me! How incredibly good you are!

SOLNESS [*urgently*]. Get up! Get up, for Heaven's sake! I think I hear somebody coming!

[*He helps her up. She staggers over to the desk.* MRS. SOLNESS *enters by the door, right. She looks thin and drawn, with traces of former beauty. Fair hair in ringlets. Elegantly dressed, all in black. She speaks rather slowly and with a plaintive voice.*]

MRS. SOLNESS [*in the doorway*]. Halvard!

SOLNESS [*turns*]. Oh, is that you, my dear?

MRS. SOLNESS [*with a glance at* KAJA]. I'm afraid I am intruding.

SOLNESS. Not at all. Miss Fosli only has a short letter to write.

MRS. SOLNESS. So I see.

SOLNESS. What did you want me for, Aline?

MRS. SOLNESS. I just wanted to say that Dr. Herdal is in the drawing-room. Perhaps you'll join us, Halvard?

SOLNESS [*looks at her suspiciously*]. H'm! Does the doctor specially want to talk to me?

MRS. SOLNESS. No, not specially. He called in to see me, but he'd like to say 'hello' to you at the same time.

SOLNESS [*laughs quietly*]. I imagine he would. Well, please ask him to wait a moment.

MRS. SOLNESS. Then you'll look in and see him later?

SOLNESS. Perhaps. Later . . . later, my dear. In a little while.

MRS. SOLNESS [*with another glance at* KAJA]. Well, don't forget, now, Halvard.

[*She withdraws, closing the door behind her.*]

KAJA [*in a low voice*]. Oh God! Oh God! I'm sure Mrs. Solness thinks badly of me!

SOLNESS. Not at all. Not more than usual, anyway. But you'd better go now, Kaja, all the same.

KAJA. Yes, yes. I *must* go now.

SOLNESS [*sternly*]. And mind you get that other matter settled for me! Do you hear!

KAJA. Oh, if it only depended on me . . .

SOLNESS. I'm telling you I want it settled. And by tomorrow at latest!

KAJA [*fearfully*]. If it can't be done any other way, I'd gladly break it off with him.

SOLNESS [*flaring up*]. Break it off! Have you gone mad! You'd break it off?

KAJA [*desperately*]. Yes, rather that than. . . . I *must* . . . I *must* stay here with you. I can't leave you! It's utterly . . . utterly impossible!

SOLNESS [*bursting out*]. But, damn it, what about Ragnar! It's Ragnar I'm . . .

KAJA [*looks at him with terror in her eyes*]. Is it mainly because of Ragnar that you . . . ?

SOLNESS [*controlling himself*]. No, no, of course not! You just don't understand. [*Gently and quietly.*] It's you I want, of course. You above all, Kaja. But that's just why you've got to get Ragnar to stay in his job. There, there . . . off you go home now.

KAJA. Yes, yes. Good night.

SOLNESS. Good night. [*As she turns to go.*] Oh, by the way. Are Ragnar's drawings in there?

KAJA. Yes, I didn't see him take them.

SOLNESS. Go in and find them for me, please. I might just glance over them.

KAJA [*happily*]. Oh yes, please do.

SOLNESS. For your sake, Kaja my dear. Well, do hurry up and get them for me, won't you?

[KAJA *hurries into the drawing office, rummages anxiously in the table drawer, takes out a folder and brings it out.*]

KAJA. Here are all the drawings.

SOLNESS. Good. Put them over there on the table.

KAJA [*putting down the folder*]. Good night then. [*Pleads.*] And think kindly of me.

SOLNESS. I always do. Good night, my dear little Kaja. [*Glances to the right.*] Off you go now!

[MRS. SOLNESS *and* DR. HERDAL *come in through the door, right. He is a stout, elderly man, with a round, good-humoured face, clean-shaven, with thinning fair hair and gold-rimmed spectacles.*]

MRS. SOLNESS [*in the doorway*]. Halvard, I can't keep the doctor waiting any longer.

SOLNESS. Well, come in, then.

MRS. SOLNESS [*to* KAJA, *who is turning down the lamp on the desk*]. Finished the letter, Miss Fosli?

KAJA [*in confusion*]. The letter . . . ?

SOLNESS. Yes, it was quite a short one.

MRS. SOLNESS. It must have been very short.

SOLNESS. You can go now, Miss Fosli. And see you are in good time in the morning.

KAJA. I will. Good night, Mrs. Solness.

[*She goes out through the hall door.*]

MRS. SOLNESS. How nice for you, Halvard, that you managed to find that girl.

SOLNESS. It is rather. She's useful in all sorts of ways.

MRS. SOLNESS. She seems to be.

DR. HERDAL. Good at book-keeping, too?

SOLNESS. Well . . . at least she's had a fair amount of training over the last two years. She's also pleasant and willing in every way.

MRS. SOLNESS. Yes, *that* must be very agreeable. . . .

SOLNESS. It is. Especially when one doesn't exactly enjoy a glut of that kind of thing.

MRS. SOLNESS [*mildly reproachful*]. How can you say that, Halvard?

SOLNESS. Oh no, no, Aline dear. You must forgive me.

MRS. SOLNESS. It's nothing.—Well, Doctor, you'll look in again later and have tea with us?

DR. HERDAL. As soon as I've made my call, I'll be back.

MRS. SOLNESS. Thank you.

[*She goes out through the door, right.*]

SOLNESS. Are you in a hurry, Doctor?

DR. HERDAL. No, not at all.

SOLNESS. Could I have a word with you?

DR. HERDAL. With pleasure.

SOLNESS. Let's sit down. [*He beckons to the doctor to take the rocking-chair, and himself takes the armchair. Looks searchingly at him.*] Tell me. . . . Did you notice anything about Aline?

DR. HERDAL. Just now, while she was in here, you mean?

SOLNESS. Yes. In her manner towards me. Did you notice anything?

DR. HERDAL [*smiles*]. Well, dash it . . . one couldn't very well help noticing that your wife . . . hm! . . .

SOLNESS. Well?

DR. HERDAL. . . . . That your wife isn't particularly enamoured of this Miss Fosli.

SOLNESS. Is that all? I've noticed that myself.

DR. HERDAL. Not that that's so very surprising.

SOLNESS. What?

DR. HERDAL. That she doesn't exactly like your having another woman beside you all day long.

SOLNESS. No, no, you may be right. Aline, too. But that's something that just cannot be helped.

DR. HERDAL. Couldn't you get yourself a male clerk?

SOLNESS. Grab the first man who came along? No, thank you—I wouldn't want that.

DR. HERDAL. But if your wife . . . ? Being so frail . . . What if she can't face up to this situation?

SOLNESS. Then, by God, that's just too bad! That's what I feel like saying, at least. I *must* keep Kaja Fosli. Nobody else will do, but her.

DR. HERDAL. Nobody else?

SOLNESS [*shortly*]. No, nobody.

DR. HERDAL [*pulling his chair closer*]. Listen to me, Mr. Solness. May I ask you a question about a rather confidential matter?

SOLNESS. Certainly.

DR. HERDAL. You know . . . women have a damned keen intuition about certain things. . . .

SOLNESS. They have. That's very true. But . . . ?

DR. HERDAL. Well, now listen. If your wife can't stand this Kaja Fosli at any price . . .

SOLNESS. Well, what of it?

DR. HERDAL. . . . Might she not in some way have certain . . . certain slight grounds for this instinctive dislike?

SOLNESS [*looks at him and rises*]. Aha!

DR. HERDAL. Don't take offence! But hasn't she?

SOLNESS [*curtly and firmly*]. No.

DR. HERDAL. No grounds whatsoever?

SOLNESS. None, apart from her own suspicious nature.

DR. HERDAL. I know you've known a good many women in your life.

SOLNESS. Yes, I have.

DR. HERDAL. And been pretty fond of some of them?

SOLNESS. Yes, I have that.

DR. HERDAL. But in the case of Miss Fosli . . . ? Nothing of that sort enters into it?

SOLNESS. No, nothing at all—not on *my* side.

DR. HERDAL. And on hers?

SOLNESS. I don't think you've any right to ask that, Dr. Herdal.

DR. HERDAL. We began by talking about your wife's intuition.

SOLNESS. That's true. And for that matter . . . [*Drops his voice.*] In one sense, Aline's intuition, as you call it . . . in fact hasn't let her down.

DR. HERDAL. Well—there we are!

SOLNESS [*sits*]. Dr. Herdal . . . I am now going to tell you a strange story. If you would care to listen to it?

DR. HERDAL. I like listening to strange stories.

SOLNESS. Very well. I dare say you remember that I took Knut Brovik and his son into my employ just after the old man had completely failed in business.

DR. HERDAL. I remember something of the kind, yes.

SOLNESS. Because actually they are both pretty clever, you know.

They both have ability, in their different ways. But then the son took it into his head to get engaged. And then, of course, he began thinking of getting married . . . and of setting up on his own as a builder. They all get ideas like that, young people nowadays.

DR. HERDAL [*laughs*]. Yes, it's an obsession with them—this wanting to be together.

SOLNESS. Well. But that didn't suit *my* book at all. I needed Ragnar myself. And the old man, too. He's so extraordinarily clever at working out stresses and strains and cubic contents . . . and all that damned rigmarole, you know.

DR. HERDAL. I dare say that's also all part of the job.

SOLNESS. It is, indeed. But Ragnar—he was absolutely intent on setting up on his own. There was no arguing with him.

DR. HERDAL. Yet he's stayed with you all the same.

SOLNESS. Yes, and I'll tell you why. One day this girl, Kaja Fosli, called in to see them for something. She'd never been here before. And when I saw how completely infatuated with each other those two were, I had an idea: if I could somehow get her into the office here, maybe Ragnar would stay, too.

DR. HERDAL. That was a fair assumption.

SOLNESS. Yes, but I never dropped the slightest hint of this at the time. I just stood and looked at her—wishing with all my soul that I had her here. Then I made one or two pleasant little remarks to her, about one thing and another. Then off she went.

DR. HERDAL. Well?

SOLNESS. Well then, the next day, in the evening after old Brovik and Ragnar had gone home, she came back here to me, and acted as though I had come to some sort of arrangement with her.

DR. HERDAL. Arrangement? What about?

SOLNESS. About the very thing I'd been wishing for. But about which I hadn't said a single word.

DR. HERDAL. Very odd.

SOLNESS. Yes, wasn't it? And then she wanted to be told what work she would be doing. Whether she could start straight away the next morning. Things like that.

DR. HERDAL. Don't you think she did it so that she could be near her young man?

SOLNESS. That also occurred to me at first. But no, that wasn't it. She seemed to drift right away from him—once she was here working for me.

DR. HERDAL. Drifted over to you?

SOLNESS. Yes, completely. I can tell she can feel me looking at her, even when her back's turned. I've only got to go near her, and at once she is all shaking and trembling. What do you make of that?

DR. HERDAL. H'm! I dare say that could be explained.

SOLNESS. Well, but what about that other matter? Her believing I'd *spoken* to her of things I'd only wished for—silently? Inwardly? To myself? Can you explain that to me, Dr. Herdal?

DR. HERDAL. No, that I can't offer to do.

SOLNESS. I might have guessed. That's why I've never felt like talking about it before.—But now, you see, it's becoming such a damned nuisance. Day after day I've got to walk about here pretending I. . . . And it's not fair on her, poor thing. [*Vehemently.*] But there's nothing else I *can* do! Because if she runs away from me—then away goes Ragnar, too.

DR. HERDAL. You've said nothing of all this to your wife?

SOLNESS. No.

DR. HERDAL. Why on earth don't you?

SOLNESS [*looking intently at him, and speaking in a low voice*]. Because I somehow . . . enjoy the mortification of letting Aline do me an injustice.

DR. HERDAL [*shaking his head*]. I don't understand a single, blessed word of all this.

SOLNESS. Oh, yes. You see it's rather like paying off a tiny instalment on a huge immeasurable debt. . . .

DR. HERDAL. To your wife?

SOLNESS. Yes. And that always eases one's mind a little. One can breathe more freely for a while, you understand.

DR. HERDAL. No, I'm damned if I understand a word. . . .

SOLNESS [*breaks off and gets up again*]. Well, well—then let's not talk any more about it. [*He wanders across the room, comes back and stops beside the table, and looks at the doctor with a sly smile.*] You must be thinking that you've got me nicely launched now, eh, Doctor?

DR. HERDAL [*rather crossly*]. Nicely launched? I still don't understand you in the slightest, Mr. Solness.

SOLNESS. Oh, come now, why not admit it? I see it all too clearly.

DR. HERDAL. *What* do you see?

SOLNESS [*slowly and quietly*]. That you come snooping round here to keep an eye on me.

DR. HERDAL. *I* do! Why on earth should I want to do that?

SOLNESS. Because you think I'm . . . [*Flaring up.*] Well, damn it, you think the same about me as Aline does.

DR. HERDAL. And what does *she* think about you, then?

SOLNESS [*controlling himself again*]. She's begun to think I'm . . . so to speak . . . ill.

DR. HERDAL. Ill! You! She's never said a single word about that to me. What's supposed to be wrong with you, my dear fellow?

SOLNESS [*leans over the back of the chair and whispers*]. Aline thinks I'm mad. That's what she thinks.

DR. HERDAL [*rising*]. But my dear Mr. Solness . . . !

SOLNESS. Yes, she does, by thunder! That's how it is. And she's got you to believe it, too. Oh, I assure you, Doctor, it's quite plain to me you do . . . quite plain. I'm not so easily fooled, let me tell you.

DR. HERDAL [*looks at him astounded*]. Never, Mr. Solness . . . never once has such a thought occurred to me.

SOLNESS [*with an incredulous smile*]. Indeed? Really not?

DR. HERDAL. No, never! Nor to your wife either, I'm sure. I think I could almost swear to that.

SOLNESS. Well, perhaps you'd better not. You see, in a way . . . she might have good grounds for thinking so.

DR. HERDAL. Well, now, really I must say . . . !

SOLNESS [*with a gesture of his hand, interrupts*]. All right, my dear Doctor . . . let's not pursue this any further. It's best we agree to differ. [*Switches to a mood of quiet amusement.*] But tell me, Doctor . . . hm! . . .

DR. HERDAL. Yes?

SOLNESS. Since you don't think I'm . . . as you might say . . . ill—or crazy—or mad, or anything like that. . . .

DR. HERDAL. You mean, what then?

SOLNESS. Then you probably imagine I'm a very happy man?

DR. HERDAL. And would that be *only* imagination?

SOLNESS [*laughs*]. No, no! Of course not! Heaven forbid! Think what it is to be Solness, the master builder! Halvard Solness! Oh yes, I'm grateful all right!

DR. HERDAL. Well, I must say *I* reckon you've had quite incredible luck on your side.

SOLNESS [*suppressing a sad smile*]. Yes, I have. I can't complain.

DR. HERDAL. First, that ghastly old fortress of a house of yours went and burnt down. That was a real bit of luck.

SOLNESS [*seriously*]. It was Aline's family home that burnt down. Remember that.

DR. HERDAL. Yes, it must have been a sad loss to her.

SOLNESS. She's never got over it, not to this very day. Not in all these twelve or thirteen years.

DR. HERDAL. The thing that followed must have been the worst blow of all for her.

SOLNESS. The two things together.

DR. HERDAL. But you yourself . . . you saw your chance and took it. Started out as a poor country lad, and now look at you—at the top of your profession. Yes indeed, Mr. Solness, you certainly have had all the luck.

SOLNESS [*glances nervously at him*]. Yes. That's what makes me feel so horribly afraid.

DR. HERDAL. Afraid? Because you have all the luck?

SOLNESS. Night and day it terrifies me . . . terrifies me. Some day, you see, that luck must change.

DR. HERDAL. Nonsense! What is going to change it?

SOLNESS [*firmly and definitely*]. Youth is.

DR. HERDAL. Puh! Youth! I wouldn't have said you were exactly decrepit yet. Oh no! I'd say you were more firmly established here now than you've ever been.

SOLNESS. The turn is coming. I can sense it. I feel it getting nearer. Somebody or other is going to demand: Make way for me! And then all the others will come storming up, threatening and shouting: Get out of the way! Get out of the way! Yes, just you watch, Doctor! One of these days, youth is going to come here beating on the door. . . .

DR. HERDAL [*laughs*]. Well, good Lord, what of it?

SOLNESS. What of it? Just that that will mean the end of Master Builder Solness. [*There is a knock on the door, left. He starts.*] What's that! Did you hear something?

DR. HERDAL. Somebody's knocking.

SOLNESS [*loudly*]. Come in!

[HILDE WANGEL *comes in by the door from the hall. She is of medium height, lithe, of slim build. Slightly tanned by the sun. She wears walking clothes, with her skirt hitched up, a sailor's collar open at the neck, and a small sailor hat on her head. She has a rucksack on her back, a plaid in a strap, and a long alpenstock.*]

HILDE WANGEL [*walks across to* SOLNESS, *her eyes shining and happy*]. Good evening!

SOLNESS [*looks uncertainly at her*]. Good evening. . . .

HILDE [*laughing*]. I do believe you don't recognize me.

SOLNESS. Well . . . in actual fact . . . just for the moment. . . .

DR. HERDAL [*approaches her*]. But I recognize you, young lady. . . .

HILDE [*delighted*]. Well, if it isn't . . .

DR. HERDAL. It most certainly is. [*To* SOLNESS.] We met earlier this summer at one of those hostels up in the mountains. [*To* HILDE.] What happened to the other ladies?

HILDE. Oh, they went further west.

DR. HERDAL. I don't think they liked us making all that noise in the evening.

HILDE. No, I'm sure they didn't.

DR. HERDAL [*wagging his finger*]. Moreover, it cannot be denied that you *did* rather flirt with us a little.

HILDE. Well, it was much more fun than sitting knitting socks with all those old ladies.

DR. HERDAL [*laughs*]. I entirely agree.

SOLNESS. Have you just come to town this evening?

HILDE. Yes, I've just arrived.

DR. HERDAL. All alone, Miss Wangel?

HILDE. Certainly!

SOLNESS. Wangel? Is your name Wangel?

HILDE [*looks at him with amused surprise*]. Of course it is.

SOLNESS. Could you by any chance be the daughter of the doctor up at Lysanger?

HILDE [*as before*]. Yes. Who else would I be the daughter of?

SOLNESS. Well, so that's where we met each other. The summer I was up there building a tower on the old church.

HILDE [*more seriously*]. Yes, that was the occasion.

SOLNESS. Well, that's a long time ago.

HILDE [*looking steadily at him*]. Ten years ago exactly.

SOLNESS. I imagine you were only a child at the time.

HILDE [*casually*]. About twelve or thirteen, at any rate.

DR. HERDAL. Is this the first time you've been to town, Miss Wangel?

HILDE. Yes, it is.

SOLNESS. And perhaps you don't know anybody here?

HILDE. Nobody but you. Oh, and your wife.

SOLNESS. So you know *her*, too?

HILDE. Only slightly. I met her when she was spending a few days up in the mountains for her health. . . .

SOLNESS. Ah, up *there*.

HILDE. She said I must be sure to call on her if ever I was in town. [*Smiles.*] Not that that was necessary.

SOLNESS. Odd that she never mentioned it. . . .

[HILDE *puts her stick down by the stove, takes off her rucksack and puts it and the plaid on the sofa.* DR. HERDAL *moves across to help her.* SOLNESS *stands looking at her.*]

HILDE [*going up to him*]. May I ask if I can stay the night?

SOLNESS. I'm sure that can be arranged.

HILDE. Because I haven't any other clothes apart from what I've got on. Oh, and a set of underclothes in my rucksack. But they'll need washing—they're filthy.

SOLNESS. That's easily managed. I'll just tell my wife. . . .

DR. HERDAL. Meanwhile I'll go and see my patient.

SOLNESS. Yes, do that. And you'll be looking in again later.

DR. HERDAL [*merrily, with a glance at* HILDE]. You're damned right I shall. [*Laughs.*] So you were right in your forecast after all, Mr. Solness!

SOLNESS. In what way?

DR. HERDAL. Youth *has* come knocking at your door.

SOLNESS [*cheerfully*]. Yes, but in rather a different way.

DR. HERDAL. It is indeed! No doubt about it!

[*He goes out through the hall door.* SOLNESS *opens the door, right, and speaks into the side room.*]

SOLNESS. Aline! Could you come in, please? There's a Miss Wangel here, whom I believe you know.

MRS. SOLNESS [*appears in the doorway*]. Who is it, do you say? [*Sees* HILDE.] Oh, is it you? [*Goes across to shake hands.*] So you did come to town after all.

SOLNESS. Miss Wangel has just arrived. She is wondering if she can stay the night.

MRS. SOLNESS. Here with us? Yes, with pleasure.

SOLNESS. To get herself tidied up a little, you understand.

MRS. SOLNESS. I shall do what I can for you. It's no more than my duty. Your luggage will be coming along later, I suppose?

HILDE. I have no luggage.

MRS. SOLNESS. Well, I'm sure everything will be all right, nevertheless. Now, if you don't mind being left here with my husband for a moment, I'll see about getting a room ready for you.

SOLNESS. Can't we use one of the nurseries? They're all ready.

MRS. SOLNESS. Oh, yes. We've plenty of room *there*. [*To* HILDE.] You sit down and rest a little.

[*She goes out, right.* HILDE *wanders about the room, her hands behind her back, looking at this and that.* SOLNESS *stands down by the table, also with his hands behind his back, following her with his eyes.*]

HILDE [*stops and looks at him*]. Do you have more than one nursery, then?

SOLNESS. There are three nurseries in the house.

HILDE. That's a lot. You must have many children.

SOLNESS. No, we have no children. But now *you* can be the child while you're here.

HILDE. For tonight, yes. I won't cry. I'm going to try and sleep like a log, if I can.

SOLNESS. Yes, I imagine you must be very tired.

HILDE. No, I'm not! But it makes no difference. . . . Because it's absolutely marvellous to lie in bed like that and dream.

SOLNESS. Do you often dream at night?

HILDE. Yes, I do! Almost always.

SOLNESS. What do you dream about mostly?

HILDE. I'm not saying tonight. Some other time—perhaps.

[*She again wanders about the room, stops by the desk, and turns over some of the books and papers.*]

SOLNESS [*walks over to her*]. Looking for something?

HILDE. No, I'm just looking at all these things. [*Turns.*] Perhaps I mustn't?

SOLNESS. Please do.

HILDE. Is it you who writes in this big ledger?

SOLNESS. No, it's my book-keeper.

HILDE. A woman?

SOLNESS [*smiles*]. Yes, of course.

HILDE. And she belongs to the office?

SOLNESS. Yes.

HILDE. Is she married?

SOLNESS. No, she's single.

HILDE. I see.

SOLNESS. But I think she's getting married soon.

HILDE. That's nice for *her*.

SOLNESS. But it's not so nice for *me*. Because then I'll have nobody to help me.

HILDE. Can't you find somebody else just as good?

SOLNESS. Perhaps you'd like to stay here—and write things in the ledger?

HILDE [*looks scornfully at him*]. Not likely! No, thank you—we're not having anything of that! [*She again walks about the room and sits in the rocking-chair.* SOLNESS *also walks across to the table.* HILDE *continues as before.*] . . . There must be better things to do around here than that! [*Looks at him with a smile.*] Don't you agree?

SOLNESS. Of course. First of all you'll be wanting to go round the shops and get yourself all rigged out.

HILDE [*gaily*]. No, I rather think I'll give *that* a miss!

SOLNESS. Oh?

HILDE. Yes. You see, I've spent all my money.

SOLNESS [*laughs*]. No luggage and no money, eh?

HILDE. Neither. But, hell! What's it matter?

SOLNESS. You know, I like you for that!

HILDE. Only for *that*?

SOLNESS. That—and other things. [*Sits down in the armchair.*] Is your father still alive?

HILDE. Yes, he's alive.

SOLNESS. And now perhaps you are thinking of studying here?

HILDE. That hadn't occurred to me.

SOLNESS. But you'll be staying here some time, I dare say?

HILDE. All depends how things go. [*She sits for a moment rocking herself, looking at him half-seriously, half-smiling. Then she takes off her hat and puts it on the table in front of her.*] Mr. Solness?

SOLNESS. Yes?

HILDE. Are you very forgetful?

SOLNESS. Forgetful? Not as far as I know.

HILDE. Don't you want to talk to me at all about what happened up there?

SOLNESS [*momentarily startled*]. Up at Lysanger? [*Casually.*] Well, there wasn't all that much to talk about, I don't think.

HILDE [*looks reproachfully at him*]. How can you sit there and say a thing like that!

SOLNESS. Well, suppose *you* talk to me about it, then.

HILDE. When the tower was finished, there were great goings-on in town.

SOLNESS. Yes, I shan't forget that day so easily.

HILDE. Won't you? That *is* nice of you!

SOLNESS. Nice?

HILDE. There was a band in the churchyard. And hundreds and hundreds of people. We schoolgirls were dressed in white. And all of us had flags.

SOLNESS. Ah yes, those flags! Those I do remember.

HILDE. Then you climbed straight up the scaffolding. Right to the very top. And you had a big wreath with you. And you hung that wreath right on the top of the weathercock.

SOLNESS [*curtly interrupting*]. I used to do that in those days. It's an old custom.

HILDE. It was wonderfully exciting, standing down there and looking up at you. Imagine now—if he were to fall! The master builder himself!

SOLNESS [*as though dismissing the matter*]. Yes, yes, and it might very easily have happened. Because one of those little devils in white was shouting and yelling at me so much. . . .

HILDE [*her eyes sparkling with joy*]. 'Hurrah for Mr. Solness!' 'Hurrah for the master builder!' Yes!

SOLNESS. . . . And waving and flapping her flag so much that I . . . that I almost grew dizzy at the sight of it.

HILDE [*more quietly, seriously*]. That little devil—was *me*.

SOLNESS [*looking fixedly at her*]. I can see it was now. It *must* have been you.

HILDE [*once more animated*]. It was marvellous—terribly exciting!
I couldn't believe any builder in the world could have built such an
enormously high tower. And then you yourself went and stood
right at the very top! As large as life! And not even the slightest bit
dizzy. The very thought of it made me sort of . . . dizzy.

SOLNESS. What made you so sure that I wasn't . . . ?

HILDE [*dismissing the idea*]. Oh, don't be silly! I felt it inside me. For
otherwise you couldn't have stood up there singing.

SOLNESS [*looks at her in amazement*]. Singing? I sang?

HILDE. You most certainly did.

SOLNESS [*shaking his head*]. I've never sung a note in my life.

HILDE. Yes, you have. You sang then. It sounded like harps in the air.

SOLNESS [*thoughtfully*]. There's something very strange about this.

HILDE [*is silent a moment, looks at him, and says in a low voice*]. But it
was then—afterwards—that the real thing happened.

SOLNESS. The real thing?

HILDE [*sparkling and animated*]. Surely I don't have to remind you about
that?

SOLNESS. Yes, please! Remind me a little about that, too.

HILDE. Don't you remember they gave a big dinner for you at the
club?

SOLNESS. Ah, yes. That must have been the same evening. Because
I left the next morning.

HILDE. And after the club you were invited home to us.

SOLNESS. That's quite right, Miss Wangel. It's amazing how well you
have remembered all these little details.

HILDE. Little details! I like that! Was it merely a little detail that I
happened to be alone in the room when you arrived?

SOLNESS. Were you?

HILDE [*without answering him*]. You didn't call me a little devil that time.

SOLNESS. I don't suppose I did.

HILDE. You said that I looked lovely in my white dress. That I looked like a little princess.

SOLNESS. And I'm sure you did, Miss Wangel. Added to the fact that . . . I felt so light and free that day.

HILDE. And then you said that when I grew up I should be *your* princess.

SOLNESS [*laughs a little*]. Well, well. . . . Did I say that, too?

HILDE. Yes, you did. And when I asked how long I had to wait, you said you'd come back in ten years—like a troll—and carry me off. To Spain or somewhere. And there you promised you'd buy me a kingdom.

SOLNESS [*as before*]. Well, after a good dinner you're not always in a mood to count your coppers. But did I really say all this?

HILDE [*laughing quietly*]. Yes. And you also said what this kingdom would be called.

SOLNESS. Well?

HILDE. It was to be called the Kingdom of Orangia, you said.

SOLNESS. Well, that's an appetizing sort of name.

HILDE. I didn't like it a bit. It sounded as if you were trying to make fun of me.

SOLNESS. I'm sure that wasn't my intention.

HILDE. Indeed I should hope not. Considering what you did after that. . . .

SOLNESS. What on earth did I do after that?

HILDE. Oh, I might have known you'd say you'd forgotten that, too! Surely one couldn't help remembering a thing like that!

SOLNESS. Well, just give me a little hint, and I might. . . . Well?

HILDE [*looks steadily at him*]. You went and kissed me, Mr. Solness.

SOLNESS [*open-mouthed, rises from his chair*]. I *did*!

HILDE. Yes, you did. You took me in your arms and bent me backwards and kissed me. Many times.

SOLNESS. Really now, my dear Miss Wangel . . . !

HILDE [*getting up*]. You're not going to deny it!

SOLNESS. I certainly do deny it!

HILDE [*looks scornfully at him*]. Well, well!

> [*She turns and walks slowly across to the stove, where she remains standing, motionless, her back turned, and her hands clasped behind her. Short pause.*]

SOLNESS [*walks warily up behind her*]. Miss Wangel . . . ? [HILDE *remains silent and motionless.*] Don't stand there like a statue. All this you've just told me—it must be something you've dreamt. [*Puts his hand on her arm.*] Listen, now . . . [HILDE *makes an impatient gesture with her arm.* SOLNESS *speaks as though a thought suddenly strikes him.*] Or . . . wait a moment! There's more in this than meets the eye, I tell you. [HILDE *does not move.* SOLNESS *speaks quietly but emphatically.*] I must have *thought* it all. I must have willed it . . . wished it . . . desired it. And then. . . . Mightn't that be the explanation? [HILDE *remains silent.* SOLNESS *speaks impatiently.*] All right, damn it . . . ! So I *did* do it then!

HILDE [*turns her head a little without actually looking at him*]. Then you admit it?

SOLNESS. Yes, anything you like.

HILDE. That you put your arms round me?

SOLNESS. Yes.

HILDE. And bent me back?

SOLNESS. Right back.

HILDE. And kissed me?

SOLNESS. Yes, I did.

HILDE. Many times?

SOLNESS. As many as you like.

HILDE [*quickly turns to face him, her eyes once again shining with happiness*]. There, you see! I finally got it out of you!

SOLNESS [*with a faint smile*]. Yes. Imagine me forgetting a thing like that.

HILDE [*walks away from him, again a little sulky*]. Oh, I suppose you must have kissed many women in your time.

SOLNESS. No, you mustn't believe that of me. [HILDE *sits in the armchair, while* SOLNESS *stands leaning against the rocking-chair, watching her intently.*] Miss Wangel?

HILDE. Yes?

SOLNESS. What happened then? What followed... between you and me?

HILDE. Nothing followed. You know that very well. Because then all the other guests arrived, and ... Pah!

SOLNESS. That's right. The others arrived. Fancy me forgetting *that* as well.

HILDE. Oh, you haven't forgotten anything. You just felt a bit ashamed. One doesn't forget a thing like that, I know.

SOLNESS. No, one wouldn't think so.

HILDE [*looks at him vivaciously again*]. Or maybe you've also forgotten what date it was?

SOLNESS. What date ... ?

HILDE. Yes, what date was it when you hung the wreath on the tower? Well? Tell me—quickly!

SOLNESS. Hm! The actual date I'm afraid I've forgotten. All I know is it was ten years ago. Some time in the autumn.

HILDE [*nods slowly several times*]. It was ten years ago. The nineteenth of September.

SOLNESS. Yes, it must have been about then. Fancy you remembering that as well! [*Stops.*] But wait a moment ... ! Today's the nineteenth of September.

HILDE. It is indeed. And the ten years are up. And you didn't come ... as you promised me you would.

SOLNESS. Promised you? Threatened you, you mean probably?

HILDE. I didn't think of it as a threat.

SOLNESS. Well then, I was probably fooling.

HILDE. Was that all you wanted to do? Make a fool of me?

SOLNESS. Or joking, probably. Heavens above, I can't remember now. But it must have been something like that. After all, you were only a child at the time.

HILDE. Ah, maybe I wasn't such a child as all that! Not such a babe as you think.

SOLNESS [*looks searchingly at her*]. Did you honestly think in all seriousness that I'd come back?

HILDE [*with a half-suppressed roguish smile*]. Of course! I expected *that* much of you.

SOLNESS. That I'd come to your home and carry you off with me?

HILDE. Just like a troll—yes!

SOLNESS. And make you a princess?

HILDE. That's what you promised.

SOLNESS. And give you a kingdom too?

HILDE [*looks up at the ceiling*]. Why not? It didn't actually have to be an ordinary, real kingdom.

SOLNESS. But something else just as good?

HILDE. Yes, at least as good. [*Looks at him for a moment.*] If you could build the highest church tower in the world, I thought to myself, then surely you'd be able to arrange some kind of kingdom or other.

SOLNESS [*shaking his head*]. I don't really follow you, Miss Wangel.

HILDE. Don't you? It seems simple enough to me.

SOLNESS. No, I just can't make out if you mean all you say. Or whether you are just joking. . . .

HILDE [*smiles*]. My turn to make a fool of you, perhaps?

SOLNESS. Exactly. To make . . . fools of us both. [*Looks at her.*] Did you know that I was married?

HILDE. Yes, I've known it all along. Why do you ask that?

SOLNESS [*casually*]. Oh, I was just wondering. [*Looks earnestly at her and says quietly.*] Why have you come?

HILDE. Because I want my kingdom. The time's up.

SOLNESS [*with an involuntary laugh*]. Ha! That's good!

HILDE [*gaily*]. Bring out my kingdom, master builder! [*Raps with her finger.*] My kingdom on the table!

SOLNESS [*pushes the rocking-chair closer and sits down*]. Seriously—why have you come? What in fact do you want here?

HILDE. Oh, first I want to go round and look at all the things you've built.

SOLNESS. That's going to keep you pretty busy.

HILDE. Yes, I know you've built an awful lot.

SOLNESS. I have. Especially in recent years.

HILDE. Many church towers, too? Great high ones, I mean?

SOLNESS. No, I don't build church towers any more. Nor churches either.

HILDE. What do you build now, then?

SOLNESS. Homes for people.

HILDE [*pensively*]. Couldn't you . . . try putting some kind of tower on them too?

SOLNESS [*starts*]. What do you mean by that?

HILDE. I mean . . . something pointing . . . right up into the air. With a weathercock on top at a great dizzy height.

SOLNESS [*muses a little*]. Strange you should say that. That's what I want to do more than anything.

HILDE [*impatiently*]. Then why don't you?

SOLNESS [*shakes his head*]. Because people don't want that.

HILDE. Fancy not wanting it!

SOLNESS [*in a lighter vein*]. But now I'm building a new house for myself. Just across the way here.

HILDE. For yourself?

SOLNESS. Yes. It's just about ready. And *it's* got a tower.

HILDE. A high tower?

SOLNESS. Yes.

HILDE. Very high?

SOLNESS. People are sure to say it's too high. For a house.

HILDE. I'll be out first thing in the morning to see that tower.

SOLNESS [*sits with his hand on his cheek gazing at her*]. Tell me, Miss Wangel . . . what's your name? Your first name, I mean?

HILDE. My name's Hilde, of course.

SOLNESS [*as before*]. Hilde? Really?

HILDE. Don't you remember? You called me Hilde yourself. The day you—misbehaved.

SOLNESS. Did I also do that?

HILDE. But that time you said 'Little Hilde'. And that I didn't like.

SOLNESS. So you didn't like that, Miss Hilde?

HILDE. No. Not on an occasion like that. But 'Princess Hilde', however. . . . That will sound rather well, I think.

SOLNESS. Yes, indeed. Princess Hilde of . . . of . . . What was to be the name of that kingdom?

HILDE. Pah! I don't want to hear any more about *that* stupid kingdom. I'm going to want a very different sort.

SOLNESS [*has leant back in the chair, still gazing at her*]. Isn't it strange. . . . The more I think about it, the more I seem to have been tormenting myself for years . . . hm!

HILDE. How?

SOLNESS. . . . Trying to identify . . . some experience I felt I must have forgotten. But I never discovered what it could have been.

HILDE. You should have tied a knot in your handkerchief, master builder.

SOLNESS. Then I'd only have gone about worrying what the knot was for.

HILDE. Ah yes, I dare say you find trolls of *that* sort, too.

SOLNESS [*getting up slowly*]. How very good it is that you've come to me now.

HILDE [*looks deep into his eyes*]. Is it good?

SOLNESS. I've been so alone here. Staring at everything, so utterly helpless. [*Lowers his voice.*] I tell you—I have begun to be so afraid, so terribly afraid, of youth.

HILDE [*snorting*]. Pah! Is youth anything to be afraid of!

SOLNESS. Yes, it is. That's why I've locked and barred myself in. [*Secretively.*] I tell you, youth will come here and beat on my door, and force its way in!

HILDE. Then I think you'd better go out and open up for youth.

SOLNESS. Open up?

HILDE. Yes. And let youth in. On friendly terms.

SOLNESS, No, no, no! Can't you see! Youth brings retribution. It is in the vanguard of change. . . . Marching under a new banner.

HILDE [*rises and looks at him and says, her mouth trembling*]. Can you use *me*, master builder.

SOLNESS. Yes, I can indeed! For you too seem to be marching under a new banner. Youth against youth . . . !

[DR. HERDAL *comes in through the hall door.*]

DR. HERDAL. Ah. . . . You and Miss Wangel still here?

SOLNESS. Yes. We have had many things to talk about, we two.

HILDE. Things old and new.

DR. HERDAL. Have you now!

HILDE. And it's been such fun. Mr. Solness has a quite incredible memory. He remembers everything, right down to the final detail.

[MRS. SOLNESS *comes in by the door, right.*]

MRS. SOLNESS. There we are now, Miss Wangel. Your room is ready.

HILDE. Oh, how very kind of you!

SOLNESS [*to his wife*]. The nursery?

MRS. SOLNESS. Yes. The middle one. But we must have something to eat first.

SOLNESS [*nods to* HILDE]. So Hilde sleeps in the nursery.

MRS. SOLNESS [*looks at him*]. Hilde?

SOLNESS. Yes, Miss Wangel is called Hilde. I used to know her when she was a child.

MRS. SOLNESS. Did you now, Halvard! Well, come along in. Supper's ready.

[*She takes* DR. HERDAL'*s arm and goes out with him, right. Meanwhile* HILDE *has gathered her things together.*]

HILDE [*softly and quickly to* SOLNESS]. Was it true what you said? Can you use me in some way?

SOLNESS [*taking her things from her*]. You are the very one I have needed most.

HILDE [*looks at him in joy and wonder and clasps her hands*]. Oh, praise be . . . !

SOLNESS [*tense*]. Well?

HILDE. Then I *have* my kingdom!

SOLNESS [*involuntarily*]. Hilde . . . !

HILDE [*again her mouth trembling*]. Almost—I was going to say.

[*She goes out, right.* SOLNESS *follows her.*]

ACT TWO

One of the smaller sitting-rooms in SOLNESS's *house; pleasantly furnished. In the back wall is a glass door giving out on to the verandah and the garden. Across the right corner is a large bay window, in which stand plant-holders. Corresponding to this, in the left corner, is a bay containing a small door papered like the wall. In each of the side walls is an ordinary door. Downstage right, a console table with a large mirror. Flowers and plants in rich profusion. Downstage left, a sofa with a table and chairs. Further back, a bookcase. Well out into the room, in front of the bay window, a small table and a couple of chairs. It is early in the day.*

SOLNESS is sitting at the small table, with RAGNAR BROVIK's *folder open in front of him. He turns over the drawings, and looks closely at some of them.* MRS. SOLNESS *walks noiselessly about with a little watering-can, watering the flowers. She is dressed in black, as before. Her hat, coat, and parasol are lying on a chair by the mirror.* SOLNESS *follows her occasionally with his eyes without her noticing. Neither of them speaks.*

KAJA FOSLI quietly enters by the door on the left.

SOLNESS [*turning his head and speaking casually*]. Oh, it's you, is it?

KAJA. I just wanted to let you know I'd arrived.

SOLNESS. Yes, yes, very good. Isn't Ragnar there too?

KAJA. No, not yet. He had to stay and wait for the doctor. But he's coming along later to ask you about . . .

SOLNESS. How is the old man today?

KAJA. Bad. He says he's very sorry but he'll have to stay in bed today.

SOLNESS. Of course he must. But you'd better get on with your work now.

KAJA. Yes. [*Stops by the door.*] Will you be wanting to speak to Ragnar when he comes?

SOLNESS. No—not particularly.

[KAJA *goes out again, left.* SOLNESS *remains sitting, looking through the drawings.*]

MRS. SOLNESS [*over by the plants*]. I shouldn't wonder if he, too, died.

SOLNESS [*looks at her*]. He too? Who else do you mean?

MRS. SOLNESS. Ah yes. Old Mr. Brovik—he's also going to die now, Halvard. You'll see.

SOLNESS. Aline dear, don't you think you should go for a little walk?

MRS. SOLNESS. Yes, I suppose I should.

[*She carries on attending to the flowers.*]

SOLNESS [*bent over the drawings*]. Is she still asleep?

MRS. SOLNESS [*looks at him*]. Is it Miss Wangel you are sitting there thinking about.

SOLNESS [*carelessly*]. I just happened to think of her.

MRS. SOLNESS. Miss Wangel was up long ago.

SOLNESS. Was she indeed?

MRS. SOLNESS. When I looked in, she was sitting there seeing to her things.

[*She steps in front of the mirror and begins slowly to put her hat on.*]

SOLNESS [*after a short pause*]. So we did find a use for one of the nurseries after all, Aline.

MRS. SOLNESS. Yes, we did.

SOLNESS. And I think it's better that way than having everything standing empty.

MRS. SOLNESS. The emptiness is dreadful. You are right.

SOLNESS [*closes the folder, rises and walks over to her*]. You'll see, Aline— from now on things are going to be better. Much nicer. Life's going to be easier—especially for *you*.

MRS. SOLNESS [*looks at him*]. From now on?

SOLNESS. Yes. Believe me, Aline . . .

MRS. SOLNESS. You mean—because *she's* come?

SOLNESS [*controlling himself*]. What I mean of course is . . . once we've moved into the new house.

MRS. SOLNESS [*taking her coat*]. You think so, Halvard? That things will be any better *then*?

SOLNESS. I can't honestly see why not. Surely you believe they will, too?

MRS. SOLNESS. Where that new house is concerned, I can't believe anything.

SOLNESS [*displeased*]. I am very sorry to hear it. Because it's mainly for your sake I've built it.

[*He goes to help her on with her coat.*]

MRS. SOLNESS [*moves away*]. You already do far too much for my sake.

SOLNESS [*with some vehemence*]. Now, now, you mustn't say things like that, Aline! I can't bear to hear you say things like that.

MRS. SOLNESS. Very well, Halvard, I won't say them.

SOLNESS. But I meant what I said. You'll see—you are going to find everything very nice over in the new place.

MRS. SOLNESS. Oh, God! Nice . . . for me!

SOLNESS [*eagerly*]. Yes, yes, you will! I am sure you will. You know . . . all sorts of things there are going to remind you of what was once your . . .

MRS. SOLNESS. Of what had once been Father's and Mother's. And which was all burnt down.

SOLNESS [*in a low voice*]. Yes, yes, poor Aline. That was a dreadful blow for you.

MRS. SOLNESS [*cries out in grief*]. Build as much as you will, Halvard— you can never build another real home for me!

SOLNESS [*walks across the room*]. Then for God's sake let's say no more about it.

MRS. SOLNESS. We never do talk about it, generally. You just avoid the subject . . .

SOLNESS [*halts abruptly and looks at her*]. I do? And why should I do that? Avoid the subject?

MRS. SOLNESS. Oh, Halvard, I understand you so well. It's because you want to spare me. And to show me you forgive me—as far as you ever can.

SOLNESS [*stares in astonishment*]. Forgive *you*! You really mean you yourself, Aline!

MRS. SOLNESS. Of course it's myself I mean.

SOLNESS [*involuntarily to himself*]. That too!

MRS. SOLNESS. As for the old house—what happened was meant to be. Heavens, when fate strikes . . .

SOLNESS. Yes, you are right. There's no escaping fate—as they say.

MRS. SOLNESS. But the terrible things that followed the fire . . . ! *That's* something I can never . . . never . . . never . . .

SOLNESS [*vehemently*]. Don't think about it, Aline!

MRS. SOLNESS. I must think about it. And talk about it sometimes, too. Because I don't think I can bear it any longer. Knowing I can never forgive myself . . .

SOLNESS [*exclaiming*]. Yourself!

MRS. SOLNESS. Yes, because really I had two loyalties. One to you, and one to the children. I should have been hard. Not let the horror of it overwhelm me. Or grief either, because my home was burnt down. [*Wrings her hands.*] Oh, if only I *could* have, Halvard!

SOLNESS [*gently, moved, comes towards her*]. Aline . . . you must promise me you'll never again think these thoughts. . . . Please, promise me that, my dear!

MRS. SOLNESS. Oh, God! . . . Promise! promise! Anybody can promise anything. . . .

SOLNESS [*clenches his hands and walks across the room*]. Oh, this is hopeless! Never so much as a glint of the sun! Not a glimmer of light ever enters this home!

MRS. SOLNESS. This is no home, Halvard.

SOLNESS. Ah, no, you're right there. And God knows, perhaps you're right to think it's not going to be any better for us in the new house either.

MRS. SOLNESS. It never will. Just as empty . . . just as desolate there as it is here.

SOLNESS [*vehemently*]. Then why on earth have we built it? Can you tell me that?

MRS. SOLNESS. No, that you must answer yourself.

SOLNESS [*glances at her suspiciously*]. What do you mean by *that*, Aline?

MRS. SOLNESS. What do I mean?

SOLNESS. Yes, damn it! You said it so strangely. As though you were insinuating something.

MRS. SOLNESS. No, I assure you . . .

SOLNESS [*goes closer*]. Oh, I know how things are, thank you very much. I've got eyes *and* I've got ears, Aline! Believe you me!

MRS. SOLNESS. But what is all this? What is it?

SOLNESS [*stands in front of her*]. You always manage to find some sly, hidden meaning even in my most innocent remarks, don't you?

MRS. SOLNESS. Do I? Do *I* do that?

SOLNESS [*laughs*]. Ha! ha! ha! But that's only natural, Aline! When you've got to cope with a sick man in the house. . . .

MRS. SOLNESS [*alarmed*]. Sick? Are you sick, Halvard?

SOLNESS [*shouts*]. A madman then! A lunatic! Call me what you will.

MRS. SOLNESS [*fumbles for the back of the chair and sits down*]. Halvard . . . for God's sake . . . !

SOLNESS. But you're wrong, both of you. Both you and the doctor. There's nothing like that wrong with me. [*He walks up and down the room.* MRS. SOLNESS *follows him anxiously with her eyes. Then he walks across to her and says calmly.*] Actually, there's absolutely nothing wrong with me.

MRS. SOLNESS. No, of course not. But what's troubling you, then?

SOLNESS. Just that sometimes I feel as if I'm cracking up under this terrible burden of debt. . . .

MRS. SOLNESS. Debt, you say? But you're not in debt to anyone, Halvard!

SOLNESS [*quietly, with emotion*]. Endlessly in debt to you . . . to you . . . to you, Aline.

MRS. SOLNESS [*slowly rising*]. What is behind all this? You might as well tell me at once.

SOLNESS. There's nothing behind it. I've never done you any wrong. Never knowingly, never deliberately, that is. And yet—I feel weighed down by a great crushing sense of guilt.

MRS. SOLNESS. Guilt . . . on my account?

SOLNESS. Mainly on your account.

MRS. SOLNESS. Then you are . . . sick after all, Halvard.

SOLNESS [*heavily*]. I suppose I must be. Or something of the kind. [*He looks towards the door, right, which opens.*] Ah! Now things look brighter.

[HILDE WANGEL *comes in. She has made one or two changes in her dress and let down her skirt.*]

HILDE. Good morning, master builder!

SOLNESS [*nods*]. Slept well?

HILDE. Marvellously well! Like a child in a cradle. Oh, I lay there and stretched myself like . . . like a princess!

SOLNESS [*smiling a little*]. Quite comfortable, then.

HILDE. I should say so!

SOLNESS. And I imagine you dreamt, too.

HILDE. Yes. But that was horrid.

SOLNESS. Oh?

HILDE. Yes, because I dreamt I was falling over a terribly high, steep cliff. Don't you ever have that dream yourself?

SOLNESS. Why yes . . . now and then . . .

HILDE. It's very exciting . . . as you go falling, falling . . .

SOLNESS. It makes me feel as if my blood is running cold.

HILDE. Do you tuck your knees up under you as you fall?

SOLNESS. Yes, as high as I possibly can.

HILDE. So do I.

MRS. SOLNESS [*picks up her parasol*]. I think I must go to town now, Halvard. [*To* HILDE.] And I'll try and bring you back a few things you might need.

HILDE [*goes to throw her arms round her neck*]. Oh my dearest, sweetest Mrs. Solness! Really this is too kind of you! Frightfully kind . . .

MRS. SOLNESS [*deprecatingly, as she frees herself*]. Not at all. It's no more than my duty. I'm very glad to do it.

HILDE [*offended, pouts*]. Actually, I don't see why I can't go into town as I am—now that I've got my things looking smart again. Or maybe you think I can't?

MRS. SOLNESS. To tell you the truth, I fancy one or two people might stare at you a little.

HILDE [*snorting*]. Pooh! Is that all! I think that'd be fun!

SOLNESS [*with ill-concealed irritability*]. Yes, but people might start thinking *you* were mad too, you see.

HILDE. Mad? Are there such a lot of mad people in this town?

SOLNESS [*points to his forehead*]. Here you see one, at any rate.

HILDE. You—master builder!

MRS. SOLNESS. Oh, really now, my dear Halvard!

SOLNESS. Haven't you realized that yet?

HILDE. No, I haven't actually. [*Thinks a moment, then gives a little laugh.*] Well, maybe there was one little thing, in fact.

SOLNESS. There you are, you see, Aline!

MRS. SOLNESS. And what sort of thing might that be, Miss Wangel?

HILDE. I'm not telling.

SOLNESS. Oh, please do!

HILDE. No, thank you—I'm not as mad as all that!

MRS. SOLNESS. When you and Miss Wangel are alone, she'll probably tell you, Halvard.

SOLNESS. Oh, you think so?

MRS. SOLNESS. Yes, of course. Because you've known her so long. Ever since she was a child . . . you say.

[*She goes out by the door, left.*]

HILDE [*after a moment*]. Can't your wife bring herself to like me just a little.

SOLNESS. Did she give you that impression?

HILDE. Couldn't you see it?

SOLNESS [*evasively*]. Aline's become rather withdrawn these last few years.

HILDE. Has she?

SOLNESS. If only you could get to know her properly. . . . Because really she's so kind . . . and so good . . . and fundamentally such a fine person. . . .

HILDE [*impatiently*]. But if she's all these things—why did she have to say all that about duty?

SOLNESS. About duty?

HILDE. Yes, she said she'd go out and buy some things for me. Because it was her *duty*, she said. Oh, I can't stand that nasty, horrid word!

SOLNESS. Why not?

HILDE. Because it sounds so cold and sharp and prickly. Duty, duty, duty! Don't you think so, too? That it seems to sting you?

SOLNESS. Hm! I haven't really thought about it.

HILDE. It does! And if she's as nice as you say she is—why should she say a thing like that?

SOLNESS. But, good Lord, what should she have said?

HILDE. She could have said she wanted to do it because she liked me such a frightful lot. She might have said something along those lines. Something that was really warm and sincere, don't you see?

SOLNESS [*looking at her*]. Is that the way you want things?

HILDE. Yes, I do. [*She walks about the room, stops by the bookcase and looks at the books.*] What a lot of books you have.

SOLNESS. Oh, I've collected quite a few.

HILDE. Do you read all these books?

SOLNESS. There was a time when I used to try. Do you read?

HILDE. No! Never! Not any more. I can't really see any point in it.

SOLNESS. That's precisely how I feel, too.

[HILDE *wanders about a little, stops by the small table, opens the folder and turns over some of the papers.*]

HILDE. Did you do all these plans?

SOLNESS. No, they were done by a young assistant of mine.

HILDE. Somebody you have trained yourself?

SOLNESS. Oh yes, I dare say he's learnt a thing or two from me.

HILDE [*sits down*]. Then he's probably very clever? [*Looks for a moment at a drawing.*] Isn't he?

SOLNESS. Oh, not too bad. I can use him. . . .

HILDE. Yes, indeed! He must be frightfully clever.

SOLNESS. You mean you can tell that from his drawings?

HILDE. What? From these bits and pieces? No. But if he's been a pupil of *yours* . . .

SOLNESS. Oh, *that*! Plenty of people have been pupils of mine. But that didn't necessarily make them anything very much.

HILDE [*looks at him and shakes her head*]. Honestly, I can't understand how you can be so stupid.

SOLNESS. Stupid? Do you think I'm so very stupid?

HILDE. I certainly do. If you're to go and let yourself train all these people. . . .

SOLNESS [*starts*]. Well? And why not?

HILDE [*gets up, half in earnest, half laughingly*]. Oh, no, master builder! What's the point of that! Nobody but you should be allowed to build. You should do it all alone. Do everything yourself. Now you know.

SOLNESS [*involuntarily*]. Hilde . . . !

HILDE. Well?

SOLNESS. What on earth made you say that?

HILDE. Why? Do you think I'm completely mad to think that?

SOLNESS. No, that's not what I meant. But now I'll tell you something.

HILDE. Well?

SOLNESS. Here alone . . . in my own secret thoughts . . . I am myself obsessed by that very same idea.

HILDE. Well, I should say that's pretty natural.

SOLNESS [*watching her rather closely*]. And doubtless you'd already noticed it?

HILDE. As a matter of fact I hadn't.

SOLNESS. But just now . . . when you said you thought I was . . . a bit queer? There was one thing, you said. . . .

HILDE. Oh, I was thinking of something quite different.

SOLNESS. What were you thinking?

HILDE. Never you mind.

SOLNESS [*walks across the room*]. All right . . . as you wish. [*Halts by the bay.*] Come over here. I want to show you something.

HILDE [*goes closer*]. What?

SOLNESS. See there? Over in the garden . . . ?

HILDE. Yes?

SOLNESS [*pointing*]. Just beyond where they've been quarrying . . .

HILDE. That new house, you mean.

SOLNESS. The one being built, yes. It's nearly finished.

HILDE. That's a very high tower it's got, isn't it?

SOLNESS. The scaffolding's still up.

HILDE. Is that your new house?

SOLNESS. Yes.

HILDE. The house you are going to move into soon?

SOLNESS. Yes.

HILDE [*looks at him*]. Are there nurseries in that house too?

SOLNESS. Three, like here.

HILDE. And no children.

SOLNESS. No, and never will be.

HILDE [*with a half smile*]. Well, isn't it like I said, then . . . ?

SOLNESS. What do you mean?

HILDE. That you are a little . . . mad, after all.

SOLNESS. Was that what you had in mind?

HILDE. Yes. All those empty nurseries where I was sleeping.

SOLNESS [*drops his voice*]. We did have children . . . Aline and I.

HILDE [*looks intently at him*]. Did you?

SOLNESS. Two little boys. Both the same age.

HILDE. Twins.

SOLNESS. Yes, twins. It's about eleven or twelve years ago now.

HILDE [*cautiously*]. And they are both . . . ? You don't have the twins any longer?

SOLNESS [*with quiet emotion*]. We only had them about three weeks.

Scarcely that. [*Bursts out.*] Oh, Hilde, you don't know how glad I am that you've come! At last I have somebody I can talk to.

HILDE. Can't you talk to . . . to *her*?

SOLNESS. Not about this. Not as I want to . . . and need to. [*Sadly.*] And not about much else, either.

HILDE [*in a low voice*]. Was that all you meant when you said you needed me?

SOLNESS. Mainly that. Yesterday, at least. Today I'm not so certain . . . [*Breaking off.*] Let's sit down over here, Hilde. You sit there on the sofa . . . then you can see the garden. [HILDE *sits down in the corner of the sofa.* SOLNESS *pulls up a chair.*] Would you like to hear about it?

HILDE. Yes, I'd love to sit and listen to you.

SOLNESS [*sits down*]. Then I'll tell you all about it.

HILDE. Now I can look at both you and the garden, master builder. So tell me! Now!

SOLNESS [*points to the bay window*]. Over there, on that high ground . . . where you can see the new house . . .

HILDE. Yes?

SOLNESS. . . . That was where Aline and I lived for the first few years. In those days there was an old house up there that had belonged to her mother. And which we inherited. Along with the whole of that enormous garden, too.

HILDE. Was there a tower on that house as well?

SOLNESS. No, nothing like that. It was a great, ugly, dark barn of a place to look at. But it was pretty cosy and comfortable inside.

HILDE. What did you do, then? Pull the whole thing down?

SOLNESS. No. It burnt down.

HILDE. All of it?

SOLNESS. Yes.

HILDE. Was it a great blow to you?

SOLNESS. It depends how you look at it. That fire was the making of me as a builder . . .

HILDE. Well, but . . . ?

SOLNESS. We had only just got our two little boys . . .

HILDE. The poor little twins.

SOLNESS. They were so sturdy and healthy when they were born. You could positively see them growing from one day to the next.

HILDE. Babies grow fast the first few days.

SOLNESS. A prettier sight you couldn't wish to see—Aline lying there with the two of them. But then came the night of the fire . . .

HILDE [*tense*]. What happened? Tell me! Was anyone burnt?

SOLNESS. No, that wasn't it. They got everybody safely out of the house. . . .

HILDE. Well, what then . . . ?

SOLNESS. Aline suffered a terrible shock. The alarm . . . the scramble to get out . . . the pandemonium . . . and on top of it all the freezing night air. . . . For they had to be carried out just as they were. Both she and the children.

HILDE. And this was too much for them?

SOLNESS. No, not for *them*. But Aline started running a fever. And that affected her milk. She insisted on feeding them herself. It was her duty, she said. And both our little boys . . . [*Clenches his hands.*] . . . They both . . .

HILDE. They didn't survive that?

SOLNESS. No, *that* they didn't survive. That was what took them from us.

HILDE. That must have been terribly hard for you.

SOLNESS. Hard enough for me. But ten times harder for Aline. [*Clenches his hands in silent fury.*] Ah, why do such things happen in this world! [*Curtly and firmly.*] From the day I lost them I've never wanted to build another church.

HILDE. Perhaps not even that church tower of ours, either.

SOLNESS. Not really. I know I was glad and relieved when that tower was finished.

HILDE. *I* know that, too.

SOLNESS. And now I never build anything of that sort any more— never! No churches, and no church towers!

HILDE [*nods slowly*]. Only houses for people to live in.

SOLNESS. Homes for human beings, Hilde.

HILDE. But homes with high towers and spires.

SOLNESS. Those for preference. [*On a lighter note.*] So you see—as I said before—that fire was the thing that made me. As a master builder, I mean.

HILDE. Why don't you call yourself an architect, like the rest?

SOLNESS. I never really had the proper training. Most of what I know I've taught myself.

HILDE. But you made your way to the top, all the same, master builder.

SOLNESS. Yes, thanks to that fire. I divided up most of the grounds into building sites. And *there* I could build exactly the way I wanted. From then on I never looked back.

HILDE [*looks searchingly at him*]. You must surely be a very happy man. The way things have gone for you.

SOLNESS [*darkly*]. Happy? You say that, too? Just like all the others.

HILDE. Well, I feel you *must* be. If only you could stop thinking about those two little boys. . . .

SOLNESS [*slowly*]. Those two little boys . . . they are not so easily forgotten, Hilde.

HILDE [*a little uncertainly*]. Do they still weigh so heavily on you—after all these years?

SOLNESS [*looking steadily at her, without answering*]. A happy man, you said . . .

HILDE. Well, *aren't* you? Apart from that?

SOLNESS [*still looking at her*]. When I was telling you all that business about the fire . . .

HILDE. Well?

SOLNESS. Wasn't there one particular thought that struck you?

HILDE [*tries hard to think*]. No. What have you got in mind?

SOLNESS [*with quiet emphasis*]. That fire, and that alone, was the thing that gave me the chance to build homes. Warm, cheerful, comfortable homes, where fathers and mothers and their children could live together, secure and happy, and feeling that it's good to be alive. And more than anything to belong to each other—in great things and in small.

HILDE [*eagerly*]. Well then, doesn't it make you very happy knowing you can make such lovely homes?

SOLNESS. But the price, Hilde! The terrible price I've had to pay that this might be so.

HILDE. But isn't that also something you can surmount?

SOLNESS. No. To be able to build homes for other people, I have had to renounce . . . for ever renounce . . . any hope of having a home of my own. I mean a home with children. Or even with a father and mother.

HILDE [*cautiously*]. But did you *have* to? For ever, did you say?

SOLNESS [*nods slowly*]. That was the price of 'happiness' people are always talking about. [*With a heavy sigh.*] That happiness . . . hm . . . that happiness wasn't to be got any cheaper, Hilde.

HILDE [*as before*]. But couldn't things still turn out all right?

SOLNESS. Never in this world. Never. That's another consequence of the fire. And of Aline's illness afterwards.

HILDE [*looks at him with an indefinable expression*]. Yet you still go on building all these nurseries.

SOLNESS [*earnestly*]. Haven't you ever noticed, Hilde, how seductive, how inviting . . . the impossible is?

HILDE [*ponders*]. The impossible? [*Eagerly.*] Why yes! Do you feel that too?

SOLNESS. Yes, I do.

HILDE. So you've also something of the troll in you?

SOLNESS. What do you mean—troll?

HILDE. Well, what would *you* call a thing like that?

SOLNESS [*gets up*]. All right, just as you say. [*Vehemently.*] But is it any wonder I'm becoming like a troll . . . the way things are going for me! The way *everything* is . . . everlastingly!

HILDE. How do you mean?

SOLNESS [*in a low voice with inward emotion*]. Mark well what I'm telling you, Hilde. Everything I've managed to achieve, everything I've built and created . . . all the beauty and security, the comfort and the good cheer . . . all the magnificence, even . . . [*Clenches his hands.*] Oh, the very thought of it is terrible . . . !

HILDE. What is so terrible?

SOLNESS. All this I somehow have to make up for. Pay for. Not in money. But in human happiness. And not with my own happiness alone. But also with others'. Don't you see that, Hilde! That's the price my status as an artist has cost me—and others. And every single day I have to stand by and watch this price being paid for me anew. Over and over again—endlessly!

HILDE [*rises and looks fixedly at him*]. You must be thinking of . . . of *her*!

SOLNESS. Yes. Above all of Aline. You see Aline had her vocation in life, too. Quite as much as I had mine. [*His voice trembles.*] But her vocation had to be ruined . . . crushed, smashed to pieces . . . so that mine could go marching on to . . . to some kind of great victory. Because, you know, Aline . . . had a talent for building, too.

HILDE. She had! For building?

SOLNESS [*shakes his head*]. Not houses and towers and spires . . . Not the kind of thing I play about with . . .

HILDE. What, then?

SOLNESS [*softly, with emotion*]. A talent for building children's souls,

Hilde. So building their souls that they might grow straight and fine, nobly and beautifully formed, to their full human stature. That was where Aline's talent lay. And look now where it lies. Unused . . . and for ever unusable. No earthly use for anything. . . . Like a charred heap of ruins.

HILDE. Yes, but even if this is true . . . ?

SOLNESS. It is true. It is. I know it is.

HILDE. Well, even so, you aren't in any way to blame.

SOLNESS [*fixes his eyes on her and nods slowly*]. Ah, that is precisely the great and terrible question. That is the doubt that nags me, day and night.

HILDE. That!

SOLNESS. Well, let's suppose I *was* to blame. In a sort of way.

HILDE. You! For the fire!

SOLNESS. For the whole thing. For everything. . . . And yet . . . I may also be completely innocent.

HILDE [*looks at him with troubled eyes*]. Oh, master builder! If you can say things like that, you must be . . . ill, after all.

SOLNESS. Hm! . . . Don't suppose I'll ever be exactly bursting with health in *that* respect.

[RAGNAR BROVIK *cautiously opens the small door in the corner, left.* HILDE *walks across the room.*]

RAGNAR [*as he sees* HILDE]. Oh, I beg your pardon, Mr. Solness.

[*He is about to withdraw.*]

SOLNESS. No, no, please don't go. Let's get it settled.

RAGNAR. Ah yes . . . if we could!

SOLNESS. Your father's no better, I hear.

RAGNAR. Father is sinking fast now. That's why I beg of you . . . please write something nice on one of my drawings. Something for Father to read before he . . .

SOLNESS [*vehemently*]. I don't want to hear any more about these drawings of yours!

RAGNAR. Have you looked at them?

SOLNESS. Yes, I have.

RAGNAR. And they're no good? And *I'm* no good either?

SOLNESS [*evasively*]. Stay on here with me, Ragnar. You can have everything just the way you want it. Then you can marry Kaja. Live without a care. Perhaps even happily. Only don't think of building on your own.

RAGNAR. Ah, well . . . then I'd better go home and tell Father this. I promised him I would. *Shall* I tell Father this . . . before he dies?

SOLNESS [*with a moan*]. Oh, tell him . . . tell him what you like. What do I care! Best say nothing at all! [*Bursts out.*] There's nothing else I *can* do, Ragnar!

RAGNAR. Then can I take the drawings with me?

SOLNESS. Yes, take them . . . take them away. They're on the table there.

RAGNAR [*walks across*]. Thanks.

HILDE [*placing her hand on the folder*]. No, leave them.

SOLNESS. Why?

HILDE. Because I want to look at them, too.

SOLNESS. But you *have*. [*To* RAGNAR.] Well then, leave them there.

RAGNAR. All right.

SOLNESS. And now straight home to your father.

RAGNAR. Yes, I suppose I'd better.

SOLNESS [*as if in desperation*]. Ragnar, you *mustn't* ask me to do things I *can't* do. Do you hear me, Ragnar! You mustn't.

RAGNAR. No, no. Excuse me. . . .

[*He bows and goes out by the corner door.* HILDE *walks across and sits on a chair by the mirror.*]

HILDE [*looks angrily at* SOLNESS]. That was a nasty thing to do.

SOLNESS. You think so, too?

HILDE. Really very nasty indeed. And hard and wicked and cruel.

SOLNESS. Oh, you don't understand my position.

HILDE. All the same . . . No, you shouldn't be like that.

SOLNESS. You said yourself just now that I was the only one who should be allowed to build.

HILDE. *I* can say things like that. But not *you*.

SOLNESS. Who better than I? Considering the price I've had to pay to get where I am.

HILDE. Oh yes . . . you mean your domestic bliss . . . or whatever you call it.

SOLNESS. And with it my peace of mind.

HILDE [*rises*]. Peace of mind! [*Feelingly.*] Ah yes, you're right! . . . Poor master builder! . . . You must be thinking that . . .

SOLNESS [*with a quiet chuckle*]. You just sit down again, Hilde, and I'll tell you something funny.

HILDE [*expectantly, sits down*]. Well?

SOLNESS. It all sounds so absurdly trivial. You see, the whole thing comes down in the end to a crack in the chimney.

HILDE. Is that all?

SOLNESS. Yes, to begin with.

[*He moves a chair closer to* HILDE's *and sits down.*]

HILDE [*impatiently slapping her knee*]. So there was this crack in the chimney?

SOLNESS. Long, long before the fire, I had noticed the crack in the flue. Every time I was in the loft, I looked to see if it was still there.

HILDE. And it was?

SOLNESS. Yes. Because nobody else knew about it.

HILDE. And you didn't say anything?

SOLNESS. No, I didn't.

HILDE. Never thought about repairing it?

SOLNESS. I thought about it . . . but it never got any further than that. Every time I thought I'd get on with it, a hand seemed to reach out and stop me. Not today, I'd think. Tomorrow. So nothing ever got done.

HILDE. Yes, but why did you always keep putting it off?

SOLNESS. Because I'd got an idea. [*Slowly, and in a low voice.*] Through that little black crack in the chimney I might perhaps make my way—to success as a builder.

HILDE [*staring into space*]. That must have been exciting.

SOLNESS. Irresistible almost. Utterly irresistible. At that time, the whole thing seemed so simple, so trivial. I wanted it to happen in winter some time. Just before dinner. I would be out for a drive in the sleigh with Aline. The people at home would have had great fires going in the stoves . . .

HILDE. Of course, it would be fearfully cold that day, wouldn't it?

SOLNESS. Fairly bitter, yes. And they would want the place nice and warm for Aline to come back to.

HILDE. I imagine she feels the cold, rather.

SOLNESS. She does. And then on our way home we would see the smoke.

HILDE. Just the smoke?

SOLNESS. First the smoke. But when we reached the front gates, the whole of that great wooden box would be a roaring mass of flames. . . . That's how I wanted it to be, you see.

HILDE. Oh, why in Heaven's name couldn't it have happened like that!

SOLNESS. Ah, you may well ask, Hilde.

HILDE. But tell me, master builder. Are you absolutely certain the fire was caused by the crack in the chimney?

SOLNESS. On the contrary, I am quite sure the crack in the chimney had nothing to do with the fire.

HILDE. What!

SOLNESS. It has been clearly established that the fire broke out in a cupboard—in an entirely different part of the house.

HILDE. Then why all this moaning about the crack in the chimney?

SOLNESS. May I go on talking to you a little longer, Hilde?

HILDE. Yes, if only you'll try and talk sensibly. . . .

SOLNESS. I'll try.

[*He moves his chair closer.*]

HILDE. Come on! Out with it, master builder.

SOLNESS [*confidentially*]. Don't you believe too, Hilde, that you find certain people have been singled out, specially chosen, gifted with the power and the ability to *want* something, to *desire* something, to *will* something . . . so insistently . . . and so ruthlessly . . . that they inevitably get it in the end? Don't you believe that?

HILDE [*with an inscrutable expression in her eyes*]. If that is so, we'll see some day . . . if I am one of the chosen.

SOLNESS. One doesn't achieve such great things *alone*. Oh, no. One has to have . . . helpers and servants . . . if anything's to come of it. But they never come of their own accord. One has to summon them, imperiously, inwardly, you understand.

HILDE. Who are these helpers and servants?

SOLNESS. Oh, we can talk about that some other time. Let's keep to the matter of the fire for the present.

HILDE. Don't you think that fire would have occurred anyway—even if you hadn't wished for it?

SOLNESS. If old Knut Brovik had owned the house, it would never have burnt down quite so conveniently for *him*. I'm quite certain of that. He doesn't know how to call upon these helpers . . . nor upon the servants, either. [*Gets up restlessly.*] You see, Hilde . . . I *am* actually the one who's to blame for those two little boys having to pay with their lives. And perhaps I'm to blame too for Aline never becoming what she could and should have been. And what she most of all wanted to be.

HILDE. Yes, but if it's only these helpers and servants who . . . ?

SOLNESS. Who called on the helpers and servants? *I* did! And they came and did my bidding. [*In rising excitement.*] That's what people call being lucky. But let me tell you what that sort of luck feels like! It feels as if my breast were a great expanse of raw flesh. And these helpers and servants go flaying off skin from other people's bodies to patch *my* wound. Yet the wound never heals . . . never! Oh, if only you knew how it sometimes burns and throbs.

HILDE [*looks attentively at him*]. You *are* ill, master builder. Very ill, I rather think.

SOLNESS. Say *mad*. For that's what you mean.

HILDE. No, I don't think there's anything much wrong with your reason.

SOLNESS. *What*, then? Out with it!

HILDE. What I'm wondering is whether you weren't born with rather a fragile conscience.

SOLNESS. Fragile conscience? What the devil's that?

HILDE. I mean your conscience is actually very fragile. Sort of delicate. Won't stand up to things. Can't bear much weight.

SOLNESS [*growling*]. H'm. What should one's conscience be like then, may I ask?

HILDE. In your case I should want to see a conscience that was . . . well, thoroughly robust.

SOLNESS. Robust, eh? Well. Have *you* a robust conscience, I wonder?

HILDE. Yes, I think so. I've never noticed it wasn't.

SOLNESS. Probably hasn't been particularly tested, I imagine.

HILDE [*with a trembling of the lips*]. Oh, leaving Father wasn't all that easy. I'm terribly fond of him.

SOLNESS. Oh, come! When it's just for a month or two . . .

HILDE. I'll probably never go back home again.

SOLNESS. Never? Why did you leave him, then?

HILDE [*half serious, half in jest*]. Aren't you forgetting again that the ten years are up?   ●

SOLNESS. Oh, nonsense! Was there something wrong at home? Eh?

HILDE [*utterly serious*]. Something inside me forced me, drove me here. Drew me, tempted me, too.

SOLNESS [*eagerly*]. There you are! There you are, Hilde! There's a troll in you, too. Just as in me. And it's the troll in us, you see, that calls on the powers outside. Then we *have* to give in—whether we like it or not.

HILDE. I rather think you are right, master builder.

SOLNESS [*walking about the room*]. It's fantastic the number of devils there are in the world you never even *see*, Hilde!

HILDE. Devils, too?

SOLNESS [*stops*]. Good devils and bad devils. Blond devils and dark devils! If only you could be sure which kind had hold of you—the light ones or the dark! [*Walks about.*] Ha! There'd be no bother then.

HILDE [*follows him with her eyes*]. Or if one had a really tough and vigorous conscience. So that one *dared* to do what one *wanted*.

SOLNESS [*halts by the console table*]. I think in this respect most people are just as cowardly as I am.

HILDE. Could be.

SOLNESS [*leans against the table*]. In the sagas . . . Have you read any of these old sagas?

HILDE. Oh, yes! In the days when I used to read books, I . . .

SOLNESS. The sagas are all about the vikings who sailed to foreign lands and plundered and burned and killed . . .

HILDE. And carried off women . . .

SOLNESS. And held them captive . . .

HILDE. Took them home with them in their ships . . .

SOLNESS. And behaved towards them like . . . like the worst of trolls.

HILDE [*staring straight ahead with half-veiled eyes*]. I think that must be exciting.

SOLNESS [*with a short, gruff laugh*]. Taking women, you mean?

HILDE. *Being* taken.

SOLNESS [*looks at her for a moment*]. Indeed.

HILDE [*as though breaking off her thoughts*]. But you were saying about these vikings, master builder . . . ?

SOLNESS. Ah, yes. Those fellows now—they had robust consciences all right. They hadn't lost any of their appetite when they got home. Happy as children they were, too. As for the women—very often they wouldn't hear tell of leaving them. Can you understand that sort of thing, Hilde?

HILDE. I understand these women perfectly.

SOLNESS. Aha! Perhaps you'd do the same yourself?

HILDE. Why not?

SOLNESS. Live . . . of your own free will . . . with a wild brute like that?

HILDE. If he was a brute I'd grown really fond of, I . . .

SOLNESS. *Could* you grow fond of a man like that?

HILDE. Good Lord, you can't always help whom you get fond of, can you?

SOLNESS [*looks thoughtfully at her*]. No . . . I dare say it's the troll within us decides *that*.

HILDE [*with a half laugh*]. Along with all those other blessed devils you know so well. The fair ones and the dark ones.

SOLNESS [*warmly and quietly*]. I hope the devils choose kindly for you, Hilde.

HILDE. They have chosen for me, already. Once and for all.

SOLNESS [*looks intently at her*]. Hilde . . . you are like some wild forest bird.

HILDE. Far from it. I don't hide myself away in the bushes.

SOLNESS. No, no. There's maybe more of the bird of prey in you.

HILDE. Yes . . . perhaps. [*With great vehemence.*] And why not a bird of prey! Why shouldn't I go hunting, too? Take the prey I want? If I can get my claws into it. And hold it firm.

SOLNESS. Hilde . . . do you know what you are?

HILDE. Yes, I'm some strange kind of bird.

SOLNESS. No. You are like the early dawn. When I look at you, it's as though I were looking at the sunrise.

HILDE. Tell me, master builder—are you sure you have never called to me? Inwardly, I mean?

SOLNESS [*quietly and slowly*]. I rather think I must have.

HILDE. What do you want of me?

SOLNESS. You are youth, Hilde.

HILDE [*smiling*]. That youth you are so afraid of?

SOLNESS [*nods slowly*]. And to which in my heart I am drawn so sorely.

[HILDE *rises, walks over to the little table and picks up* RAGNAR BROVIK's *folder.*]

HILDE [*holding the folder out to him*]. Now what about these drawings. . . .

SOLNESS [*curtly, waving it aside*]. Put those things away! I've seen enough of them.

HILDE. Yes, but you're going to endorse them for him, aren't you?

SOLNESS. Endorse them! Never in this world.

HILDE. With that poor old man lying at death's door! Can't you do him and his son this one kindness before they are parted? Then perhaps he might get the commission to build it, too.

SOLNESS. Yes, that's precisely what he would do. He'll have made sure of that all right, our fine young friend.

HILDE. But, good Lord, even if he has, couldn't you tell a white lie for once—just a little one?

SOLNESS. Lie? [*Furious.*] Hilde—get those damn drawings out of my sight!

HILDE [*withdraws the folder a little*]. Now, now—don't bite me. You talk about trolls. I think you are behaving a bit like a troll yourself. [*Looks round.*] Where do you keep your pen and ink?

SOLNESS. Don't keep any in here.

HILDE [*walks to the door*]. But that girl will have some out here. . . .

SOLNESS. Stay where you are, Hilde! . . . You wanted me to tell a lie, you said. Well, I suppose I might, for his poor old father's sake. Because . . . I broke him once. Smashed him.

HILDE. Him, too?

SOLNESS. I needed room for myself. But this Ragnar . . . he must never on any account be allowed to get ahead.

HILDE. Poor boy, he's not likely to, is he? If he isn't much good, then . . .

SOLNESS [*comes closer, looks at her and whispers*]. Once Ragnar Brovik gets started, he'll have me down in the dust. He'll break me . . . just as I broke his father.

HILDE. Break *you*? So he *is* good?

SOLNESS. He's good all right, don't you worry! He represents youth standing there ready to beat upon my door. Ready to finish off Master Builder Solness.

HILDE [*looks at him with quiet reproach*]. And yet you wanted to shut him out. For shame, master builder!

SOLNESS. It's cost me enough already, this battle I've fought. Besides, I'm afraid the helpers and servants might not obey me any more.

HILDE. Then you'll just have to manage on your own. Nothing else for it.

SOLNESS. Hopeless, Hilde. My luck will turn. Sooner or later. Retribution is inexorable.

HILDE [*fearfully, holding her hands over her ears*]. Don't say things like that! Do you want to kill me! Do you want to rob me of more than life itself!

SOLNESS. And what is that?

HILDE. To see you great. See you with a garland in your hand. High, high up on a church tower. [*Calm again.*] So get out your pencil. You must surely have a pencil on you?

SOLNESS [*takes out his notebook*]. I have one here.

HILDE [*putting the folder on the table*]. Good. Now we'll both sit down here, master builder. [SOLNESS *sits at the table.* HILDE, *behind him, leans over the back of the chair.*] And now we'll write on the drawings. Something really nice and really kind we'll write. For this nasty old Roar, or whatever his name is.

SOLNESS [*writes a few words, turns his head and looks up at her*]. Tell me one thing, Hilde.

HILDE. Yes?

SOLNESS. If you've in fact been waiting for me all these ten years . . .

HILDE. Well?

SOLNESS. Why didn't you write to me? Then I could have answered you.

HILDE [*swiftly*]. No, no, no! That's just what I didn't want.

SOLNESS. Why not?

HILDE. I was afraid that might spoil everything. . . . But we were going to write something on the drawings, master builder.

SOLNESS. So we were.

HILDE [*leaning over him and watching as he writes*]. Very kind and generous. Oh, how I hate . . . how I hate this . . . Roald.

SOLNESS [*writing*]. Have you never really *cared* for anyone, Hilde?

HILDE [*in a hard voice*]. What did you say?

SOLNESS. I asked whether you'd ever really cared for anyone.

HILDE. Anyone else, I suppose you mean?

SOLNESS [*looks up at her*]. For anyone else, yes. Haven't you ever? All these ten years? Never?

HILDE. Oh yes, now and again. When I was really furious with you for not coming.

SOLNESS. So you have taken an interest in other people?

HILDE. A little. For a week or so. Good Lord, master builder, you know how things are.

SOLNESS. Hilde . . . what have you come here for?

HILDE. Don't waste time on chattering. All this time that poor old man might be dying.

SOLNESS. Answer me, Hilde. What do you want of me?

HILDE. I want my kingdom.

SOLNESS. H'm. . . .

[*He glances quickly at the door, left, and then goes on writing on the drawings.* MRS. SOLNESS *comes in at that moment; she is carrying some parcels.*]

MRS. SOLNESS. I've brought a few of the things for you myself, Miss Wangel. The larger parcels are being delivered later.

HILDE. Oh, really how extremely kind of you!

MRS. SOLNESS. No more than my duty. Nothing else.

SOLNESS [*reading through what he has written*]. Aline!

MRS. SOLNESS. Yes?

SOLNESS. Did you notice whether the girl—the book-keeper was out there?

MRS. SOLNESS. Yes, of course she was.

SOLNESS [*puts the drawings in the folder*]. H'm. . . .

MRS. SOLNESS. She was standing by the desk—as she always is when I walk through the room.

SOLNESS [*gets up*]. Then I'll just give this to her. And tell her that . . .

HILDE [*takes the folder from him*]. Oh, no! That pleasure is mine! [*She walks towards the door but turns.*] What's she called?

SOLNESS. She's called Miss Fosli.

HILDE. Ugh, that sounds so cold! Her first name, I mean?

SOLNESS. Kaja—I think.

HILDE [*opens the door and shouts out*]. Kaja! Come in here! Hurry! The master builder wants to speak to you.

[KAJA FOSLI *appears at the door.*]

KAJA [*looks at him, terrified*]. Here I am. . . .

HILDE [*hands her the folder*]. Look, Kaja! You can take these now. The master builder has written something on them.

KAJA. Oh, at last!

SOLNESS. Take them to the old man as quickly as you can.

KAJA. I'll take them home at once.

SOLNESS. Yes, do that. And this means Ragnar can do the building.

KAJA. Oh, please can he come and thank you for everything . . . ?

SOLNESS [*hard*]. I want no thanks. You can tell him that from me.

KAJA. Yes, I'll . . .

SOLNESS. And tell him at the same time that from now on I've no more use for him. Or for you either.

KAJA [*softly, tremulously*]. Not for me either!

SOLNESS. You'll have other things to think about now. And to look after. And isn't that just as it should be? Now, off home you go with those drawings, Miss Fosli. Quickly! Do you hear!

KAJA [*as before*]. Yes, Mr. Solness.

[*She goes out.*]

MRS. SOLNESS. Heavens, what shifty eyes that girl has.

SOLNESS. What? That poor little creature?

MRS. SOLNESS. Ah, I've got eyes to see, Halvard. . . . Are you really giving them notice?

SOLNESS. Yes.

MRS. SOLNESS. The girl, too?

SOLNESS. Isn't that what you wanted?

MRS. SOLNESS. But how will you manage without *her* . . . ? Ah, yes! You've probably somebody else up your sleeve, Halvard.

HILDE [*gaily*]. Well, I wouldn't be much good behind a desk, anyway.

SOLNESS. Now, now . . . things will work out somehow, Aline. You just give your mind now to the business of moving into the new house, as soon as possible. This evening we'll have the topping-out . . . [*Turns to* HILDE.] We'll put the wreath right high up on the very top of the tower. What do you say to *that*, Miss Hilde?

HILDE [*looks at him with glistening eyes*]. It'll be absolutely marvellous to see you so high up again!

SOLNESS. Me!

MRS. SOLNESS. Dear God, Miss Wangel, put that out of your mind! My husband . . . ! When he gets so dizzy?

HILDE. Dizzy! No, surely not!

MRS. SOLNESS. Oh, he does.

HILDE. But I've seen him myself right at the top of a high church tower.

MRS. SOLNESS. Yes, I've heard people say that. But it's quite impossible. . . .

SOLNESS [*vehemently*]. Impossible . . . yes, impossible! But I did it, all the same.

MRS. SOLNESS. How can you say that, Halvard? You can't even bear to go out on to the first floor balcony here. You've always been like that.

SOLNESS. You might see something different tonight.

MRS. SOLNESS [*in alarm*]. No, no, no! Please God, don't let me ever see such a thing! I'll send for the doctor immediately. He'll put a stop to it.

SOLNESS. But, Aline . . . !

MRS. SOLNESS. I will. Because you're ill, Halvard. There's no other explanation! Oh, God! Oh, God!

[*She goes quickly out, right.*]

HILDE [*looks intently at him*]. *Is* it true, or isn't it?

SOLNESS. That I get dizzy?

HILDE. That *my* master builder dare not . . . cannot climb as high as he builds?

SOLNESS. Is that the way you see it?

HILDE. Yes.

SOLNESS. I'm beginning to think no part of me is safe from you.

HILDE [*looks towards the bay window*]. Up there. Right up there. . . .

SOLNESS. You could live in the topmost room in the tower, Hilde. . . . Could live there like a princess.

HILDE [*flatly, between earnest and jest*]. Yes, that's what you promised me.

SOLNESS. *Did* I, in fact?

HILDE. For shame, master builder! You said I was to be a princess. That you would give me a kingdom. And then you took me and . . . Well!

SOLNESS [*cautiously*]. Are you quite sure it isn't some kind of dream . . . some fantasy that's taken hold of you.

HILDE [*sharply*]. You mean you didn't do it?

SOLNESS. Don't really know . . . [*More quietly.*] But one thing I do know now, and that is that I . . .

HILDE. That you . . . ? Say it!

SOLNESS. . . . That I ought to have done it.

HILDE [*bursts out gaily*]. You could never be dizzy!

SOLNESS. Tonight we'll put up the wreath . . . Princess Hilde.

HILDE [*with a bitter grimace*]. Over your new home . . . yes.

SOLNESS. Over the new house. Which will never be a home for me.

[*He goes out through the garden door.*]

HILDE [*stares straight ahead with half-closed eyes and whispers to herself; the only words heard are:*] . . . terribly exciting. . . .

ACT THREE

A large broad verandah belonging to SOLNESS'S *house. Left, part of the house can be seen, with a door leading out on to the verandah. Right, the railings of the verandah. At the back, a flight of steps leads down from the narrow end of the verandah to the garden below. Tall old trees in the garden extend their branches over the verandah and towards the house. Extreme right, in among the trees, a glimpse is caught of the lower part of the new villa, with scaffolding round the tower section. In the background, the garden is bounded by an old wooden fence. Beyond the fence is a street with mean dilapidated cottages.*

Sunlit clouds against the evening sky. On the verandah by the wall of the house stands a garden bench, in front of which is a long table. On the other side of the table an armchair and some stools. All the furniture is wickerwork.

MRS. SOLNESS, *wrapped in a large white crêpe shawl, sits resting in the armchair gazing out to the right.*

After a moment HILDE WANGEL *comes up the steps from the garden. She is dressed as before and is wearing her hat. On her breast she wears a little bunch of small garden flowers.*

MRS. SOLNESS [*turning her head slightly*]. Been for a walk in the garden, Miss Wangel?

HILDE. Yes, I've been down there having a look round.

MRS. SOLNESS. And found some flowers too, I see.

HILDE. Yes, I have! There are lots and lots of them, down in among the bushes.

MRS. SOLNESS. Oh, *are* there? Still? I hardly ever go down there.

HILDE [*approaching*]. What? I imagined you rushing down there every day.

MRS. SOLNESS [*with a faint smile*]. I don't 'rush' anywhere. Not any more.

HILDE. But don't you go every so often, just to look in on all the lovely things down there?

MRS. SOLNESS. It's all become so remote. I am almost afraid to look at it again.

HILDE. Your own garden?

MRS. SOLNESS. I don't feel it *is* mine any more.

HILDE. Oh, come now . . . ?

MRS. SOLNESS. No, no it isn't. Not like it was in Mother's and Father's day. They've taken such an awful lot of the garden away, Miss Wangel. Do you know, they've split it all up and gone and built houses on it, for a lot of strangers! People I don't even know. And they sit there in their windows looking at me.

HILDE [*brightly*]. Mrs. Solness?

MRS. SOLNESS. Yes?

HILDE. May I stay here beside you for a little while?

MRS. SOLNESS. Certainly, if you would like to.

[HILDE *moves a stool across to the armchair and sits down.*]

HILDE. Ah! Here you can really sit and sun yourself. Like a cat.

MRS. SOLNESS [*places her hand gently on* HILDE's *neck*]. How nice you wanting to sit beside *me.* I thought you were going in to see my husband.

HILDE. What would I want with him?

MRS. SOLNESS. To help him, I suppose.

HILDE. No, thank you. Anyway he isn't in. He's over there with the workmen. But he looked so fierce that I didn't dare speak to him.

MRS. SOLNESS. Oh, he's very mild and gentle, really.

HILDE. *He* is!

MRS. SOLNESS. You still don't know him properly yet, Miss Wangel.

HILDE [*looks affectionately at her*]. Are you glad you're moving into the new house?

MRS. SOLNESS. I should be glad, really. It's what Halvard wants. . . .

HILDE. Oh, not just for that, surely.

MRS. SOLNESS. Oh yes, Miss Wangel. After all it's my duty—doing what *he* wants. Just that it's often rather hard to make oneself fit in.

HILDE. Yes, that must be hard.

MRS. SOLNESS. Believe me, it is. And when you're only a poor creature like myself. . . .

HILDE. When you have gone through as much as you have, you mean. . . .

MRS. SOLNESS. How do you know about that?

HILDE. Your husband told me.

MRS. SOLNESS. He rarely talks about these things to me. Yes, indeed, I've been through a great deal in my lifetime, Miss Wangel.

HILDE [*looks at her sympathetically and nods slowly*]. Poor Mrs. Solness. First there was that fire . . .

MRS. SOLNESS [*with a sigh*]. Yes, I lost everything.

HILDE. Then worse was to follow.

MRS. SOLNESS [*looks questioningly at her*]. Worse?

HILDE. The worst thing of all.

MRS. SOLNESS. What do you mean?

HILDE [*softly*]. You lost your two little boys.

MRS. SOLNESS. Oh, them, yes. Well, you know, that was something else again. That was an act of destiny. One must learn to accept such things and be thankful.

HILDE. Do you do that?

MRS. SOLNESS. Not always, I'm afraid. I know very well that it's my duty. But I can't.

HILDE. Ah, well. I think that's understandable.

MRS. SOLNESS. Time and time again I have to tell myself that it was a just punishment . . .

HILDE. How?

MRS. SOLNESS. Because I wasn't resolute enough in misfortune.

HILDE. But I don't understand. . . .

MRS. SOLNESS. No, no, Miss Wangel. . . . Don't talk to me any more about my two little boys. We need not be sad about them. They are happy where they are—so happy now. No, it's the small losses in life that cut deep into the heart. Losing things that other people think nothing of.

HILDE [*puts her arms on* MRS. SOLNESS's *knee and looks affectionately up at her*]. Dear Mrs. Solness, tell me! What things?

MRS. SOLNESS. Just little things. Like I said. All the old portraits on the walls were burnt. And all the old silk dresses were burnt. Things that had been in the family for years and years. And all Mother's and Grandmother's lace—that was burnt too. And even the jewels! [*Sadly.*] And all the dolls.

HILDE. The dolls?

MRS. SOLNESS [*choking with tears*]. I had nine lovely dolls.

HILDE. And they were burnt too?

MRS. SOLNESS. All of them. Oh, I found that hard—so hard.

HILDE. Had you put them all away, then? From when you were little?

MRS. SOLNESS. Not put away. The dolls and I had gone on living together.

HILDE. After you had grown up?

MRS. SOLNESS. Yes, long after that.

HILDE. And after you were married, too?

MRS. SOLNESS. Oh, yes. As long as he didn't see, it was . . . But then they all got burnt, poor things. Nobody thought of saving *them*. Oh, it's so sad when you think about it. Now, you mustn't laugh at me, Miss Wangel.

HILDE. I'm not laughing.

MRS. SOLNESS. Because in a way they too were living things, you know. I carried them under my heart. Like little unborn children.

[DR. HERDAL, *hat in hand, comes out through the door and catches sight of* MRS. SOLNESS *and* HILDE.]

DR. HERDAL. You'll catch cold sitting out here, Mrs. Solness.

MRS. SOLNESS. It seems nice and warm out here today.

DR. HERDAL. Ah, well. But is there something the matter? You sent me a note.

MRS. SOLNESS [*gets up*]. There's something I must talk to you about.

DR. HERDAL. Very well. Then perhaps we'd better go inside. [*To* HILDE.] In your mountaineering kit again today, Miss Wangel?

HILDE [*gaily, as she rises*]. Rather! In full regalia! But there's no climbing and breaking my neck for me today. We two will sit nicely down below and watch, Doctor.

DR. HERDAL. What are we supposed to watch?

MRS. SOLNESS [*in a low and terrified voice, to* HILDE]. Hush, hush, for Heaven's sake! He's coming! Try and persuade him to give up this idea. And do let us be friends, Miss Wangel. Can't we?

HILDE [*throws her arms impetuously round* MRS. SOLNESS's *neck*]. Oh, if only we could.

MRS. SOLNESS [*freeing herself gently*]. There, there! Here he is, Doctor! I'd like a word with you.

DR. HERDAL. Is it about him?

MRS. SOLNESS. Yes, it's about him. Come inside.

[*She and the doctor go into the house. A moment later* SOLNESS *comes up the steps from the garden.* HILDE's *face takes on a serious expression.*]

SOLNESS [*glances towards the door of the house, which is cautiously closed from inside*]. Have you noticed, Hilde, that as soon as I come, she goes.

HILDE. I have noticed that your coming makes her go.

SOLNESS. Perhaps. But I can't help that. [*Looks attentively at her.*] Are you cold, Hilde? You look as if you are.

HILDE. I've just emerged from a tomb.

SOLNESS. What do you mean?

HILDE. That the frost has seized my bones, master builder.

SOLNESS [*slowly*]. I think I understand. . . .

HILDE. What are you doing up here?

SOLNESS. I saw you from over there.

HILDE. Then you must have seen her too?

SOLNESS. I knew she'd go the moment I came.

HILDE. Does it hurt you very much—the way she avoids you?

SOLNESS. In one way it's a kind of relief.

HILDE. That you don't have to face her?

SOLNESS. Yes.

HILDE. That you're not constantly being reminded how hard she's taking it—this about the two boys.

SOLNESS. Yes. Chiefly that.

[HILDE *walks across the verandah with her hands clasped behind her back, stands by the railing and looks out over the garden.*]

SOLNESS [*after a short pause*]. Were you talking with her for long?

[HILDE *stands motionless and does not answer.*]

SOLNESS. I said, was it for long?

[HILDE *is silent as before.*]

SOLNESS. What did she talk about, Hilde?

[HILDE *remains silent.*]

SOLNESS. Poor Aline! It was probably about the boys.

[HILDE *shudders nervously, then she nods rapidly several times.*]

SOLNESS. She'll never get over it. Never, never get over it. [*He comes closer.*] Now you're standing there like a statue again. You also stood like that last night.

HILDE [*turns and looks at him with large serious eyes*]. I want to leave.

SOLNESS [*sharply*]. Leave!

HILDE. Yes.

SOLNESS. But I won't let you!

HILDE. What is there for me to do here now?

SOLNESS. Just stay here, Hilde!

HILDE [*looks him up and down*]. Oh yes, thank you very much. But it wouldn't stop at *that*.

SOLNESS [*impulsively*]. So much the better!

HILDE [*vehemently*]. I can't hurt someone I *know*! Can't take what belongs to her.

SOLNESS. Who says you will?

HILDE [*continuing*]. A stranger, yes! That's something quite different! Somebody I'd never set eyes on. But anybody I'd been close to . . . ! No! No! Ugh!

SOLNESS. But I've never suggested anything else!

HILDE. Oh, master builder, you know very well what would happen. And that's why I'm leaving.

SOLNESS. And what will happen to me when you are gone? What will I have to live for? Afterwards?

HILDE [*with the enigmatic expression in her eyes*]. There's no need to worry about *you*. You have your duty towards her. Live for that duty.

SOLNESS. Too late. These powers . . . these . . . these . . .

HILDE. . . . Devils . . .

SOLNESS. Yes, devils! And the troll in me too. They have drained her of all her life's blood. [*Laughs despairingly.*] And it was for my sake they did it! Yes! [*Heavily.*] And now she is dead—on my account. And here I am, chained alive to this dead woman. [*In wild anguish.*] Me . . . a man who *cannot* live a joyless life!

HILDE [*walks round the table and sits down on the bench, her elbows on the table and her head in her hands; she sits a moment looking at him*]. What are you going to build next?

SOLNESS [*shakes his head*]. I don't think I'll be building very much more.

HILDE. No more cheerful family homes? For mother and father and the children.

SOLNESS. God knows if there'll be any call for that kind of thing from now on.

HILDE. Poor master builder! When for ten years you've given your whole life to that very thing.

SOLNESS. Yes, you may well say that, Hilde.

HILDE [*breaking out*]. Oh, this whole business is so stupid, so absolutely stupid!

SOLNESS. What is?

HILDE. This not daring to reach out and lay hold on happiness. On life! Just because standing in the way happens to be somebody one knows!

SOLNESS. Somebody one has no right to push aside.

HILDE. I only wonder if one really does have the right, in fact? Yet even so. . . . Oh, if only one could fall asleep and leave the whole sorry business behind!

[*She lays her arms flat down upon the table, rests the left side of her head on her hands and shuts her eyes.*]

SOLNESS [*turns the armchair round and sits down by the table*]. Did you have a cheerful happy home—in your father's house, Hilde?

HILDE [*motionless and answering as though half asleep*]. All I had was a cage.

SOLNESS. And you don't want to go back there again?

HILDE [*as before*]. A forest bird never wants a cage.

SOLNESS. Preferring to swoop through the empty sky . . .

HILDE [*continuing as before*]. To swoop upon its prey . . .

SOLNESS [*resting his gaze upon her*]. Ah, any man with a bit of viking spirit . . .

HILDE [*in an ordinary voice, opening her eyes but not moving*]. And what else? Tell me that!

SOLNESS. A robust conscience.

[HILDE *sits up animatedly on the bench. Her eyes again glisten happily.*]

HILDE [*nods to him*]. I know what you'll build next time!

SOLNESS. Then you know more than I do, Hilde.

HILDE. Yes. But these master builders—they're so stupid, you know.

SOLNESS. So what will it be?

HILDE [*nods again*]. The castle.

SOLNESS. What castle?

HILDE. *My* castle, of course.

SOLNESS. You want a castle now?

HILDE. You owe me a kingdom, don't you?

SOLNESS. That's what you keep telling me.

HILDE. Well then! You owe me this kingdom. And surely any kingdom carries a castle with it, doesn't it?

SOLNESS [*more and more animatedly*]. Yes, that's generally the way.

HILDE. Good! Then build it for me! Quickly!

SOLNESS [*laughs*]. This very minute, eh?

HILDE. Of course! Time's up! Ten years. And I'm not waiting any longer. So—bring out the castle, master builder!

SOLNESS. It's no easy matter owing *you* anything, Hilde.

HILDE. You should have thought of that before. Now it's too late. So! [*Beating on the table.*] Out with the castle! It's *my* castle! I want it at once!

SOLNESS [*more seriously, leans over towards her with his arms on the table*]. How do you picture this castle, Hilde?

[*Her expression slowly changes, and she seems to be gazing deep into her own soul.*]

HILDE [*slowly*]. My castle shall stand on high ground. Very high it must stand. And open to all sides. So I can see into the far, far distance.

SOLNESS. With a high tower, I suppose?

HILDE. A tremendously high tower. And at the very top of the tower there's to be a balcony. And out up there I shall stand . . .

SOLNESS [*involuntarily clutches at his forehead*]. How you can enjoy standing at such a dizzy height . . .

HILDE. But of course! That's where I shall stand looking at the others —at those who build churches. And homes for father and mother and the children. And you can also come up and have a look.

SOLNESS [*in a low voice*]. Will the master builder be allowed to come up to his princess?

HILDE. If the master builder wishes it.

SOLNESS [*more softly*]. Then I think the master builder will come.

HILDE [*nods*]. The master builder—he will come.

SOLNESS. But he'll never build again. Poor old master builder!

HILDE [*animatedly*]. Yes, he will! We two will do it together. And we'll build the loveliest . . . quite the loveliest thing in all the world.

SOLNESS [*tense*]. Hilde! Tell me what that is!

HILDE [*looks at him with a smile, shakes her head a little, pouts, and speaks to him as though to a child*]. These master builders—what very, very stupid people they are.

SOLNESS. Yes, of course they're stupid. But tell me what it is! What is it that's quite the loveliest thing in all the world. Which we two are to build together?

HILDE [*is silent for a moment and then says with an enigmatic expression in her eyes*]. Castles in the air.

SOLNESS. Castles in the air?

HILDE [*nods*]. Yes, castles in the air! Do you know what a castle in the air is?

SOLNESS. From what you say, it's the loveliest thing in the world.

HILDE [*rises abruptly and makes a gesture of repudiation with her hand*]. Yes, yes, of course! Castles in the air—they're so easy to take refuge in. So easy to build, too . . . [*Looks scornfully at him.*] Particularly for master builders with . . . weak nerves.

SOLNESS [*rises*]. After today we two will build together, Hilde.

HILDE [*with a doubting smile*]. A *proper* castle in the air?

SOLNESS. Yes, with a real foundation.

[RAGNAR BROVIK *comes out of the house. He is carrying a large green wreath with flowers and silk ribbons.*]

HILDE [*with a cry of joy*]. The wreath! Oh, how absolutely marvellous this is going to be!

SOLNESS [*surprised*]. How is it *you* are bringing the wreath, Ragnar?

RAGNAR. I promised the foreman I would.

SOLNESS [*relieved*]. Then your father must be a little better?

RAGNAR. No.

SOLNESS. Didn't what I wrote make him feel any better?

RAGNAR. It came too late.

SOLNESS. Too late!

RAGNAR. He was no longer conscious when she got back with it. He had had a stroke.

SOLNESS. Then you must go home to him. You must look after your father!

RAGNAR. He doesn't need me any more.

SOLNESS. But surely you ought to be with him.

RAGNAR. She's sitting by the bed.

SOLNESS [*somewhat uncertainly*]. Kaja?

RAGNAR [*looks darkly at him*]. Yes, Kaja.

SOLNESS. Go home, Ragnar. Be with him and with her. Let *me* have the wreath.

RAGNAR [*suppressing a mocking smile*]. You're not thinking of doing it yourself...?

SOLNESS. I want to take it down there myself. [*Takes the wreath from him.*] Now go home. We don't need you today.

RAGNAR. I know you don't need me after this. But today I'm staying.

SOLNESS. All right, stay, if you really want to.

HILDE [*by the railings*]. Master builder! I'm going to stand here and watch you.

SOLNESS. Watch me!

HILDE. It's going to be terribly exciting.

SOLNESS [*in a low voice*]. We'll talk about that later, Hilde.

[*He takes the wreath and goes down the steps and across the garden.*]

HILDE [*looks after him and then turns to* RAGNAR]. I think you might at least have thanked him.

RAGNAR. Thanked him? Me thank *him*?

HILDE. Yes, you really should!

RAGNAR. More likely you are the one I ought to thank.

HILDE. How can you say a thing like that?

RAGNAR [*without answering her*]. But just you beware! You don't know him properly yet.

HILDE [*fierily*]. I know him better than anybody!

RAGNAR [*laughs bitterly*]. Thank him! The man who held me down year after year! The man who undermined my father's faith in me. Who made me lose faith in myself.... And all that just to...!

HILDE [*as though suspecting something*]. To what...? Tell me! Quickly!

RAGNAR. Just to be able to keep her for himself.

HILDE [*with a sudden movement towards him*]. That girl at the desk!

RAGNAR. Yes.

HILDE [*threateningly, with clenched hands*]. It's not true! You're lying!

RAGNAR. I wouldn't have believed it either, until today—when she told me herself.

HILDE [*as though beside herself*]. What did she say? I want to know! Now! This minute!

RAGNAR. She said that he has taken control of her mind—utterly and completely. Taken possession of all her thoughts. She says she can never escape him. That she wants to stay here where *he* is. . . .

HILDE [*with flashing eyes*]. She won't get the chance!

RAGNAR [*inquiringly*]. Who says she won't?

HILDE [*quickly*]. He'll say she won't!

RAGNAR. Ah, yes—I understand everything now. After this she'd be nothing but a nuisance.

HILDE. You don't understand anything—if you can say a thing like that! No! I'll tell you why he held on to her.

RAGNAR. Why?

HILDE. To keep *you*.

RAGNAR. Did he tell you this?

HILDE. No, but it's true! It must be true. [*Wildly.*] I want it to be true! I *want* it to be!

RAGNAR. And as soon as you came, he let her go.

HILDE. It was *you* he let go! You! Why should he bother himself about girls like her?

RAGNAR [*reflecting*]. Could he really have been afraid of me all this time?

HILDE. *He* afraid! I think you flatter yourself.

RAGNAR. He must have realized long ago that I had something. Anyway, don't you see that's precisely what he is—*afraid*!

HILDE. Him! Don't make me laugh!

RAGNAR. In his own way he *is* afraid. The great master builder! Things like spoiling other people's lives—the way he spoilt my father's and mine—he's not afraid of *that*. But a little thing like climbing up a bit of scaffolding—you watch him steer well clear of that!

HILDE. Ah, you should have seen him way up high, high as I once saw him—so high it left your senses reeling!

RAGNAR. Did you see that?

HILDE. I certainly did. Free and proud he stood there, tying the wreath to the weathercock!

RAGNAR. I knew he'd risked it *once* in his life. One solitary occasion. We've often talked about it among ourselves. But no power on earth would get him to do it again.

HILDE. He'll do it again today!

RAGNAR [*scornfully*]. That's what you think!

HILDE. We'll see him!

RAGNAR. We won't! Neither of us will ever live to see that!

HILDE [*vehemently, beside herself*]. I *will*! I *will* see it! I *must* see it!

RAGNAR. He won't do it. He simply *daren't* do it. Because he's now got this fatal flaw—this great master builder of ours!

[MRS. SOLNESS *comes out of the house on to the verandah.*]

MRS. SOLNESS [*looking around her*]. Isn't he here? Where's he gone?

RAGNAR. Mr. Solness is over there with the workmen.

HILDE. He took the wreath.

MRS. SOLNESS [*in terror*]. He took the wreath! Oh God! Oh God! Brovik—you must go down to him! Get him to come back here!

RAGNAR. Shall I tell him you want to speak to him?

MRS. SOLNESS. Oh yes, please do! No, no! Don't say *I* want him! Tell him there's somebody here. Say he must come at once.

RAGNAR. Very well. I'll do that, Mrs. Solness.

[*He goes down the steps and away through the garden.*]

MRS. SOLNESS. Oh, Miss Wangel, you can't imagine the dread I go through on his account.

HILDE. But what's so frightening about this?

MRS. SOLNESS. Oh, surely you see. Suppose he meant it! Suppose he takes it into his head to climb the scaffolding!

HILDE [*excitedly*]. Do you think he will?

MRS. SOLNESS. Oh, you never know what he's going to do. He's capable of doing absolutely anything!

HILDE. Ah! So you too think he's possibly a bit—er . . . ?

MRS. SOLNESS. I no longer know what to think. The doctor has told me so many different things, and when I remember some of the other things I've heard him say, and put two and two together . . .

[DR. HERDAL *puts his head in through the doorway.*]

DR. HERDAL. Isn't he coming soon?

MRS. SOLNESS. Yes, I think so. He's been sent for.

DR. HERDAL [*approaches*]. But hadn't you better go inside, Mrs. Solness. . . .

MRS. SOLNESS. No, no! I'll stay out here and wait for Halvard.

DR. HERDAL. But there are some ladies here to see you . . .

MRS. SOLNESS. Oh, my God! Why must it be now!

DR. HERDAL. They say they want to watch the ceremony.

MRS. SOLNESS. Ah, well, I suppose I'd better go in and see them. It's my duty.

HILDE. Can't you ask these ladies to go away?

MRS. SOLNESS. No, I couldn't possibly do that. Now they've come, it's my duty to receive them. You wait out here, though . . . so you can be here when he comes.

DR. HERDAL. And try to keep him talking as long as possible. . . .

MRS. SOLNESS. Yes, please do, dear Miss Wangel. Hold on to him as tightly as you can.

HILDE. Wouldn't it be best if you did this yourself?

MRS. SOLNESS. Oh dear, yes! It is *my* duty, really. But when one is so beset by duties . . .

DR. HERDAL [*looking towards the garden*]. He's coming!

MRS. SOLNESS. And here am I, having to go in.

DR. HERDAL [*to* HILDE]. Don't say anything about my being here.

HILDE. Oh, no! I think I can find other things to talk to Mr. Solness about.

MRS. SOLNESS. And do please hold tight on to him. I think *you* can do that best.

[MRS. SOLNESS *and* DR. HERDAL *go into the house.* HILDE *remains behind, standing on the verandah.* SOLNESS *comes up the steps from the garden.*]

SOLNESS. They tell me somebody wants me.

HILDE. Yes, master builder. Me.

SOLNESS. Oh, it's you, Hilde. I was afraid it might be Aline and the doctor.

HILDE. You seem pretty afraid altogether!

SOLNESS. You think so?

HILDE. Yes. People are saying that you are afraid of climbing . . . up the scaffolding, for instance.

SOLNESS. Well, that's a different matter.

HILDE. Then you are afraid to do it?

SOLNESS. Yes, I am.

HILDE. Afraid you might fall and dash yourself to pieces?

SOLNESS. No, not that.

HILDE. What, then?

SOLNESS. I am afraid of retribution, Hilde.

HILDE. Retribution? [*Shakes her head.*] I don't understand.

SOLNESS. Sit down. And I'll tell you something.

HILDE. Yes, do! Quickly!

[*She sits down on a stool by the railing and looks expectantly at him.*]

SOLNESS [*throwing his hat on the table*]. You know that I first began by building churches.

HILDE [*nods*]. I know that.

SOLNESS. You see, I was brought up in a God-fearing home out in the country. That's why I thought building churches was the worthiest thing I could do.

HILDE. Yes, yes.

SOLNESS. And I think I can say that I built those humble little churches with such honesty and sincerity and devotion that . . .

HILDE. Well?

SOLNESS. Well . . . that I think He should have been pleased with me.

HILDE. He? Which he?

SOLNESS. He for whom the churches were intended, of course! He, whose honour and glory they were meant to serve.

HILDE. I see! But are you so sure that . . . He wasn't . . . pleased with you?

SOLNESS [*scornfully*]. *He* pleased with *me*! How can you say things like that, Hilde? He who has let loose this troll within me to rampage about as it will? He who bade them all be ready night and day to minister to me . . . all these . . . these . . .

HILDE. Devils . . .

SOLNESS. Yes, of both kinds. Oh no, I was soon made to realize that He wasn't pleased with me. [*Mysteriously.*] In fact, you know, that's why He let the old house burn down.

HILDE. Was that the reason?

SOLNESS. Yes, don't you see? He wanted to give me the chance of becoming a complete master of my craft, so that I could build ever more splendid churches for Him. At first I didn't understand what He was getting at. Then suddenly I realized.

HILDE. When was that?

SOLNESS. It was when I built that church tower up at Lysanger.

HILDE. That's what I thought.

SOLNESS. You see, Hilde, up there in a strange place where I had time to think, I was able to turn things over in my mind. It was then I realized why He had taken my little children from me. It was so that I should have nothing else to cling to. No love or happiness or anything like that, you see. I was to be a master builder, and that was all. I was to spend my whole life building for Him. [*Laughs.*] But that idea didn't come to much.

HILDE. What did you do then?

SOLNESS. First, I scrutinized myself . . . examined myself . . .

HILDE. And then?

SOLNESS. Then—just as He had—I did the *impossible*.

HILDE. The impossible?

SOLNESS. Never before had I been able to stand heights. But that day I could.

HILDE [*leaps up*]. Yes, yes, you could!

SOLNESS. And as I stood there on high, at the very top, and as I hung the wreath on the weathercock, I spoke to Him: Listen to me, Almighty One! From this day forward, I too will be free. A master builder free in his own field, as you are in yours. Never again will I build churches for you. Only homes for the people.

HILDE [*with wide glistening eyes*]. *That* was the song I heard in the air!

SOLNESS. But He got His own back later on.

HILDE. What do you mean by that?

SOLNESS [*looks at her despondently*]. Building homes for the people isn't worth a brass farthing, Hilde.

HILDE. What makes you say that now?

SOLNESS. Because now I see that people have no use for these homes of theirs. It doesn't help them to be happy. And I probably wouldn't have had any use for a home like that, either. Even if I'd owned one. [*Laughs quietly and bitterly.*] And now, looking back, what does it all add up to? In fact, I've built nothing. Nor did I really sacrifice anything for the chance to build. Nothing! Absolutely nothing!

HILDE. You're not going to build anything else after this?

SOLNESS [*animatedly*]. Oh yes, I am! I am just about to begin!

HILDE. What's it to be? Tell me quickly!

SOLNESS. The one thing I think can contain human happiness—that's what I'm going to build now.

HILDE [*looks fixedly at him*]. Master builder, you mean our castles in the air.

SOLNESS. Yes. Castles in the air.

HILDE. I'm afraid your mind would reel before we got half-way.

SOLNESS. Not if I can go hand in hand with *you*, Hilde.

HILDE [*with suppressed venom*]. Only me? Won't there be several of us?

SOLNESS. Who else?

HILDE. Oh, that Kaja out of the office. Poor thing, aren't you going to take her along with you, too?

SOLNESS. Ah! So that's what Aline was sitting here talking to you about.

HILDE. *Is* it true, or isn't it?

SOLNESS [*angrily*]. I won't answer that! You must believe in me, implicitly!

HILDE. For ten years I have believed in you, utterly and completely.

SOLNESS. You must go on believing!

HILDE. Then let me see you standing on high again!

SOLNESS [*sadly*]. Oh, Hilde . . . I can't do a thing like that every day.

HILDE [*passionately*]. I want you to! [*Pleadingly.*] Just once more, master builder! Do the *impossible* once more!

OLNESS [*stands and looks deep into her eyes*]. If I try it, Hilde, I shall stands up there and speak to Him as I did last time.

HILDE [*with rising excitement*]. What will you say to Him?

SOLNESS. I shall say to him: Hear me, Great and Mighty Lord! Judge me as you will. But henceforth I shall build one thing only, quite the loveliest thing in the whole world . . .

HILDE [*carried away*]. Yes . . . Yes . . . Yes!

SOLNESS. . . . Build it together with the princess I love . . .

HILDE. Yes, tell Him that! Tell Him that!

SOLNESS. Yes. And then I shall say to Him: Now I go down to take her in my arms and kiss her . . .

HILDE. . . . Many times! Say that!

SOLNESS. . . . Many, many times, I shall say.

HILDE. And then . . . ?

SOLNESS. Then I shall wave my hat and come down to earth . . . and do as I told Him.

HILDE [*with arms outstretched*]. Now I see you again as you were when there was a song in the air!

SOLNESS [*looks at her with bowed head*]. How did you become as you are, Hilde?

HILDE. How did you make me as I am?

SOLNESS [*abruptly and firmly*]. The princess shall have her castle.

HILDE [*joyfully clapping her hands*]. Oh, master builder . . . ! My lovely, lovely castle! Our castle in the air!

SOLNESS. On its firm foundation.

[*In the street a crowd of people have gathered; they can be glimpsed indistinctly through the trees. The sound of a brass band can be heard in the distance behind the new house.* MRS. SOLNESS, *wearing a fur round her neck,* DR. HERDAL, *with her white shawl over his arm, and several ladies come out on to the verandah.* RAGNAR BROVIK *comes up at that moment from the garden.*]

MRS. SOLNESS [*to* RAGNAR]. Is there going to be a band?

RAGNAR. Yes. The band of the builders' union! [*To* SOLNESS.] The foreman asked me to tell you he's ready to go up with the wreath.

SOLNESS [*takes his hat*]. Good. I'll go down myself.

MRS. SOLNESS [*anxiously*]. What do you want down there, Halvard?

SOLNESS [*curtly*]. I must be down there among the men.

MRS. SOLNESS. Yes, down there. Down below.

SOLNESS. That's where I generally am, aren't I? In the ordinary way.

[*He goes down the steps and across the garden.*]

MRS. SOLNESS [*calls after him over the railing*]. But tell the man to be careful as he's climbing up! Promise me, Halvard!

DR. HERDAL [*to* MRS. SOLNESS]. There, I was right, you see. He's given up those wild ideas.

MRS. SOLNESS. Oh, what a relief! Twice we've had workmen falling down. Both of them dashed to pieces instantly. [*Turns to* HILDE.] Thank you, Miss Wangel, for keeping such a tight hold on him. I'm sure *I'd* never have managed him.

DR. HERDAL [*gaily*]. Yes, yes, Miss Wangel! You know how to hold tight on to somebody when you set your mind to it!

[MRS. SOLNESS *and* DR. HERDAL *walk over to the ladies, who stand by the steps looking out over the garden.* HILDE *remains standing by the railing in the foreground.* RAGNAR *walks over to her.*]

RAGNAR. [*with suppressed laughter, in a low voice*]. Miss Wangel. . . . Do you see all those young people down in the street?

HILDE. Yes.

RAGNAR. They are all the other builders in training, come to watch the master.

HILDE. What do they want to watch him for?

RAGNAR. They want to see him too scared to climb his own building.

HILDE. So that's what the lads want, is it?

RAGNAR [*venomously and scornfully*]. He's kept us down too long. Now we want to watch him having to stay down, too.

HILDE. That's something you won't see. Not this time.

RAGNAR [*smiles*]. Oh? Where will we see him, then?

HILDE. Right up high! High up by the weathercock is where you'll see him!

RAGNAR [*laughs*]. Him! Don't you believe it!

HILDE. He means to get to the top. And that's where you'll see him.

RAGNAR. He means to, yes! I'm prepared to believe that. But he just *can't* do it. He'll be dizzy long before he's got half-way. He'll have to crawl down again on his hands and knees!

DR. HERDAL [*pointing*]. Look! There goes the foreman up the ladder.

MRS. SOLNESS. And he's got the wreath to carry as well. Oh, let's hope he takes care!

RAGNAR [*stares incredulously and cries out*]. But surely that's . . .

HILDE [*with a shout of joy*]. It's the master builder himself!

MRS. SOLNESS [*shouts out in terror*]. Yes, it's Halvard! Oh my God . . . ! Halvard! Halvard!

DR. HERDAL. Shh! Don't shout to him!

MRS. SOLNESS [*almost beside herself*]. I must go to him! I must get him down again!

DR. HERDAL [*holding her back*]. Everybody keep still! Not a sound!

HILDE [*motionless, following* SOLNESS *with her eyes*]. Climbing, climbing. Higher and higher! Look! Just look!

RAGNAR [*breathlessly*]. He *must* turn back now! There's no other way.

HILDE. Climbing, climbing. He's nearly at the top.

MRS. SOLNESS. Oh, I shall die of terror. I can't bear to watch!

DR. HERDAL. Don't look at him then.

HILDE. There he is, standing on the very top plank! Right at the top!

DR. HERDAL. Nobody move! Do you hear!

HILDE [*in quiet jubilation*]. At last! At last! Now I see him great and free again!

RAGNAR [*almost speechless*]. But this is . . .

HILDE. This is the way I've seen him all these ten years. How confident he looks standing there! Terribly exciting, all the same! Look at him! Now he's hanging the wreath over the spire!

RAGNAR. I feel as though I am witnessing something utterly impossible.

HILDE. Yes! What he is doing now *is* impossible! [*With that enigmatic expression in her eyes.*] Can you see anybody else up there with him?

RAGNAR. There is nobody else.

HILDE. Yes, there is. He is disputing with someone.

RAGNAR. You are wrong.

HILDE. Don't you hear a song in the air, either?

RAGNAR. It must be the wind in the tree-tops.

HILDE. *I* hear a song. A mighty song! [*Cries in wild jubilation.*] Look! Look! Now he's waving his hat! He's waving to us down here! Oh, let's wave back to him! Now, now he's done it! [*Snatches the white shawl from the doctor, waves it about and shouts up in the air.*] Hurrah for the master builder!

DR. HERDAL. Stop it! Stop it! For God's sake . . . !

[*The ladies on the verandah wave their handkerchiefs, and the people in the street join in the cheering. There is a sudden silence, and then there is a cry of terror from the crowd. A human body and some planks and poles can be indistinctly glimpsed plunging down among the trees.*]

MRS. SOLNESS AND THE LADIES [*together*]. He is falling! He is falling!

[MRS. SOLNESS *sways and falls back in a faint; amid cries and confusion, the ladies catch her. The crowd in the street breaks down the fence and rushes into the garden.* DR. HERDAL *also hurries down there. Short pause.*]

HILDE [*continues to stare upwards, as though turned to stone*]. My master builder!

RAGNAR [*supporting himself trembling against the railing*]. He must have been dashed to pieces. Killed instantaneously.

ONE OF THE LADIES [*as* MRS. SOLNESS *is carried into the house*]. Run to the doctor . . .

RAGNAR. I can't move . . .

ANOTHER LADY. Then shout to somebody!

RAGNAR [*tries to shout*]. How is it? Is he alive?

A VOICE [*down in the garden*]. The master builder is dead!

OTHER VOICES [*nearer*]. His head is all smashed in. . . . He fell right into the quarry.

HILDE [*turns to* RAGNAR *and says quietly*]. I can't see him up there now.

RAGNAR. This is terrible. So in fact he couldn't do it.

HILDE [*with a kind of quiet, bewildered triumph*]. But he got right to the top. And I heard harps in the air. [*Waves the shawl upwards and shouts with a wild intensity.*] My . . . my . . . master builder!

The Oxford World's Classics Website

www.worldsclassics.co.uk

- Information about new titles
- Explore the full range of Oxford World's Classics
- Links to other literary sites and the main OUP webpage
- Imaginative competitions, with bookish prizes
- Peruse the Oxford World's Classics Magazine
- Articles by editors
- Extracts from Introductions
- A forum for discussion and feedback on the series
- Special information for teachers and lecturers

www.worldsclassics.co.uk

American Literature

British and Irish Literature

Children's Literature

Classics and Ancient Literature

Colonial Literature

Eastern Literature

European Literature

History

Medieval Literature

Oxford English Drama

Poetry

Philosophy

Politics

Religion

The Oxford Shakespeare

A complete list of Oxford Paperbacks, including Oxford World's Classics, Oxford Shakespeare, Oxford Drama, and Oxford Paperback Reference, is available in the UK from the Academic Division Publicity Department, Oxford University Press, Great Clarendon Street, Oxford OX2 6DP.

In the USA, complete lists are available from the Paperbacks Marketing Manager, Oxford University Press, 198 Madison Avenue, New York, NY 10016.

Oxford Paperbacks are available from all good bookshops. In case of difficulty, customers in the UK can order direct from Oxford University Press Bookshop, Freepost, 116 High Street, Oxford OX1 4BR, enclosing full payment. Please add 10 per cent of published price for postage and packing.